BROTHERS IN ARMS

Southwestern Writers Collection Series

The Southwestern Writers Collection Series originates from the Southwestern Writers Collection, an archive and literary center established at Southwest Texas State University to celebrate the region's writers and literary heritage.

BROTHERS IN ARMS

A JOURNEY FROM WAR TO PEACE

WILLIAM BROYLES, JR.

UNIVERSITY OF TEXAS PRESS

AUSTIN

Requests for permission to reproduce material from this work
should be sent to Permissions, University of Texas Press,
P.O. Box 7819, Austin, TX 78713-7819.

♾ The paper used in this publication meets the
minimum requirements of American National Standard
for Information Sciences—Permanence of Paper for
Printed Library Materials, ANSI Z39.48-1984.

Broyles, William.
Brothers in arms : a journey from war to peace / by William Broyles, Jr.
    p.   cm.—(Southwestern writers collection series)
Includes bibliographical references.
ISBN 0-292-70849-1 (pbk. : alk. paper)
1. Vietnam—Description and travel.   2. Vietnamese Conflict, 1961–1975.
3. Broyles, William—Journeys—Vietnam.   I. Title.   II. Series.
DS556.39.B76   1996
959.704′38—dc20
                                                        96-30814

CONTENTS

ACKNOWLEDGMENTS

This book is the story of a journey in search of some basic truths about war and peace, and why love and laughter thrive so near to death. It is part memoir, part narrative, part history. Almost twenty years have passed since I began, and a good many people helped me along the way. I am grateful to them all, and offer the excuse of a poor memory to anyone whose contributions I fail to acknowledge.

Many veterans of the Vietnam War helped in different ways in the course of my writing this book, among them Tom Bird, Charles Clements, Bernard Edelman, Arthur Egendorf, Jack Fuller, Winston Groom, Robert Kerrey, Robert Muller, Robert Nylen, Tim O'Brien, Al Santoli, Robert Santos, Tom Tomasie-wicz, James Webb, John Wheeler III, and General William C. Westmoreland. Several of them have written their own books, and most would probably disagree with at least some of what appears in this one. No matter. All of us were there.

James Fallows and Paul Burka read the entire manuscript and made valuable suggestions throughout. I also received useful comments from Andrew Cockburn, James Dingeman, John Gregory Dunne, Peter Goldman, Harry Hurt III, Nima Isham, Jonathan Kirsch, Nicholas Lemann, Jan Lodal, Allen Matusow, Terry McDonell, Al Reinert, William Shawcross, and Meredith White, as well as from Kurt Vonnegut, who shared with me some reminiscences of World War II.

William Whitworth, Jack Beatty, and Sue Parilla of *The Atlantic* contributed editorial insight to portions of the book, as did Lee Eisenberg and David Hirshey of *Esquire.* At Alfred Knopf, Bob Gottlieb was an inspiration in shaping the manuscript, and Mel Rosenthal and Mary Maguire gave me much assistance. My agent, Lynn Nesbit, always seemed to see the light at the end of the tunnel, even when I could not.

Ted Slate of the *Newsweek* library gave me research help, and Frank Gibney, Jr., of *Newsweek*'s Bangkok bureau came to my rescue on more than one occasion. Retired Brigadier General Edwin Simmons made available the resources of the Marine Corps Historical Center in Washington, D.C., where Jack Shulimson and Colonel John Miller were generous with their time and knowledge.

I could not have made my return journey to Vietnam in 1984 without the many Vietnamese who persuaded their unfathomable bureaucracy to allow my unorthodox itinerary, and who gave me invaluable aid along the way. I owe special thanks to Tran Trong Khanh in New York City, Duong Minh and Nguyen Van Thuan in Hanoi, Tran Hien in Da Nang, and Nguyen Phuong Nam and Tran Van Viet in Saigon. Le Luong Minh traveled with me the length and breadth of Vietnam, never losing his patience or his good humor as he helped me see what has become of his country. Many other men and women helped me inside Vietnam, some at considerable risk to themselves. It would not be prudent to mention their names, but I have not forgotten them.

Among the international community in Hanoi and Saigon, several people were particularly generous, among them Michael Flaks of the International Committee for the Red Cross, Wendy and Michael Wood of the British Embassy, Catherine von Heidenstam of the Swedish Embassy, and Charles De Nerciat of Agence France Presse and his wife, Mary Sun.

As my radioman during the war, Jeff Hiers kept me alive. During the writing of this book his flawless memory, irreverent humor, and constant encouragement kept me going.

I have only begun to understand how much Vietnam affected my family. While I was in the war, my parents and my sister suffered the daily pain and uncertainty, the fear of the telephone call late at night, that is a part of staying behind. This book is a small way of thanking them for their support through that year, and throughout my life.

My wife Sybil's good judgment, clear thinking, and visual imagination improved each page of this book, just as her love and patience made it possible. For the past two years she and my children have had the double burden of living with both an old soldier and a writer. They deserved better, but then again, so did we all.

W.B.

PREFACE TO THE NEW EDITION

This book is based on two journeys I made to Vietnam, one in war, the other in peace. The first was in 1969, when I spent a year there as a young Marine Corps lieutenant during the war. When I returned in 1984, the country where I had fought had vanished. Only my memories of it remained, fixed and immutable, or so I thought. Since then Vietnam has changed even more, but it still has a troubling, powerful pull on our memories and on our foreign policy. We lost something there. *Brothers in Arms* grew from my quest to go back and find it.

When I first saw Vietnam I was immediately drunk on the green strange savage sweetness of it. I was leading a platoon of marines, which meant I saw the country with my face in the mud, struggling with fear, desperately trying to be worthy of the teenage Americans under my command. I lay in the jungles in the black fecund Asian night, watching astronauts streak by in the sky high above me. They knew more about the moon than I knew about this mysterious land where we wandered about, clinging to our ideals and our weapons, utterly lost. We were young and scared and we gave each other everything we had.

Then I was assigned to the generals commanding my division. After breakfast we flew high above the countryside in our helicopters, occasionally swooping down on some battlefield or pacification program. In the evening we dined on Navy china and entertained ourselves with a movie or a game of Ping-Pong. We talked strategy. The big picture. It was a somewhat different perspective than I had when my face was in the mud.

In 1984 I made my second journey to Vietnam; to my knowledge, I was the first veteran to return to the actual battlefields of the war. The war was over. We had lost. No one seemed quite to understand why. I went to make sense of my first experience, and, as much as I could, to probe the deeper mysteries of war itself and what it does to the men and women who fight it—how war gets hold of young men and doesn't let go, how its images sear into our souls and suck the color from all experience after it.

I also went back to meet my enemies. I wanted to see face to face the men and women I had fought against: the generals who ran the war, the soldiers whose muzzle flashes winked at me in the monsoon nights. I talked strategies with the old men who ran Hanoi's war. They told me how the war looked from their side and what political and military strategies they used to fight us. Their views are still among the most reliable source material available in English on the ideology, experience, and strategies of the other side.

Everywhere I went, from the Chinese border to the Mekong Delta, I met veterans of the war. But I most wanted to meet the soldiers I had fought against in the hills and paddies between Da Nang and the Ho Chi Minh Trail, the ones who knew the same bloody ground I did. In the flickering light of lanterns, fueled by rice wine and surrounded by entire villages, we shared the experience of having tried to kill each other. And on a dusty road I met a woman whose husband was most likely killed by my platoon, perhaps by me. There is no greater divide among human beings than that, but I saw no hatred in her eyes. She did not expect me to feel guilt. That was during the war, she said. The war is over now. Life goes on.

I had expected Vietnam to be the same. But life had indeed gone on. The bases were dismantled and overgrown, the battlefields become forest or paddy or village once again. Birds sang. Schoolchildren played. For so many of us Americans, the war, whether a source of pride and strength or shame and despair, was like a piece of shrapnel, still working its way to the surface, troubling our sleep. Despite their victory, most of the Vietnamese war veterans I met felt discarded and unappreciated. No one wanted to hear their war stories—except me.

Since 1984 much has changed in Vietnam. Westerners and Japanese flood the streets of Hanoi and Saigon. The Stalinist police state is finally being disassembled. Propaganda has become more muted. Saigon has become once again a vibrant commercial center. The natural energies of the Vietnamese people are enriching their country as well as our own. Revisiting the war has become something of a tourist industry, and the places I discovered are now required stops. Bicycle tours amble down the Ho Chi Minh Trail. Tour buses disgorge their passengers at the tunnels of Cu Chi.

One particular spot—China Beach—has become a major tourist attraction, and I am partly to blame. During the war I had gone there with my platoon for a couple of days of in-country R&R. We were given clean clothes, a spot on the beach, and all the beer and steaks we wanted. For a couple of days, we were out of the war. Next door was an evacuation hospital, with, it was rumored, real American nurses. When I later worked with the generals, I visited wounded men in that hospital, met some of the nurses, and was struck by their courage, dedication, and bawdy black humor.

After I wrote this book I realized that I had left out an important piece of the puzzle—the men and women who went to heal and help. From their experience I helped create the television series *China Beach*. Outside Los Angeles we built a replica of an evacuation hospital and an R&R center like the ones from the real China Beach. The set was so eerily real that at times I felt I was back in the war. But of course the blood washed off, the wounded went to lunch, the dead got up and played football. I wished with all my heart that the wounded and dead from the real war could so easily have been saved.

After a few years of working with *China Beach*, my memories and dreams of the real war became confused with the make-believe images of television. In a similar way, the farther Vietnam fades from immediate memory the more its specific nature gives way to the universal, timeless experience of war: the loss of innocence, the conquering of fear, the power of comradeship, the hopelessness of death, the occasional triumph of hope, the roles of randomness and fate.

As I reread *Brothers in Arms* I remembered, however, that during my second trip to Vietnam my former enemies and I spent most of our time talking about specifics. What was it like, I wanted to know, living in those tunnels, bombed by B-52s, strafed by Spookies, burned by napalm, seared by white phosphorous? They wanted to know what it was like to fear the night, to trust no one, to want so badly to go home. We talked about how awful the food was, how cold and wet we were, how it was the best and worst time of our lives.

I am drawn to those parts of this book that deal with personal experience. Distance does that. The issues that divided the Philistines from the Israelites 4,000 years ago have faded, but we are forever entranced by the story of the young shepherd boy who found the courage to slay a giant with a stone.

I did my best to give this personal experience its necessary context of history, politics, and ideology—the combustible forces that kept the war going. But at the core of this book is my struggle to make sense of the powerful appeal of war: why men love it so much, why it endures as part of the human experience. Its evocation of my own experience is as honest as I could be. And the men I served with are still the finest I have ever known—the brothers I never had.

The memories of the war continue to trouble and/or inspire those who fought it. And no one seems to have learned its lessons.

William Broyles, Jr.
April 1996

Used by permission of David Lindroth

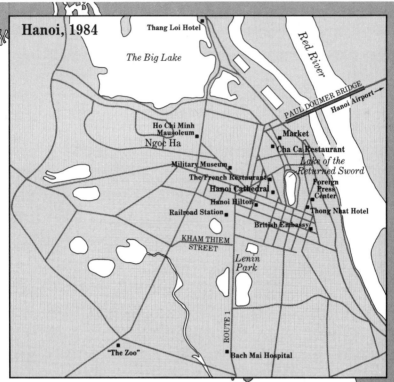

Hanoi, 1984

Thang Loi Hotel

The Big Lake

Red River

PAUL DOUMER BRIDGE

Hanoi Airport →

Ho Chi Minh Mausoleum

Ngoc Ha

Market

Cha Ca Restaurant

Military Museum

The French Restaurant

Hanoi Cathedral

Lake of the Returned Sword

Foreign Press Center

Hanoi Hilton

Thong Nhat Hotel

Railroad Station

British Embassy

KHAM THIEM STREET

ROUTE 1

Lenin Park

"The Zoo"

Bach Mai Hospital

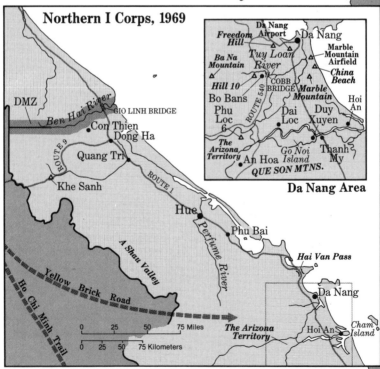

Northern I Corps, 1969

DMZ

Ben Hai River

GIO LINH BRIDGE

Con Thien

Dong Ha

ROUTE 9

Quang Tri

ROUTE 1

Khe Sanh

Hue

Phu Bai

A Shau Valley

Perfume River

Hai Van Pass

Yellow Brick Road

Ho Chi Minh Trail

Da Nang

Cham Island

Hoi An

The Arizona Territory

| 0 | 25 | 50 | 75 Miles |
| 0 | 25 | 50 | 75 Kilometers |

Da Nang Area

Da Nang Airport

Freedom Hill

Da Nang

Ba Na Mountain

Tuy Loan River

Marble Mountain Airfield

China Beach

Hill 10

COBB BRIDGE

Marble Mountain

ROUTE 540

Bo Bans

Phu Loc 6

Dai Loc

Duy Xuyen

Hoi An

The Arizona Territory

An Hoa

Go Noi Island

Thanh My

QUE SON MTNS.

Used by permission of David Lindroth

BROTHERS IN ARMS

PROLOGUE:
1969

The water in the rice paddy was chest-deep. We waded across in single file, holding our rifles over our heads. Our packs were heavy and pushed our feet deep into the mud. In the paddies barefoot boys on the backs of water buffalo fished with long poles. In the fields women gathered rice, while in the shade of a banyan tree girls wove bamboo reeds into a lattice fence. Young men from the local militia, their rifles slung casually over their shoulders, waved at us, the cigarettes in their hands trailing puffs of smoke. Children played tag on their way to school. Old women in black pajamas crouched by the path—gossiping and spitting blood-red betel juice onto the ground.

We crossed the paddy, left the last village behind, and headed toward the mountains. By midmorning we were in a free-fire zone. Our mission was to cut across the contour lines on the map, looking for fresh trails out of the mountains. We spent the day going up and down hills, but all we found were some faint footprints on an old trail. The elephant grass was thick and razor sharp—our arms were bleeding from dozens of cuts. Every hour or so we stopped to pull off leeches.

On the way back we followed the river. The air was hot and still and the jungle closed in around us. The only sound was our own breathing, and the occasional scraping of a branch along a man's cartridge belt. Suddenly, the column stopped. Everyone went down. From the point a hand signal came back, each man repeating it.

Lieutenant up.

The message stopped with me. I was the lieutenant. The point man had found a small hole hidden in some grass. I popped a smoke grenade and dropped it down the hole. Smoke poured out, and after a minute or so began to filter up from the riverbank. An old log and some brush had been arranged to conceal a larger hole—a tunnel entrance. We had to explore the tunnel, then blow it up. I caught the eye of the squad leader and moved my hand in the shape of an arc. Without a word, he motioned his men into positions around the tunnel entrance.

The point man, a Cajun from Louisiana named Thibodeaux, was a natural soldier. Because he was so good I tended to give him the most difficult jobs, like walking point. Or going down in tunnels. I trusted him totally. I looked at him, then at the tunnel.

He shook his head and his lips formed the words "No way, José."

That was it. If he didn't feel right about going, then I couldn't send him. Tomasiewicz, the squad leader, was from Chicago—another natural soldier. Like Thibodeaux, he was nineteen. I looked at him. He shook his head too. That meant one thing.

I pulled off my cartridge belt. Thibodeaux handed me two sticks of C-4 plastic explosive. Tomasiewicz took a blasting cap out of his pocket, fastened it to a length of fuse, then—casually risking losing his jaw—crimped it down with his teeth. He fastened the fuse igniter to the other end of the fuse and pushed the blasting cap deep into the stick of C-4. I tested my flashlight and took my .45 off safety.

After cutting off a long strand of elephant grass, I crawled down the bank. At the tunnel entrance I waved the elephant grass carefully, feeling for that slight resistance that would mean a trip wire.

I felt nothing.

It was a sensible precaution, but trip wires weren't the only way to detonate a mine or a booby trap. A Bouncing Betty could be set in the ground, ready to pop into the air and explode at groin level. Or an artillery shell with a pressure detonator could be buried at the entrance. If it were, my men wouldn't find enough pieces of me to fill a matchbox. Inside the tunnel poisonous snakes might be hung from the ceiling. A pit might lie beneath the floor, lined with sharpened stakes—perhaps with poison on the tips. Or men might be inside—men with rifles, knives, grenades, or even spears—waiting for the marine who would come groping around a bend in the darkness, helpless.

The tunnels were part of the special terror of Vietnam. In our minds the enemy wasn't another soldier, a man like us. He was mysterious and elusive—a vision from the unknown, a bogeyman with terrible powers rising up out of the earth. Vietnam was a nightmare war, the deepest childhood fears come true. In Vietnam the monster really was under the bed, the tunnel really did suddenly open in your bedroom wall. The primitive methods that the enemy adopted in the face of our technology made him that much more formidable. We controlled the air, so he went underground—and emerged to control the night.

The friendly peasants of the day became menacing and lethal after dark, as if our own subconscious were rising up against us in our sleep. The protection of our modern selves was stripped away. Our technology, our air superiority, our firepower, all were useless. The very earth itself became the enemy. We fought a darkness we could neither penetrate nor understand. The only other place I had ever been so scared was in my own bedroom, when I was a boy and my imagination attacked me in the night.

I looked up from the tunnel entrance and saw Hiers, my radioman. He grinned and gave me the thumbs up.

It was all happening so quickly that I hardly had time to wonder just what I was doing here and why I was going into that tunnel, alone. I hardly had time to be afraid. But I had time enough.

I took a breath and went into the tunnel. It was narrow and tight, designed for men much smaller than I. Crawling with my arms fully extended in front of me, I held the flashlight in one hand, my pistol in the other. I pushed forward with my feet and, when I could, my elbows. Dirt covered my face and filled my nostrils with its dankness. I left my flashlight off. There was no point announcing my arrival.

The tunnel turned sharply, then went down and up again. I had lost all sense of direction. Suddenly the ceiling lifted off my back and the walls moved away from my ribs. I sensed space around me. I lay still, my legs still held tight in the narrow passage, my heart pounding in my throat.

Something was terribly wrong.

I felt something else.

I felt someone else.

Someone else was in that tunnel. I could feel his heart beating, his lungs working, his eyelashes blinking. I could feel the curve of the trigger on his finger—or was it the heft of a grenade in his hand? The sweat on my body turned cold.

Very slowly, I began to back out of the tunnel, pushing with the heels of my hands. I tried not to breathe, then to take tiny gulps. I was sweating so heavily that the dirt on my face and body had turned to mud. After a few feet I stopped and lay motionless. I heard nothing. I could no longer feel that other presence.

I started crawling again. Finally, other hands grabbed my feet and pulled me out. I took a handful of river water and washed the mud from my eyes, my nose, my mouth.

"Anything down there, Lieutenant?" Tomasiewicz asked.

I shook my head. I felt a bond with that other human being down in that tunnel. How long had he been there, in the darkness? What was he like? Did he write poetry? Was he married? I didn't want to share him, even with my men.

Once it was known there was someone there, then the whole bureaucracy of the war would come into play—reports, body counts, publicity. This war was fought not for a hill or a bridge or a capital, or even for a cause; it was fought to keep score. I didn't want that other human being on our scorecard. I had played those games, and would play them again—but this encounter in the dark, under the earth, was part of something different. I couldn't say why then, and I'm not really sure now. But I said nothing.

Tomasiewicz gave me more C-4 and I went back into the tunnel. When I judged I was close to the large room, I set the C-4 down, and backed out until the fuse was fully extended. I pulled the fuse igniter, and scrambled out of the tunnel again. We waited for the explosion. There was only a dull pop. A dud.

We made another plastic charge and I went into the tunnel for the third time. I crawled to the old charge and carried it with me a few yards farther, to the entrance to the large chamber. I lay there quietly, hoping to feel nothing.

The presence was still there. Why hadn't he left?

"Didi!" I whispered. *"Didi mau!"* Go away! Go away fast!

I should not have warned him. He was my enemy. I was supposed to kill him. But it was not so easy. I felt a powerful connection to him.

I also knew what I had to do. I pushed the C-4 explosive into the wall of the narrow tunnel, a few feet back from the entrance to the room. After stretching out the fuse, I pulled the igniter and pushed myself out. My arms could hardly move. I had barely got past the entrance and into the clean air when the charges went off with a muffled thud.

We made our way back in silence. When we arrived, I took off my wet and filthy clothes, but I could not get the dirt of the tunnel off my skin. I sat on a C-ration box and wrote a letter home as the light faded and the night patrols prepared to go out. I described going down in the tunnel, but I said nothing about the presence I had encountered there.

I had already begun to bury him in my memory, just as I had most likely buried him in the earth.

1

WHY GO BACK?

I fought in Vietnam, but I understood little of what going to war had meant for me and for the men I fought beside. About what it meant for the men and women we fought against—our enemies—I knew nothing.

For years I was content in my ignorance. My life was in the future, not the past. For me, the war was over, or so I thought. But no one who goes to war as a young man comes home in one piece. War marks the men and women who are caught up in it for life. It visits them in the hour before sleeping; it comes to them—bringing grief, pride, shame, and even laughter—in the casual moments of everyday life. It never goes away.

When the Vietnam Veterans Memorial in Washington was dedicated in the autumn of 1982, I was absorbed in the now-forgotten crises of editing *Newsweek*. At the last minute, I decided to go to Washington for the dedication. I stood in front of the long black wall, gazing at names like Sai G. Lew, Glenn F. Cashdollar, Kenyu Shimabukuru, Famous L. Lane, Max Lieberman, Thomas L. Little Sun, Salvatore J. Piscitello, and Savas Escamillo Trevino: American names, drawn from every culture in the world—each name a father or a son, a husband or a friend who never came home. So many names—my emotions were overwhelmed.

I was surrounded by other men who stared at the names, reached out and touched them, washed them with their tears. Some of them were grandfathers now. They wore camouflage fatigues and bush hats, or nylon vests with their unit's name on the back. One man in a three-piece suit had a battered helmet on his head. Some of the men wore old uniforms wrinkled and dotted with moth holes, as if they had been pulled from the attic for this occasion. There were cowboys and union men and Hell's Angels and members of bowling teams; doctors and lawyers and diplomats and accountants; men who walked with canes and too many men in wheelchairs. Time and again I saw women point out a name to their children, then turn away, shoulders shaking, while the children carefully made a rubbing of the name.

Most of these veterans had volunteered as teenagers to fight in Vietnam. In their world, that was what patriotic Americans did. I was different. I was drafted at the age of twenty-four, and I had spent the previous three years doing my best to avoid military service. I believed it would be wrong for me to fight in Vietnam. The war would set me behind my peers, would place me in danger, and, oh yes, was immoral and all that. In 1968 I was a student at Oxford, and I watched the BBC as young Americans died in the streets of Hue during the Tet Offensive. Those boys were like the friends I had grown up with in a small town in Texas. They were fighting a war while my friends from college and I went on with our lives. I thought my country was wrong in Vietnam, but I began to suspect that I was using that conviction to excuse my selfishness and my fears.

When I came back to America from Oxford, I took my pre-induction physical in Newark. There were a hundred and fifty of us—four whites, the rest blacks. The white men carried X rays and other evidence of medical "problems" and were gone in half an hour. For the young black men, on the other hand, the Army was their escape from the Newark ghetto. They wanted in, not out. When I left Newark that day I realized I could no longer act as if my education and social class had given me special privileges. I set out to find some solution that would allow me to live—and to live with myself.

A few months later I was in the Marine Corps, preparing to study Chinese in Monterey, California, and then to serve out my three years translating documents in Washington, D.C. Instead —to my considerable surprise—when the orders were issued I was sent to Vietnam to command an infantry platoon in the foothills west of Da Nang. Throughout my year in Vietnam I kept wanting to tell my superiors—anyone—that I wasn't supposed to be there, that people like me didn't fight this kind of war. But I quickly learned just how adaptable I could be, particularly when other men wanted to kill me. The war became what I did. Instead of getting up in the morning, picking up my briefcase, and going to the law firm, I got up in the morning, picked up my rifle, and went to war. A year later, I came home.

For a while after I returned I resented my peers who had avoided the war and got on with their careers. I felt more in common with the antiwar activists who had become conscientious objectors or gone to prison. Vietnam changed them as it changed the men who fought it. But political protest simply isn't as intense as war; the stakes aren't as high. And the protesters didn't seem to suffer the great extremes of pain, belligerence, and nostalgia I kept seeing in veterans. The veterans had loved their country, and it had not loved them back.

I also didn't feel that much in common with the veterans who couldn't seem to put the war behind them. Perhaps that was because I was older than most of the men who fought the war, or because I saw less combat, or because I had done reasonably well after I came home. I didn't know the reason. I only knew that I had lost touch with the men I had fought beside and that for me the war had become a memory—some old medals and a faded bush hat I could show my son on a quiet day.

But in the presence of those names on the wall, I saw Vietnam as if I'd left it only yesterday. I remembered the first time I was under fire, the first dead man I saw, the bloody floors of medevac helicopters, the heat, the mud, the leeches, and the fear. I remembered the way we gambled for C rations, read each other's mail, sang rock-and-roll at twilight before the patrols went out. I remembered how we laughed when March went to sleep on ambush and fell into the river, and when Broman hid in a rolled-up rug while the MPs raided a house of some disrepute. I remembered how beautiful the country was, how it smelled, and how its people looked, the children with clear skin and innocent brown eyes, the old men squatting on the paddy dikes, the young women in billowing *ao dais*, graceful as deer.

I remembered slogging through the paddies in flak jackets, boots, and helmets, our bodies shot full of immunizations, our water purified. We pushed our way into mysterious villages hidden behind walls of bamboo as thick as time. At night in the mountains, I would watch the track of satellites making their way around the earth. Other Americans were on the moon, sent there by the same American can-do spirit that had sent us to Vietnam, and using the same technology that was so useless there. Those astronauts were the first men to leave the earth for another celestial body, but they knew more about the moon than we knew about Vietnam. We were strangers on our own planet, alone and afraid. We were blown about like rice husks on the wind.

All we had was each other, and the strange culture we had created. Vietnam was the first rock-and-roll war, a weird mix of sex, drugs, music, violence, and idealism that was the dark mirror of the sixties. For the men who fought there, it was also an intense sharing of comradeship and trust, a Woodstock with weapons. In spite of all the moral and political confusion, in spite of the horror and shame of war, we knew that by our own lights we had done something good, and we clung to that belief even when the war and its warriors were out of fashion.

Vietnam was a different sort of war, but not as different from other wars as many of its veterans think. The Confederate soldier also fought well in a dubious cause and lost; the British

Tommy in World War I lived and died in a war where courage and death changed nothing and only the war won. But in most wars the soldier knows where the battlefield is. In Vietnam the war was everywhere. In most wars the soldier knows who his enemy is. In Vietnam it was difficult to tell which Vietnamese were our friends and which our foes, and too easy to give up trying.

A soldier's best weapon is not his rifle but his ability to see his enemy as an abstraction and not as another human being. The very word "enemy" conveys a mental and moral power that makes war possible, even necessary. I had never known my enemy, and I wanted to. Americans died in Vietnam for more than fifteen years, longer than in the Civil War, World War I, and World War II put together. But the people on whose behalf we were fighting, and the enemies who were so much like them, remained a mystery to the end, as elusive as that presence I had encountered in a tunnel so many years ago.

I remember one night when Da Nang was attacked by rockets. For once, we had seen a flash and knew where the enemy was. For the next two hours we witnessed the terrible miracle of American firepower. The enemy was bombed by F-4s, pounded with artillery, strafed by helicopter gunships. They were surrounded by rings of napalm, dark red fire, smoke black against the moonlight. Everyone opened up on them. The earth shook, the sky was ablaze.

When the shelling stopped, there was an eerie silence. I shivered, involuntarily. I could not imagine how anyone could have survived. And then, from the center of this scorched and mutilated piece of earth, we saw another flash. They were still there, and still fighting.

Who were they? How did they keep coming back, and why? Who were those men who stormed the American embassy in Saigon, who holed up inside the Citadel in Hue, who crept forward under B-52 strikes at Khe Sanh, who crawled through our wire and into our bases, naked and covered with mud, throwing bombs into our bunkers?

They took stunning losses; hundreds of thousands—perhaps two million—of them were killed. When wounded they had the most rudimentary medical care. For rations they carried a few balls of rice. They lived in the jungle and in tunnels, and were separated from their families for ten and even twenty years. They were my enemy, we were locked in the most intimate combat, and I knew nothing about them.

As I stood mesmerized by all those names at the wall, I saw something else. I saw my own reflection. It fell across the names like a ghost.

"Why me?"

That was the question we asked ourselves each morning as we went out on patrol in Vietnam, and each evening as the night settled around our foxholes. It is the soldier's first question. What has brought me—out of all the rich possibilities of life— here, now, to this? Is this why my mother bore me, why my parents raised me, why my girlfriend grappled with me in the back seats of borrowed Chevies? Is all my youth—throwing papers after school, doing my homework, enduring two-a-day football workouts in August—is it all come to this sorry end, to die so far away in a piece of mud?

But should the young man survive, yet witness other young men shot through with bullets, blown to pieces by shrapnel, ripped up by booby traps, should he be a witness and not a victim, then he moves on to the second question:

"Why them?"

That is the survivor's question, and I asked it at the Memorial on that cloudy November morning. I was filled with a terrible sadness at all the lives lost. But beneath that sadness I felt a deep relief, tinged with guilt: my name isn't on the wall.

And then I realized that other names weren't there—the names of the men and women we fought, our enemies. They died by the hundreds of thousands, but they remain abstractions. Who knows their names?

It takes two sides to make a war, and I still knew no more about the men we fought, that other "them," than I knew about

that presence I had encountered in a tunnel. Another human
being had come to be there, through some sequence of events,
just as I had. Was it fate? Chance? I kept wondering about the
why of it. Soldiers do that. We keep wondering why we walked
over the mine that the man behind us detonated, why we moved
just before the bullet hit the paddy dike where our head had
been, why we went to war and others didn't, why we made it
home and others did not.

I realized that even though I had been a reluctant warrior the
war was still in me, like a buried piece of shrapnel working its
way to the surface. I had to try to understand what it meant to
go to war. I had to confront what it meant to me and to my men,
but that would not be enough.

I had to reach farther. I had to reach out in that tunnel and
try to touch that other man. To know myself I had to know my
enemy.

I had to go back.

And so in the autumn of 1983 I went to the United Nations and
met with the Foreign Minister of Vietnam, Nguyen Co Thach. I
explained that I wanted to do what no American veteran had
ever done: return to Vietnam and write about the people we had
fought against. For me the war had never really ended. If I could
meet my enemy in peace, perhaps it would finally be over.

He listened politely, and said that it was an intriguing idea
and he would do what he could.

For months my request was considered, appeared on the
verge of approval, then was shelved again. I made many visits
to the offices of the Vietnamese Mission to the United Nations,
which are located in a modern apartment complex built over the
East River. I had pleasant discussions about American politics
and about Vietnam with Tran Trong Khanh, the press officer,
while a portrait of Ho Chi Minh looked down on the rented
furniture, but I never seemed to come any closer to getting my

visa. Finally, I put it out of my mind and went on with other projects. And then, in September 1984, the call came.

"Mr. William?" It was Khanh. They are no better with our names than we are with theirs.

"Yes, Khanh."

"Your visa—approved."

"Great," I said, thinking that sometime around Christmas would be ideal.

"Your visa is approved if you arrive before the end of September."

"Khanh, it's September twenty-first now."

"That is correct. There is a plane from Bangkok that flies to Hanoi on Fridays. The last Friday, I believe, is the twenty-eighth."

"I'll be on it," I said.

2

MORNING IN HANOI

I arrived in Bangkok early the next week, and went directly to the Vietnamese embassy, a small villa up Wireless Road from the palatial compound of the American embassy. On my first visit a bland official insisted not only that they did not have my visa but that they had never heard of me.

The next day I was able to meet with Tran Ngoc Thach, known as "Little Thach," in deference to his boss, Foreign Minister Nguyen Co Thach. Little Thach's eyeglasses were as thick as an old Coke bottle, and made his eyes seem as big as golf balls. We spread out the documents Khanh had given me in New York. He looked through them all, nodded his head, then asked for my passport.

While he was gone I leafed through a thick book of war photographs published in Hanoi. Page after page was filled with atrocities: Americans displaying the severed ears of dead Viet Cong, Americans dragging prisoners with ropes behind half-tracks, Americans proudly standing over bodies piled high as cordwood. The Communists* had got most of them from the bodies of American soldiers who had carried the bizarre battlefield photographs in their packs as souvenirs.

I couldn't read the words that went with the photographs, but the images clearly showed what our former enemies thought of us. I began to wonder whether this trip was a good idea.

---

*The Vietnamese I met referred to themselves with pride as Communists. I use the word throughout neither to convey pride nor as a pejorative, but merely to describe them as they describe themselves.

Little Thach returned, without my passport. "We must cable Hanoi," he said. "If everything is in order, you can pick up your visa tomorrow." "But the plane leaves tomorrow." "Yes," he said. "Good day." I returned the next morning. No passport. No visa. No Little Thach. I was told to go to the airport.

I picked up my bags and headed for the airport. To my considerable relief, my visa and my passport were waiting for me. I had no trouble finding my fellow passengers. A small group of Vietnamese men and women, all dressed in simple dark shirts, trousers, and sandals, waited in a corner of the large waiting room while the brightly dressed tourists and passengers bound for other airlines swirled through the airport.

I was one of the last passengers to board the Air Vietnam twin-engine Russian turboprop. Two seats were vacant. One was next to an old woman who was picking her teeth with a knife; they were black from betel juice. The other was beside a middle-aged man reading *Paris Match*. I sat next to him. He was a physicist on his way back to Hanoi from a scientific conference. He had left the South to attend university in Hanoi in 1953, and when the Geneva conference divided Vietnam he remained in the North. For twenty-one years, he did not see his mother and father. One of his brothers was with the Viet Cong, and a sister worked for the South Vietnamese government.

"It's not an unusual story," he said. "There are thousands and thousands like it."

The plane sat on the runway. The pilot hadn't turned on the engines and we had no air. After half an hour men were wringing the sweat out of their shirts onto the floor, babies were crying, old women appeared about to faint. I asked my new acquaintance what it was like in 1975 when the war was over and he saw his mother for the first time in more than twenty years.

"It was very sad," he said. "I could see her youth had gone. The first thing she asked me was how many children I had. I told her we had one—a daughter we named Huong Tra, after two famous rivers in the South, to show our belief that Vietnam was one country. My mother said that one girl wasn't enough. So I went back to Hanoi and about a year later my wife and I had a boy.

"Everyone is happier now. No one complains about these separations, about all the people who died. The sacrifice was worth it, for our country. But it was such a price to pay. Such a high price."

His eyes grew more intense. "You know, America owes us a debt," he said. "We have had so much suffering, for so long. None of us understands why, really. We only wanted our country united and independent. What threat were we to you?"

I didn't answer. I was feeling a certain numbness of mind come over me, the same feeling I remembered from religious revivals back in Texas. It had something to do with having only complex answers to simple questions, with being unable to bring his world and mine together.

I believed that while we began the war in idealism, we prolonged it unnecessarily, and that all the money, all the tremendous effort, and all the lives had been wasted. On the other hand, I knew that my men and I had done our jobs well there, with courage and honor, and I was proud of that. It was a contradiction, and my seatmate had exposed my own inner confusion. He knew exactly where he stood. I did not. I didn't have a simple, direct answer to his simple, direct question.

I couldn't say, "We thought you were Communists," or "We wanted to stop China," or "We wanted to give the South a chance to decide for itself," or even "I don't know."

At that moment, on that plane, those answers seemed facile and hollow. But I didn't have a better answer. If I had, I probably wouldn't have been on that plane in the first place. And so I sat in silence, the sweat pouring down my face. I was thinking this was going to be a long trip.

He picked up his *Paris Match* and began leafing through it. He came across a photograph of Jane Fonda.

"Tom Hayden was here," he said, brightening. "I met him. He is a senator now, right? Do you think he will be President someday?"

That was a question I could answer. "No," I said, as the stewardess brought us some flat beer and an orange. "No, I don't think so."

We flew into Hanoi along the route the American pilots had once taken on their missions out of Takhli and Udorn in Thailand. The Plain of Jars in Laos gave way to higher mountain jungles, with only the occasional clearing to mark the presence of man. Then we banked over the last chain of mountains, and I could see, on the horizon to the north, the long line of low mountains the American pilots called Thud Ridge, after "the Thud," their nickname for the F-105 Thunderchief.

Thud Ridge pointed down the Red River directly at Hanoi, and for those pilots Thud Ridge marked the entrance to the descent into hell. Hanoi had learned to fight back; it was protected by forests of SAMs (surface-to-air missiles), walls of flak, and hornet's nests of MiG fighter planes. And the American pilots were permitted to hit only a very limited number of targets, so the North Vietnamese quickly learned all the possible bombing runs. They were never surprised. They were always ready. No pilots had ever braved such terrible defenses before. When they flew into Hanoi the skies would be ablaze. "It looked," one pilot recalled, "like the end of the world."

But as I gazed out my tiny window the only evidence I could see of this epic combat was a few bomb craters filled with water, brown pockmarks marring the green geometry of paddy and dike. Amid the paddies were typical villages, the houses jumbled tightly together and surrounded by a thick wall of bamboo. The airport was tiny and primitive. Oxen pulling carts trudged slowly around the perimeter. Men on bicycles crossed the tarmac. The passengers from my flight were the only ones in the airport; there had been only one other flight that morning, and there would be no more that day.

The arrival formalities were surprisingly casual. I had expected the police state thoroughness of East Berlin, where I once spent almost two hours crossing the border. The East German police searched my bags and examined every paper in my wallet. They spent a good five minutes peering back and forth between me and my passport, methodically checking to be sure my ears, nose, hair, and other features matched my photograph. But instead of East Germany, I got Mexico. One guard glanced at my passport while a second guard initialed my customs form and waved me through. The process took less than a minute. My bags weren't searched; in fact, I hadn't even claimed my bags when I cleared customs.

Glancing around the rapidly emptying airport, I suddenly realized that no one had come to meet me. This gave me pause, since there were no telephones, no taxis, and I knew no one in Hanoi. I had arrived at an airport other Americans had been bombing only a few years before, in the capital of my old enemies, a nation with no diplomatic or other ties to America. I was alone, and I had no idea whether a random Vietnamese would greet an American in a spirit of hospitality or of revenge.

And then, as the last passengers were leaving the airport, a young man in a white shirt, jeans, and sandals came up, introduced himself in formal English, and apologized for being late. His name was Tien and he was from the Foreign Press Center. We loaded my bags into a new Toyota and headed for Hanoi. Thousands of people crowded the road, threshing rice, fixing bicycles, driving pigs, carrying rocks, playing games, getting their hair cut—all right on the pavement. Fishermen and hunters and schoolchildren with red scarves walked on the highway. There were oxcarts and cattle and flocks of ducks, and everywhere there were bicycles: bicycles being ridden by one, two, three, four, and even five people; bicycles carrying immense loads of rice, charcoal, lumber, and livestock. There were a few trucks, but ours was the only car. If the Toyota had a brake pedal, the driver did not discover it on this particular trip. Horn blaring, we charged through this sea of activity like a shark through a school of mullet. Out in the paddies armies of peasants were plowing, weeding, planting, reaping. Children rode water buffalo or bathed in the paddies. Women bent over with their scythes, harvesting rice like insects taking tiny bites out of a huge golden cheese. Around each house dozens of people huddled, drinking tea, gesturing with cigarettes in their hands. Groups of men busied themselves around brick kilns, charcoal racks, and primitive sawmills. It was a robust, public life, with an urban intensity, like a street in New York City.

My modern eye was accustomed to the empty landscapes of America, where the sighting of a solitary figure aboard a tractor is cause for comment. But the landscape of Vietnam is preindustrial, like a painting by Breughel, filled with men, women, children, and animals occupied with the many varied tasks of bringing forth food from the earth. I could have come to these fields a thousand years before and what I saw then would be little changed now. In our hurtling car we were on some linear mission from point A to point B; we had schedules to keep. But all around us was a different world, revolving around the cycle of birth, death, and rebirth, always repeated, seldom changing, the harvest of life deeply rooted in the harvest of rice.

But then my memory intruded. The small villages, paddy dikes, and tree lines were the same as those villages, paddy dikes, and tree lines that had once meant ambushes and death. I closed my eyes and saw green tracers coming at me. I could hear the crack of rifles, the booming of artillery, the deceptive velvet *thonk* of an incoming mortar. And I could smell all those odors of war—gunpowder, excrement, decay. The soldiers on the highway wore the same uniforms the North Vietnamese soldiers had worn when we were doing our best to kill each other. When I saw them, I had to struggle with the impulse to flee, to take cover. For a brief moment I felt naked; I wanted a rifle.

I knew how brave and resourceful the North Vietnamese soldiers were. But I couldn't understand how this backward place could have taken those boys riding placidly on the backs of water buffalo and made them antiaircraft gunners and platoon commanders, could have organized them to build and maintain a vast logistic network across 1,500 miles of trackless mountains and jungle, could have found ways to defeat every new technological weapon we developed. It simply didn't compute. In combat the North Vietnamese troops had seemed so motivated, as if history were riding on their shoulders. Tiny men, no bigger than boys, they drove out a race of giants. But this pastoral, timeless landscape that had nurtured them seemed outside of history. Nothing, I thought, ever happens here.

We arrived at the Paul Doumer Bridge, and since there was no place for the pedestrians to flee, the driver mercifully slowed down the car. Beneath us the Red River flowed by in silence. Ahead I could see the lights of Hanoi. A few minutes later, we were in the city.

With its wide streets and low pink stucco buildings, its tile roofs and green shutters, Hanoi has the look of a sleepy French provincial town. Almost nothing remains of the ancient Vietnamese city the French found when they arrived, and since their departure in 1954 little seems to have been added. To visit Hanoi is like coming upon an ancient city. The people who built it have vanished, and another race inhabits the ruins. Everywhere is a sense of crumbling, as if a layer in some future archaeological dig was already prepared and the city was settling into it as rapidly as possible.

The Vietnamese themselves seem like foreigners in Hanoi. They have the air of men wearing other men's clothes. In 1946 Ho Chi Minh had no compunction about abandoning Hanoi to the French. He knew that the strength of his country was not in the cities, and even today the Vietnamese in Hanoi retain in their hearts the conviction that they really live somewhere else. I asked dozens of them where they were from: they invariably gave me the name of their native village. We stopped in front of the Thong Nhat, the Reunification Hotel. Under the French it was called the Métropole, and it was the jewel of Hanoi. Its elevators have long since quit, and the plaster is cracked and peeling. The bar sells Russian vodka, wine, and champagne, as well as Heineken and Coke. The prices of souvenirs in the window displays are listed in dollars. Only foreigners are allowed to stay there.

The man who helped me with my luggage spent several minutes manipulating the small Russian air conditioner in my room, apparently as a hint that I was to give him a tip. I pulled out a pack of cigarettes to give him a few—as I had been advised would be necessary—but he simply reached out and took the whole pack. Since a pack of American cigarettes brings approximately 240 Vietnamese dong on the black market, I had just tipped him almost the equivalent of a month's salary.

Down in the bar some Hungarians were getting drunk while Vietnamese plainclothes police watched the evening's television dramas. I had a dinner of cucumbers, tomatoes, and roast chicken in the dining room while ceiling fans slowly turned, without noticeable effect on the still, hot air. I counted five rats wandering about as I ate my dinner. A few other guests sat at the other tables, each eating quietly, in his own world. The only sign of life in the room was a table filled with some ten or twelve boisterous Russians and their wives, most of whom appeared to have borrowed their fashion ideas from Mrs. Khrushchev.

After dinner I went walking. Only the hiss of thousands of bicycle wheels on the pavement penetrated the silence. I walked two blocks and found myself at the Lake of the Returned Sword, the physical and spiritual center of Hanoi. Thousands of Vietnamese on bicycles were silently circling the lake the way American teenagers cruise a drive-in. Lovers were sitting in the shadow of fountains and clutching each other behind bushes, the sure sign of a housing shortage.

I walked for hours around the lake, down side streets, past the cathedral and many pagodas, past houses lit only by candles or small kerosene lamps, past families sleeping by their window a few feet from the street. No one approached me. I felt invisible. About midnight I returned to my hotel, and lay sweating under the hum of the Russian air conditioner. (Three miserable days later I realized that the man who had spent so long at the controls waiting for his tip had neglected to turn on the compressor.)

Hanoi wakes up to a little music-box tune played on a loudspeaker. By six o'clock in the morning the park around the lake was filled with people doing their morning exercises, either alone or in groups. Old couples batted badminton birdies back and forth, men did Tai Chi, and runners circled the lake. My running shoes were of intense interest, since the Vietnamese were jogging in shower shoes, tennis shoes, or barefoot. Some young men playing soccer invited me to come and play. After twenty minutes we took a break and one of them asked me, in formal English, "What is your nationality? Russian?"

I bent down, in the stooped posture that came to seem natural in a world where almost no one was taller than my shoulder, and told him that I was an American. His face broke into a large grin.

"Number one!" he said.

We resumed the game, and one of the Vietnamese effortlessly kicked the ball through my legs for a goal.

An Army track team was running laps around the block, past the old air-raid shelter and beneath the huge poster of Ho Chi Minh that covers the front of the national bank. They invited me to join them. I kept up for one lap, as the old couples playing badminton cheered and the young women doing their exercises stopped to watch. But then they picked up the pace for the second lap and I coasted to a stop.

After the race the young man who won picked out a bench in the center of the park and ostentatiously did ten push-ups. I quietly lowered myself to the ground and did fifty. When I got back up I was greeted with whistles and applause. And then I remembered the truth that in war the legs are far more important than the arms, and size and strength are no match for mobility and endurance. An old man invited me to join his badminton game, and so I passed my first morning in Vietnam, playing innocent games in the park.

Later that morning I went to the Foreign Press Center, which is housed in an old French villa not far from the hotel. We entered through the back gate; two women were squatting on the ground, cooking over a small charcoal brazier, and a chicken wandered around, pecking among the rocks.

In a reception room with high ceilings, French doors, and a large portrait of Ho Chi Minh, I met my guide and the men who would coordinate the details of my visit. Duong Minh was the acting director of the Foreign Press Center. A man in his late forties, he is a smooth and efficient diplomat with a wry sense of humor and a masterful command of English idiom. To my many requests to do this and that he kept responding, "Let's not get too many irons in the fire." When I worried that a certain schedule would have me miss the thirtieth anniversary of the liberation of Hanoi, he replied, "Ah, the fish is always bigger when it is in the water."

I also met Nguyen Van Thuan, one of Duong Minh's senior aides, who would do the complicated advance work on my travels in the North. He told me that he had escorted Jane Fonda and Tom Hayden through the "liberated areas" around Quang Tri, just south of the DMZ. Thuan had been a soldier during the war and had been seriously wounded in a B-52 strike. He asked me where I had fought, and when I told him, his eyes squinted and a sly smile crossed his face. "I thought I recognized you," he said, pointing at me in mock surprise.

Tien, the young man with a shy, formal manner who had met me at the airport, was also there. Tien was just out of the Army and was serving his apprenticeship at the Press Center. He was to be my assistant guide. I was then introduced to Le Luong Minh, my guide and translator, who was to be with me throughout the trip, and who would more than earn his meager salary of 280 dong a month—about $1.20 at the black-market exchange rate.*

Minh turned out to be a good traveling companion. He had spent five years at Vietnam's embassy in Canada, and so was no stranger to the ways of the West. He was well versed in political philosophy and history, and he was also a poet and a hopeless romantic. On long drives he would recite his poetry to me ("My love is like the bamboo tree . . ."), or recount Vietnamese folk tales and legends, or quote long passages about Vietnam from the memoirs of various American political figures. He was witty, entertaining, and very, very bright. He was also completely dedicated to his country and to his ideology.

In a frank display of what really mattered, I heard that first day in Hanoi nothing about Vietnam's politics or its ideology— we talked about money; specifically, we talked about dollars. I learned how much I would pay for car rental ($0.50 a kilometer), airplane tickets to Da Nang ($150) and Saigon** ($162), and the services of the Foreign Press Center ($20 a day)—cash only, no credit cards. There was a long discussion of how the hotel and the bank had different exchange rates (the black-market, or true, exchange rate was not mentioned), culminating in a tactful effort to determine if in fact I had enough cash for all this.

*The exchange rates cited are those obtaining as of November 1984.
**Since the end of the war officially, but only officially, called Ho Chi Minh City.

The dollar is king in Vietnam. My hotel in Hanoi had a special cashier, known among the guests as Madame Dollar, who handled American currency. Whenever I paid in dollars, there would be an interlude in which each bill was subjected to intense scrutiny; if it had the slightest nick or mark, it was rejected. In three different cities I had a silver certificate dollar bill turned down because the seal was blue and not green, as on the Federal Reserve notes. The bills that passed muster were each entered, by number, in special books. I half expected them to be carried away on a silk cushion.

3

"I AM NOT A RUSSIAN"

There is no loneliness like the loneliness of a traveler with nothing to do. It struck me that first Saturday in Hanoi. I spent the morning with my hosts, but nothing was scheduled for the afternoon. I had planned to take a walk, but then it began to rain. The power was off in the hotel, so I couldn't do any reading. I did not know a soul in Hanoi. I recognized the first symptoms of traveler's despair. The only cure is to make contact with someone, anyone. I phoned the British embassy and asked for the first secretary, a man whose name I had been given by a journalist in Bangkok.

"He's not here," a pleasant female voice said, with what I took to be an English accent. "He's been transferred back to England."

Any American who has spent time alone abroad knows the delight and relief of meeting someone else who speaks English. I had no idea with whom I was talking, but the fact that we *could* talk, in a country where the English language is basically useless, was a luxury I hated to give up. As fast as I could manage, I explained who I was and that I would like to talk to her, whoever she was.

After a pause, the pleasant voice said, "Well, why don't you pop over and have some tea?"

I took down the directions and hung up. I just had time to shower and change. My shower was incapable of mixing hot and cold water for any period of time, and would switch back and forth between the two at random—which made taking a shower an exercise in alertness and quick reactions. I would wash frantically as the shower switched from hot to cold, jump out, then rinse frantically as it progressed from cold to hot, jump out, and continue until I had become scalded, chilled, exhausted, or reasonably clean.

In my careful packing for the trip I prepared myself for almost everything: I had hiking boots and a sport coat, pamphlets, books, and maps, a snakebite kit and a compass, and all manner of medicine, from malaria pills to antibiotics. But I had left my raincoat and umbrella in Bangkok, and this was the rainy season. To buy a raincoat and an umbrella in Hanoi was no simple matter. I had not yet changed any dollars into dong; and besides, there were no stores—not no stores open, but no stores, period—where umbrellas were sold. The few raincoats I had seen in the market were many sizes too small.

Many people in Hanoi relied on large plastic trash bags— which were much too valuable to be used for trash, and besides, there was no trash. The concept of garbage is unknown: nothing is thrown away. Everything is used and reused. Hanoi is a city without trash cans. And so the Vietnamese cut out holes in trash bags for the arms and head, and wear them in the rain. This was a practical solution, but somehow I did not feel it would be appropriate for me to be wandering the streets of Hanoi dressed in a garbage bag.

Fortunately, the British embassy, according to my directions, was just down the street and around the corner, so I picked up a newspaper I had brought from Thailand, put it over my head, and ran out into the monsoons of Asia. I raced down the street, leaping over huge puddles, made the turn as directed, and began peering through sheets of rain for the address. After many blocks I found the number—attached to a crumbling stucco shed where a few chickens, some dogs, and two old men huddled under the eaves.

"This British embassy?" I yelled.

They shook their heads, smiled, and shrugged.

"Embassy? Britain? England? Here? Near here?"

No response. I switched to my primitive Vietnamese. They

came to the gate. One pointed down the street. The other pointed up. They began to argue.

I pushed on. For almost an hour I wandered the streets of Hanoi. I gave up looking for the embassy, but then I discovered I didn't know how to get back to my hotel. I asked directions again and again. Not a single cyclo (bicycle cab) driver was to be found. The newspaper had long since dissolved. My shirt and trousers were plastered to my skin; my shoes were soaked and squishy. Water streamed down my face. I was cold and shivering. Curious eyes stared at me from darkened doorways. Finally I turned down yet another narrow street and saw the lake at the end of the block. From there I made it back to the hotel.

After another sporting attempt at a shower, I changed into dry clothes and called the British embassy to apologize for not arriving. No one answered. After many tries, I finally got through and explained to the pleasant voice what had happened. She promised to send her husband around at once in the Land-Rover, and fifteen minutes later Mike Wood, the first secretary, and his wife, Wendy, were offering me tea and cake in their apartment above the embassy. After an afternoon of pleasant conversation, they invited me to join them later at the Swedish disco.

The phrase "Swedish disco" had a certain, well, ring to it for me, perhaps because a Swedish disco, while an attractive proposition anywhere in the world, ranked high on my list of amenities I did not expect to find in Hanoi. I returned to the hotel for a quick meal before it was time to go. Sitting alone at my table in the dining room, I ordered curry and opened a book. But I had barely begun to eat when two of the Russian tourists appeared at my table, gesturing at me with one finger and then shaking their heads. At first I wondered if perhaps I wasn't supposed to be eating curry after all, but then I realized they were trying to tell me I shouldn't be eating alone. So I picked up my curry and went over to their table, feeling bad that I had judged these Russians so quickly.

Through a creative effort at translation, based on consulting their Russian-Vietnamese dictionary and my English-Vietnamese one, I pieced together that they were film producers from Leningrad. From their appearance that conclusion seemed implausible. I tried again, and it turned out they were factory workers from Irkutsk whose superb performance at producing something—what, I couldn't quite decipher—had earned them a vacation to the various pleasure spots in their sister socialist country.

They all seemed middle-aged but they were a hardy lot, friendly and expansive, perhaps in part because of the alarming, and growing, collection of empty vodka bottles on the table. Immediately they began offering me shots of Russian vodka, with lemonade chasers. I thanked them profusely, picked up my shot glass, and took a sip.

"*Nyet! Nyet!*" The whole table joined the chorus, even the women, who laughed and grasped their bellies. The man across from me demonstrated. He held the shot glass up at eye level, said something in Russian, and then downed it in a gulp. He then looked me in the eye, turned the shot glass upside down, and banged it down on the table.

This was serious business. I couldn't let my country down. We proceeded to down shots of vodka in progressively dramatic fashion. After half an hour the women dropped out and went back to lemonade. I kept going, eyeball to eyeball with the Soviets, none of us blinking—except to rub an occasional tear from our eyes, since the vodka had a bite like a breath of Siberian winter. I'd found a word for "friendship," so we were all drinking to *obshchestvo*.

The men then pretended to be firing guns and said, "*No khorosho, no khorosho.*" I took this to mean that war was no good, no good at all. I agreed, and drank again to *obshchestvo*.

The men laughed, patted me on the back, and then made little jokes to each other and laughed some more. After a feeble stab at discussing politics, we traded information on children and finally on ourselves. To my surprise, the Russians weren't middle-aged at all. They were mostly in their twenties; the oldest, who I had assumed was fifty or so, was in fact thirty-two. I was so incredulous he finally showed me his passport. I could almost have been their father. Life in Siberia—and all the vodka —must do that.

I was rescued by a young Swiss named Michael Flaks, the representative of the International Committee of the Red Cross in Hanoi. Wendy Wood had told him to bring me to the Swedish disco. As I left, shakily, with him, the Russians were opening another bottle. "*Obshchestvo! Obshchestvo!*" they called out to me, waving and squinting through the smoke from the cigarettes they held constantly in their lips. I smiled and waved back.

I asked Michael what the Vietnamese really thought of the Russians.

"They hate them," he replied.

It was too early for the Swedish disco, so we drove to "the French restaurant," one of two private restaurants serving foreigners in Hanoi. The streets were dark and deserted. On the way Michael taught me the single most useful Vietnamese phrase I learned, the one that brought smiles and affection and opened doors for me everywhere: *"Khong phai Lien Xo"*—"I am not a Russian."

We parked on a quiet street near the cathedral. From nowhere two boys appeared, and Michael gave them each a cigarette to watch the car. After a few minutes of searching we found the alley that led to the restaurant. The alley was dark and wet, and smelled of charcoal, urine, and garbage. We walked up some narrow stairs. Off the landing two old women watched a few pots bubble over charcoal fires. The owner, a tall, thin young man, greeted Michael, and showed us to one of a handful of tables on a balcony. A dog was asleep under my chair, and moved lazily away when I sat down. The only other diners were two young Vietnamese. The woman was dressed in neatly pressed blue jeans, high heels, and a silk blouse. Her hair was swept back from her face, and she was wearing makeup.

"Two or three years ago you would never have seen a girl like that in Hanoi," Michael whispered to me. "And you would never have seen young Vietnamese here. No one had any money, and there was nothing to buy. Now look. She's beautiful, don't you agree?"

Yes, I did. We ordered turtle soup and a bottle of French wine. Michael told me a story that was making the rounds of the Europeans in Hanoi: One night some diplomats went to the French restaurant and were offered a particularly fine bottle of wine. Word spread quickly, and soon everyone in the foreign community was talking about what a superb wine list the little restaurant suddenly had. Finally, the news reached the French ambassador, who went to the restaurant, ordered a bottle of wine—and discovered it had been stolen from his own cellar.

Through the window across the courtyard I could see a woman sewing by the light of a kerosene lantern; behind her, on the wall, was a large poster of Pope John Paul II. The owner sat down with us as I tried in vain to separate turtle meat from turtle bones. He said that he had been "too thin" to fight in the war. His biggest problem running the restaurant was "high taxes." Because of the "taxes," a euphemism for a combination of legitimate taxes and bribes, the restaurants are open only a few days a week and at odd hours.

We drove to a place I'll call the drugstore and sat down. A pleasant young man came up and asked if I wanted to change any money. I jumped at the opportunity. The bank was closed over the weekend and I had been unable to buy any dong. Since I would have a light schedule on Sunday, I could do some shopping. I only had a hundred-dollar bill, which he took away at once. I had thought to change $20 at most. The rate was 240 dong to the dollar, so for my $100 I was given 24,000 dong—neatly packed in twenty-four sets of ten 100-dong bills, with the tenth bill folded across the other nine. The whole stack was wrapped in newspaper and was thicker than the Manhattan phone book.

I felt very rich. I also felt a bit guilty. It was a tiny crime, this changing of money on the black market; and, given an official exchange rate of only 12 dong to the dollar, it was a crime routinely committed by virtually every foreigner in Hanoi. But, as it happened, my feeling of wealth was soon to diminish, while the guilt was to grow, and grow, and grow.

From the drugstore we drove to a small café near the lake. At the bar sat two Eastern Europeans with drug-blasted eyes, numbly pouring brandy from a paper sack into their coffee and looking sullen. The place was packed with *bo doi,* young Vietnamese soldiers in the uniform of my former enemies. Rock music blared from the speakers. The room was filled with smoke.

"Lien Xo," the soldier next to me said to his friend, gesturing at us in disgust. "Russian."

"Khong phai Lien Xo," I said, testing my new phrase. "I am not a Russian."

"East German?" he asked in Vietnamese, suspiciously.

"Khong. Toi nguoi My," I said. "No, I'm an American." At once everyone's eyes lit up and their faces broke out in big grins. The soldiers kept patting me on the back and putting their arms around me. They insisted I try on their helmets and caps with red stars on them. A boy of about ten came in selling black-market cigarettes, and Michael bought a pack of 555s and passed them around.

They kept repeating the same phrases: "America number one! Russia number ten!"; and "America *tot! Tot lam!"* ("America good! Very good!") They brought us glass after glass of strong, very sweet coffee, and wouldn't let us pay for anything. One soldier who was sitting with a striking young woman in jeans brought her over, motioned the soldier sitting next to me away, and sat her down beside me. She smiled and began to move against me in time to the music.

"Where you stay?" she yelled in my ear, in English.

"Thong Nhat," I replied.

She made a face. "No good. Too many police. We go in your car."

This was all a little more than I had counted on. Only a few hours before, I had been feeling the onset of traveler's loneliness; now I had overload.

"Uh, we've got to go," I said, looking for Michael.

"Okay," the young woman said, squeezing my arm. "You come here tomorrow." She took my arm and pointed at eight on my watch. "Come this time. We go someplace."

As we left, the soldiers cheered. "America number one!"

In the car I tried to explain to Michael how the scene in the café—the easy camaraderie of soldiers, the sharing of women, the smiles and slogans about America being number one—reminded me of the war. Then, even when the smiles and slogans were sincere, they were often a prelude to some scam. Anyone who truly took them seriously was likely to be parted from his money and occasionally from his life.

But these young soldiers in Hanoi seemed to be different. Their reaction to me lacked the edge of patronizing cynicism I would have expected. They had nothing to gain from their kindness to me. I was, officially, an imperialist. Hundreds of thousands of their friends and relatives had died fighting me and men like me only a decade before. My comrades had bombed their homes and their cities into rubble. Yet I was encountering what appeared to be sincere good feeling—even admiration.

I remained skeptical. I had, after all, been to Vietnam before, and I was learning again its lesson, the lesson that had first been driven home fifteen years earlier at the Marine Corps basic school in Quantico, Virginia: Reality is elusive; beware appearances. Hanoi appeared to be regimented, puritan, alien, the Marxist triumph of idea over matter. And it was. But something else was struggling to emerge from the tight cocoon of ideology and self-denial. It was something modern, something Western. And it was something I, as an American, stood for.

4

MIAs AND
THE SWEDISH DISCO

After this unexpected glimpse into the underside of Hanoi, the long-awaited Swedish disco was a disappointment. It was on the grounds of the Swedish embassy, behind the residences, the tennis courts, and the pool. The disco had been shipped prefabricated from Sweden, which was easy to believe, since it was paneled like a large sauna and felt like one inside. It came fully equipped with a sound system and strobe lights, all powered by the embassy's own generator.

On the crowded dance floor Swedish lumberjacks danced with Malaysian office workers. Central European women, cigarettes dangling from their mouths, caught German men in the gaze of their sexy, hooded eyes. One young UN worker in a Rod Stewart haircut was dancing with exaggerated poses and expressions, but the rest were vintage square. The effect was like a parody of a foreign students' prom. Because I was new, several people came up to introduce themselves. A young European tried to fill me in on the various dancers.

"That's the daughter of an Eastern European ambassador—she's the hottest number in Hanoi. And that's Hilda—she's an au pair. All the Swedish lumberjacks are finding excuses to come to Hanoi to see her. And that's Samantha—she works at a UN agency. She's fairly new. We're all after her, but unfortunately Jason over there seems to have the inside track . . ."

At that point, when I was beginning to feel I would need a program to keep everyone straight, Wendy Wood came up with a man in tow. He was Michel Amiot, a Canadian who ran the United Nations family-planning program in Vietnam.

"Wendy told me who you were," he said. "I'm amazed they let an American who fought here into Vietnam."

"So am I," I said as we shouted over a Japanese version of "Maniac."

"Will they let you go to the South?" he asked me.

"That's my whole plan," I said.

"You won't believe it. Along the beach at Da Nang you can still see the old bunkers. The graffiti are still there. 'Get some!' 'Born to raise hell.' It's eerie. And then Khe Sanh. You drive down Route 9 and it's so peaceful—there's even a farm at Khe Sanh now. But then, just off the road, over the hills, there's all this *stuff*—old guns, tanks, barbed wire—just rusting away."

"That's exactly what I've come to see," I told him. I asked him why he had wanted to go to Khe Sanh.

"Are you kidding? Khe Sanh. Hue. Dak To. Dong Ha. I know those places like I know Canada. I grew up watching the war on Canadian television. Two of my cousins were killed in Vietnam. I felt like I knew it already, from television. It's in my blood. It's my youth, it's everything."

We talked for a while about the various bases he'd seen, and then I made my farewells. It had been a long day.

"There's one other thing," he said as we stood on the landing. "I think I've seen some Americans."

A chill went through me. "What?"

"Some Americans. I think I've seen some Americans."

"Where? How many? When? How could you tell?"

"Let's not talk about it here," he said with a laugh. "It will keep till tomorrow. I'll come by the hotel and we'll have a coffee."

• • •

That night the nagging thought came back: *There may still be somebody here.* Did we commit the soldier's cardinal sin? Did we leave our comrades on the battlefield? The images of the real POWs—the bowing, the postures of submission, the stories of torture—hardly help. Are Americans, our comrades, still undergoing such treatment? The thought nests in our guilt, preys on our minds. It goes to the heart of a soldier's deepest fear—of being abandoned, of being alone.

Most men who have been in combat are no strangers to visions. I saw my share—of my own death, many times over; of being wounded, in countless ways; and, most terrifying, of being captured. We are on patrol in the mountains. Suddenly, an ambush. The air is filled with screams and yelling, with the deafening sounds of automatic weapons, the explosions of grenades. We counterattack, charging through the ambush—the shortest way out of the killing zone is right through the guns. It is chaos. I am hit in the leg.

But then the reaction force swoops in, beats back the attackers, and begins to evacuate the wounded. Before they can reach me I hear the soft *thonk* of mortars announcing a counterattack. I am alone, too close to the enemy to make a sound. Small men in green uniforms and flat helmets stream by me carrying AK-47s. One of them sees me.

Or I am walking sweep on a patrol, following the back of the man in front of me, when, in an instant, I round a bend and he is gone. I am alone, in the hostile jungle. Suddenly, all around me I hear the chatter of strange voices. The bushes begin to move.

Or I am flying in the front seat of an F-4, headed into the heavy flak of Pack VI or the Ho Chi Minh Trail. My panel flashes: a SAM is locked on me! I dive to evade it, and as I scream past the deadly flying telephone pole the gunners on the ground open up with their 57mm cannon. I'm hit and the plane is in flames. I float down alone, unnoticed and unmarked, except by the watching eyes of the enemy on the ground.

During the war these scenes, and others, constantly unreeled in my mind. Years later, early in the morning of sleepless nights, or when I'm relaxed and least expecting it, they still come back. I was lucky. I made it home. But I could have been a POW; they were my comrades. I did not believe that any POWs were left alive in Vietnam, but I wasn't going to miss the opportunity to try to make certain.

While I was in Bangkok, I arranged an appointment with the Joint Casualty Resolution Center (JCRC), which since 1973 has been in charge of investigating whether any American POWs are still held in Vietnam. I spoke to Lieutenant Colonel Paul Mather, an Air Force officer who has been negotiating with the Vietnamese off and on for more than ten years.

"I really don't know if there is anyone still there," Mather told me. "There's so much mythology about this, but we have no proof, none, that would stand up in court. We hear hundreds of secondhand accounts up in the refugee camps, but we never seem to be able to find the guy who'll say, 'I'm the one who saw them.' Still, the possibility is there. We operate on the assumption that 'it could be.' "

I asked for a case that I could try to track down when I was in Vietnam, so Mather gave me the details on one of the MIAs from the area where I fought. His name was Donald Sparks, a PFC from Iowa who was in the Americal Division. He disappeared in the Que Son Mountains southwest of Da Nang on June 7, 1969, a few months before I arrived.

Sparks's story read like one of my own nightmares. His unit was ambushed and he was wounded, but his comrades were taking heavy fire and couldn't reach him. The next day they returned, but found no trace of him. Months later, a Viet Cong deserter turned up with a letter supposedly written by Sparks in captivity. According to later reports, Sparks eventually died, but his name was not on the list of POWs who had died in captivity furnished by the Viet Cong after the Paris agreement in 1973. Since his death has yet to be confirmed, he is listed as an MIA and his case is still open.

Mather and I got down on our knees, spread out a map, and

located the coordinates where Sparks had disappeared. I made
a copy of the map, marked the spot, and took it with me to
Vietnam. I had hopes that I could get to the general area and ask
about him. I didn't expect to find anything after so many years,
but I wanted to do something.

As I left the office of the JCRC, it struck me that the vast
American war effort had come down to this: a few small offices
in Bangkok and Honolulu, where a few men come to work each
day, open up some files, and try to tie up the loose ends while
everyone else gets on with their ambitions and their careers.
There is something almost religious about the work of the JCRC:
each day they attempt to raise Lazarus from the dead. But their
operation is a backwater, and the POWs have become one of
those emotional, symbolic issues, like the fate of the Kurds or
the Baltic nations, that cool diplomats would just as soon have
go away.

I waited impatiently for Michel Amiot to arrive at the Thong
Nhat. Finally, he appeared, and we ordered glasses of sweet
coffee. Not wanting to appear too eager, I began the conversation with some small talk about life in Hanoi. As it usually did,
the conversation soon arrived at the black market.

"Have you changed money?" Michel asked me.

"Why?" I asked, cautiously.

"Oh, nothing, really," he said. "Just be careful. They don't
like it. But it's okay for us—we have immunity. You don't. And
whatever you do, don't change money at the drugstore. It's full
of informers."

I had, of course, changed money there the night before. I had
a sinking feeling, but I tried to put it aside: the POWs were far
more important than my little transgression, even if I was suddenly not so sure how little it had been. I asked Michel about the
Americans he said he had seen.

There were two. The first, a black woman, was in my opinion

most likely a métis fathered by a French African soldier, not
unlike women I was to see later around Saigon. But the second
fascinated me.

"I was in a boat," Michel said. "I had just opened a small
clinic in Song Be, and I saw this blond-haired white man in shorts
walking along the bank of the river. At first I thought he was
a Russian, but he was muttering to himself, and as I came closer
I could hear that he was muttering in English."

I was on the edge of my chair. He took a sip of his coffee. "So
what happened?" I asked.

"When he saw me watching him," he said, "he ducked into
some bushes and was gone."

I was to hear several other stories like this one: of a black
man wandering about near the Swedish paper mill in Vinh Phu
north of Hanoi, also muttering to himself in English; of the
UNICEF man digging water wells in the Mekong Delta south of
Saigon who has seen "a few" Americans wandering through the
villages. But as intriguing as these stories were, they all fell
within the category of men who might simply have stayed behind. Of the almost three million Americans who served in Vietnam, a handful might have decided to remain there—for any of
a number of reasons. During the war Americans lived underground in the back alleys of Saigon and Da Nang—junkies and
hustlers and black-market kings acting out some Conrad fantasy
that could have kept right on going after the fall of Saigon.
Others may have fallen in love and moved into hamlets with their
new families, disappearing beneath the opaque surface of Asia.
But I would have to wait until I went South to pursue those
possibilities. I hoped that once there I would be able not only to
check on Sparks but also to ask former Viet Cong about American prisoners.

Later that afternoon Tien took me to the military museum,
where we watched a sand-table reenactment of the Viet Minh's

decisive defeat of the French at the battle of Dien Bien Phu. Artillery thundered, planes took off and landed, a ring of red lights advanced inexorably on the French positions, and, finally, a Viet Minh flag popped up over the French headquarters. I was sitting next to a delegation of Cubans, so the narration was in Spanish. The Vietnamese officer escorting the Cubans was very nervous about my being there, but he relaxed as soon as Tien gave him a few of my American cigarettes.

When we went outside, crowds of children followed me as I examined the displays of Vietnamese artillery and antiaircraft weapons and the ruins of American planes. From the museum Tien and I walked to an exhibit of political cartoons, most of which consisted of crude attacks on Ronald Reagan. Again, I was followed by crowds of young people, who seemed to view the cartoons, and their message, with absolute equanimity. Each time I stopped in front of a cartoon—of the Statue of Liberty, say, brandishing MX missiles—my entourage would wait until I had moved on, then stare for long moments at the cartoon that had caught my eye, trying to figure out what I had found of interest. As at the military museum, the crowds seemed to make no connection whatsoever between me and the Americans in the propaganda cartoons. It was as if that was one reality, I was another; one official, the other personal, and there was no reason to confuse the two.

On the way to the Hanoi art museum we walked by a large compound that took up an entire city block. It was surrounded by a tall green wall. Children played in a small park in its shadow.

"What's that?" I asked Tien.

"It's the prison," he said. "What you called the Hanoi Hilton."

"Why don't you ask if I can go in and talk to the American POWs who are still there?" I asked him.

"Very good joke," he said. "There are no POWs there, of course. Now the prison is for black-market criminals—smugglers and money changers."

I looked at the wall and I remembered all those stories the POWs had told of their years of captivity. They had been in the Hanoi Hilton for serving their country—for their courage. I could be imprisoned there for changing money—for my greed. For the rest of the walk I was preoccupied with how to hide my Vietnamese currency—but there was so much of it. They *knew*, I thought. At any moment I could hear that knock on the door. The Hanoi Hilton: forever.

We wandered through the art museum, a spacious, all but deserted colonial building. More than two-thirds of the art is directly related to the wars of Vietnam—the *dau tranh*, or struggle, which defines the Vietnamese people. They struggle, therefore they exist. I was struck by one painting, the depiction of an early patriot being tortured by Chinese soldiers. They have surrounded him and are piercing his body with a dozen lances. But he lies on his side, smiling, oblivious to the pain.

This theme of martyrdom is everywhere. The pantheon of Vietnam is filled with heroes who were tortured, dismembered, and executed for the fatherland. The Vietnamese are intensely conscious of the atrocities committed against them. They have even built "atrocity museums" not unlike the Holocaust memorials in Jerusalem and Dachau, filled with photographs of Vietnamese maimed and killed during the war.

"We have suffered much," Tien told me as I gazed at the painting—but he smiled as he said it.

5

DRAGONS FROM THE SKY

I expected Hanoi to have the devastated look of East Berlin in the 1950s. Instead, the city seemed to have been sleeping soundly since the French left in 1954. The only visible damage is from decay and neglect. I asked to visit some of the areas that had been the most heavily bombed. Minh, Tien, and I set off in a black Russian Volga—the driver apologized for not being able to bring the Toyota. We drove to the outskirts of the city, to Kham Thien Street, which supposedly had been obliterated by B-52s during the Christmas bombing of 1972. We were looking for a monument to the bombing, but even after driving up and down the busy street we could not find it.

Tien got out of the car and began asking directions from women selling fruit and cigarettes on the sidewalks and from the men repairing bicycles on the corners. No luck. We were on Kham Thien Street, but the bombing might as well have happened on another planet. Finally we found our destination—a small monument in a tiny park. An old man stood by the gate, silently watching us. At the curb, a cyclo driver in shorts and shower shoes stood smoking a cigarette, waiting for his next fare. And beyond him, in the street, the great flow of humanity rushed on. The physical wound had long since healed.

"I know it looks like it was never bombed," Minh said as we drove away. "But I was here the next day. There was rubble everywhere. Bodies were lying in the street. But I never come by here now. That is all in the past."

While I was in Hanoi the city celebrated the thirtieth anniversary of its liberation from the French, but the French hardly merited a mention. The themes were the glorious war against the Americans and the imminent threat of the Chinese. For the parade the faded murals of tiny peasant girls capturing American pilots were refurbished. The city was presented a medal for its "heroic struggle" against the American bombers.

Vietnam was not one war but many wars. The war in the Mekong Delta was not like the war in the Highlands or the war near the DMZ. The war of 1965–68 was different from the war of 1969–72. The infantry had several wars, so did the pilots, and the vast majority of men in the rear had no war at all. I was an infantry officer, so I knew little of the long air war against the North. But in Hanoi and elsewhere in North Vietnam it was the air war that mattered.

The air war is known in Vietnam as the Dien Bien Phu of the Air—the decisive battle of the war. It is to Vietnam what the Battle of Britain is to the English—"their finest hour," when the home front became the battleground and every citizen became a soldier. The air war was the American equivalent of the Communists' Tet Offensive of 1968: both were dramatic assaults on the civilian population's will to fight. But while the Tet Offensive successfully separated the American people from the war effort and left the American soldiers orphans, the bombing had exactly the opposite effect. "You brought the war home to every house in the North," one general told me, "and you made the people even more united with the fighters in the South."

Many American advocates of air power now believe we failed because we did not bomb enough. We dribbled away our vastly superior power by bombing predictable targets in a sporadic, purposeless way, and we needlessly avoided crucial targets, such as the MiG airfields, which were off limits until 1967. (That produced the absurdity of American pilots cruising over the air base at Phuc Yen hoping a MiG would take off. In the air, when it was dangerous and could shoot down American planes, it was a fair target. On the ground, when it could be easily destroyed, it was off limits.)

The result, this theory goes, is that we allowed North Vietnam to believe it had survived the worst we could deliver. Wayne W. Thompson, who is writing the official Air Force history of the air war over North Vietnam, told me that if we had bombed Hanoi with B-52s in 1965 and 1966 the way we did in 1972, "their will to fight could have been seriously crippled." This argument is backed up by the POWs, who reported that their captors were panicked in 1972 by the Christmas bombing. Certainly it has its advocates among the men who fought the air war, who by and large do not have pleasant memories of how they were forced to take great risks, under complex restrictions, for dubious ends.

But the argument has one basic flaw: whatever the price of winning the war—twenty more years of fighting, another million dead, the destruction of Hanoi—the North Vietnamese were willing to pay it. That was the fallacy at the core of our strategy of graduated response; gradually increasing the pain does not necessarily affect an opponent who is willing to lose everything.

The theory of limited war, developed as a way of avoiding total war among nuclear powers, does not apply to countries who don't have nuclear weapons. North Vietnam had no threshold it would not cross. The war was a battle to the death. They had no compunction about mobilizing their whole society, about absorbing terrible destruction, about losing hundreds of thousands of lives. For them this wasn't limited war—it was total war.

I asked to see Bach Mai Hospital, which for years was on the visitors' circuit. Jane Fonda went to Bach Mai after it was bombed, and my hosts proudly displayed pictures of her standing in the rubble. I spoke with Dr. Tran Do Trinh, the deputy director of the hospital, a kindly, competent-looking man, accompanied by a young resident who also exuded confidence and purpose.

"It was the night before Christmas in 1972," Dr. Trinh told me. "Most of the hospital had been evacuated, but about two hundred and fifty of us were still here. We lived and worked in the basement under the cardiology building. I was teaching a class in mitral stenosis when we heard the antiaircraft guns begin to fire, and then the terrible noise of the B-52 bombs coming toward us like thunder. I kept lecturing—there was nothing else to do—and the students were taking notes when the bombs hit. The whole shelter collapsed. The living were mixed in with the dead. We had to break through the rubble that covered the entrances with our bare hands to bring out the wounded. It took almost two weeks to extricate all the dead, and the smell of bodies filled the hospital. Three of the students in my lecture were killed."

He shrugged, then smiled. "But war is war. We must go on."

I spent some time touring the hospital. The doctors were particularly proud of some new ultrasound machinery from the Netherlands. "We found the first three cases of left atrial myxoma in Vietnam with this machine," one doctor said. But to a casual visitor the benefits of medical technology seemed woefully uneven. Exotic heart diseases were being discovered, but there was no blood in the lab refrigerator. The patients lay two to a bed, in their own clothes. Several pieces of simple equipment stood dusty and inoperable. Supply cabinets and medicine lockers were empty.

"For two hours each day the power goes out," one Vietnamese doctor told me. "That's bad enough, but what's worse is we never know which two hours. It could be anytime—right in the middle of surgery." The hospital was a paradigm of Vietnam today: a place of stoic suffering and maddening bureaucracy, where almost nothing works—except the people, and they work incredibly hard. How, I kept thinking, did they ever get organized to win the war? How did they do it?

The hospital was rebuilt ten years ago, but by some principle of socialist decay looks to be of the same colonial vintage as all other buildings in Hanoi. If I hadn't seen the photographs, I would never have known it had been bombed.

On the way back to the hotel, the driver told stories of driving a truck down the Ho Chi Minh Trail, dodging F-4s during the day and AC-130 gunships at night. He spent eight years in Tay Ninh province, transporting rice the Viet Cong bought from South Vietnamese troops who wanted to make a nice profit on their supplies and so sold them to their enemy. "Driving in Hanoi is harder," he said, leaning on the horn.

Back at the hotel I had lunch with Judith Ladinsky, a Wisconsin gynecologist who works closely with Vietnamese hospitals, and Steve Atwood, a New York pediatrician who had been invited by Ladinsky to teach a course in pediatric care. At our table, to the best of my knowledge, were 30 percent of all the Americans in Vietnam. (In addition to two other Americans in Ladinsky's group, there was a professor doing research on Vietnamese women, a wife of a UN official, and three American immigration officials conducting interviews in Saigon.) Ladinsky is a robust woman from Madison, who met Dr. Ton That Tung, Vietnam's expert on Agent Orange, after the war. Dr. Tung invited her to Vietnam in 1980. Since then she has been back many times. She is dedicated, tireless, realistic.

"I don't feel any guilt about being an American or about the war," she said as we sat with Steve in my hotel room. Then the power went out and we were plunged into darkness. I took notes by candlelight. "That's not why I'm here. I'm here because you can't be a doctor and see such needless suffering and not want to help."

Steve Atwood told me that "visiting a Vietnamese hospital is like walking into a nineteenth-century medical textbook. The incidence of neonatal tetanus, dengue fever, rheumatic heart disease, parasites, diphtheria, polio, measles, diarrheal dehydration, it just goes on and on—they're all way above normal. These people, particularly the children, are dying from diseases we know how to cure."

He paused and looked away. When he looked back at me, his voice was filled with emotion. "I've been a doctor for a long time. I trained myself to disassociate from suffering. I thought I was hardened to everything. But the first time I went into a ward in Vietnam I was overcome with emotion, with the tragedy of it. I burst into tears."

Judith Ladinsky nodded her head. "I felt the same way. There's such an urgency here. If we could get them the supplies and the drugs, they could save thousands of lives. The doctors here are sophisticated, they work very hard, but they need so much. At the same time, doctors here are like doctors anywhere —they can't help being mesmerized by the latest technology. I'd been waiting for them to ask me for a CAT scanner—in January, they did. I just laughed.

"For what one sophisticated machine costs they could buy the drugs that would cure thousands of cases of curable diseases. They need X-ray film, gowns, blood storage—the basics. What an American hospital throws away in a day could keep Bach Mai Hospital going for a month."

When American officers and military historians talk about the Christmas bombing, they insist that it hit "the same old targets" on the outskirts of Hanoi. The difference, said Air Force historian Wayne Thompson, is that "B-52s are less accurate than the fighter-bombers we had used before. With the heavy flak and the SAMs coming up at them they could be considerably off target. It's a great credit to the B-52 crews that there were as few civilian casualties as there were. The Vietnamese say they had about twelve hundred dead. But that figure proves our point, not theirs. Just one of those B-52 raids could have killed thousands of civilians, if that had been our goal. We could have firebombed, we could have hit the center of the city. If we had wanted to destroy Hanoi, we could have wiped it out."

Having been to Hanoi, I believe he is right. But the detached way Americans discuss the air war comes from having dropped the bombs; the Vietnamese have a very different view. To them, the B-52 was not simply a bigger and more terrible bomber. It was like the death star, flying so high and so fast as to be beyond sight, beyond hearing, beyond humanity. It attacked without warning. One moment all was peaceful, the next the ground erupted as if the very earth was exploding.

To have been through a B-52 attack was the ultimate experience of the war. To have been wounded by a B-52 was a special badge of honor. Again and again the men and women I interviewed would pause in the midst of their memories, and their eyes would take on a faraway gaze. I came to expect that they were about to tell me of the time they were hit by a B-52. It was the one moment they would never forget.

"The first time we shot down a B-52," a general who had been in charge of air defenses told me, "was during the Christmas bombing. It was an occasion of great celebration throughout the country." The most popular exhibit at the war museum in Hanoi is the wreckage of a B-52, which lies in the courtyard beneath a MiG-21. Children gather around it throughout the day, staring, as if transfixed by the body of a slain beast.

In Hanoi, near the military museum, is the village of Ngoc Ha, which for generations has supplied many of the flowers sold in markets and on street corners. The city has long since grown around it, but Ngoc Ha is still a quiet island of rural Vietnam. There are no roads in the village, so Minh and I left our car at a small café and entered on foot. Open sewers ran alongside the pathways. We were looking for a pond by a school, and an old man standing in a doorway gave us directions.

He had been in Ngoc Ha in 1972, just before Christmas, when President Nixon, pursuing his "madman" negotiating ploy, sent waves of B-52s against Hanoi after the Paris peace talks had broken off in stalemate. The raids were the heaviest of the war, sortie after sortie, each plane carrying thirty tons of bombs. When it was over, the Vietnamese came back to the table and the agreement was signed.

Fifteen of these huge planes were shot down during the Christmas bombing. And on the night of December 23, one of them fell with a terrible roar into this village. The old man remembered it well.

"It was like nothing I had ever heard," he said. "Like the scream of a great dragon."

Minh and I made our way down the winding paths, stumbling in our city shoes. Finally we rounded a corner and saw a paddy filled with lotus plants, where a boy was methodically fishing and a woman waded slowly, up to her chest, picking blossoms. To the right were some simple flower nurseries made of woven bamboo, a pond, and, across the pond, a school where children were running and playing in a small yard. I could hear their voices reflected over the water. And in the middle of the pond, like a giant sail, was the tail of a B-52. The American star was faded but still visible. It reminded me of the pagoda that seems to float in the middle of the Lake of the Returned Sword, as if this were the lake of the returned plane.

I stopped two children and asked them what that was, sticking out of their pond. One, a young girl, simply shrugged her shoulders and said, "It's the B-52," as if she were saying it was the banyan tree. They were not born when it came screaming out of the night sky; it is not an object of intense fascination like the B-52 at the war museum. It is simply part of their landscape.

The Vietnamese pilots who flew against the American planes did not have an enviable mission, but they managed to shoot down one American plane for every two they lost—far better than the 1-to-20 ratio in the Korean War. There were a number of reasons for their relative success. The American F-4 and F-105 pilots were flying multipurpose fighter-bombers, while the MiG-21 was a simple, unsophisticated fighter that did its job surpassingly well. Colonel Jack Broughton, who led the Air Force's famous demonstration team, the Thunderbirds, before flying F-105s in Vietnam, wrote: "I don't think you will find a truly professional fighter pilot who would not sell his front seat in hell to be a MiG squadron commander in the face of an American fighter-bomber attack."

The MiG pilots also had a superb radar system which could vector them onto the path of American planes almost from the moment they left their bases in Thailand, Da Nang, or the South China Sea. And the Vietnamese were defending their homeland, which gave them not only a psychological boost but many options for quick landings and evasions. The MiGs were part of one of the most effective systems of antiaircraft weapons ever assembled. The American pilots never knew what to expect; in Broughton's words, they never knew whether they were going to have "a SAM day" or a "MiG day."

Few of the American pilots had great respect for the "MiG drivers," Broughton included. Many of the Vietnamese pilots had been pulled off the backs of buffalo and taught how to fly. Most of them learned to fly a jet before they learned to drive a car. But they did manage to shoot down 92 American planes, and three of them are said to have shot down B-52s, an achievement that made them heroes of the fatherland, more or less a cross between Luke Skywalker and St. George. (The Americans contend that all the B-52s lost were shot down by SAMs, since the MiGs did not carry rockets powerful enough to down one of the huge bombers.)

I asked to see one of those pilots, Pham Tuan, who went on to orbit the earth with Soviet cosmonauts. I met him one evening at the Press Center. He is tall and husky for a Vietnamese, with

an easy, athletic manner and enthusiasm I can only describe as
All-American. Pham Tuan grew up riding water buffalo in Thai
Binh province. When the Americans bombed the North for the
first time in 1964, he was seventeen. He volunteered at once and
was made a mechanic.

I asked him how the Air Force knew he could be a pilot. He
told me that the primary qualification of a fighter pilot is the
correct "will." His answer was classic Marxism, the same view
of the importance of thought over matter which had Chinese
pilots reading the quotations of Chairman Mao in order to learn
to fly a jet. Pham Tuan evidently had the correct will, and a good
deal more. After two years' training in the Soviet Union he
returned to fly MiG-21s against the American Air Force. It was
not a job that was considered to have much longevity.

"I and my comrades," he said, "had been assured that we
might have to sacrifice ourselves. I expected to be killed. The
first time I flew I couldn't find your planes. Where were they?
I was so nervous. But once I saw an American plane, I had only
one thought—to kill him. Our tactics were to make one pass,
very close, then hit with the first shot. That's what happened
with the B-52. It was December 27, 1972, the tenth night of the
Christmas bombing. Two of us took off against the B-52s. I
spotted one, got very close, then let go my rockets. My hatred,
my training, my ideology helped my aim be true. That plane was
bombing my homeland. I was glad when I hit it."

Today Pham Tuan is a colonel. He is married to an Army
doctor who spent many years in Quang Nam province, where I
fought. His trip into space has left him with some of the same
near-mystic views of our tiny planet and the futility of its wars
that some American astronauts have described. What he would
like, more than anything, is to fly into space on a joint mission
with Americans, with the sort of men he once took such joy in
shooting down.

• • •

One of the most famous photographs of the war appeared on a 1972 cover of *Life* magazine: a young girl is running down a road naked, her body still smoldering from napalm, her face twisted in shock and pain. That girl's name is Phan Thi Kim Phuuc, and she is twenty-one now. She was passing through Hanoi on her way home to Saigon from West Germany, where she underwent operations to improve the use of her left arm. I had lunch with her at the Thong Nhat. She was dressed in a modish running suit, the sleeves pulled down over her wrists, even though the day was hot.

We were joined by Thuan from the Press Center, who wore a short-sleeved shirt that left the scars on his hands and wrists clearly visible. He had been hit by a bomb from a B-52 near Dong Ha. At first, I simply did not know what to say to Kim Phuuc, so I asked Thuan about his scars.

"Two of the three B-52s missed me, but the third blasted me out of my shelter," he said. "Many of my comrades were killed. I was in a field hospital for almost four months. They thought I was going to die, but I did not—or perhaps that is debatable." He talked matter-of-factly, as if he were discussing someone else.

His immediate concern was working out my trip to Da Nang. He wanted me to drive, which cost more money. I wanted to fly, which was quicker—and cheaper. My money was disappearing at an alarming rate. This was not a problem susceptible to casual solution. I couldn't write a check—there are no banks. Vietnam doesn't honor American Express cards. First I had felt guilty over changing money on the black market; now I was getting anxious about running out of money entirely. But I didn't want to tell Thuan I couldn't afford the car, so we argued politely about the relative merits of flying versus driving.

Finally, we agreed that I would fly if reservations could be obtained. That mundane detail settled, I turned to Kim Phuuc and she told me her story. She has a round, open face, a shy smile, and a soft, quiet voice. Her hands moved with small, contained gestures as she talked.

"My village was bombed and we went to the pagoda for shelter. Usually the American planes dropped explosives, but on that day they dropped napalm. There was fire everywhere. We ran out of fear—there was something on us that burned so terribly, but we couldn't get it off. When I got to the bridge where the picture was taken I had run almost a kilometer. My clothes were burned off. I was exhausted and terrified. My aunt and my two cousins were with me, but they all died. I couldn't understand why they would do such a terrible thing to us. But I was very small then." She was nine years old.

For more than a year she was in a hospital in Saigon. Then she went back to her village in Tay Ninh and resumed her studies. A few years ago, in response to an inquiry from a German magazine, Thuan tried to find her. After a year of sending cables and visiting the area, he succeeded. "She was very surprised people would be interested in her," he said. "Many people were killed and injured during the war. She didn't feel that different from everyone else."

"I saw that picture and I began to cry," she said, rubbing her arm. "How could that be me? How could that happen to me? It seemed so unfair."

She was only a young girl when she was napalmed—a child, an innocent. Her tragedy mirrored the tragedy of the war, which made civilians combatants and their homes battlefields. Kim Phuuc lived in an area controlled by the Viet Cong, not far from the jungle headquarters of the entire Communist operation in the South. She lived in enemy territory. Unfortunately, the enemy army and leadership were invisible, while the villages were all too visible. A photographer happened to witness her moment of pain and made her a symbol of war's suffering, while hundreds of thousands of others on both sides, Thuan at our table included, who were bombed, napalmed, or otherwise killed or wounded, suffered alone and unnoticed.

Kim Phuuc has two dreams: one is to become a doctor, but she isn't sure she will succeed, because her hand isn't always steady and her stamina is poor. "But I have to keep trying," she says, rubbing her arm. The other dream is not so lofty, but more poignant. "I would like, just once," she said, "to be able to wear a short-sleeved shirt."

As I listened to her story I realized how the terrible epiphanies of one person's life, those moments when the torturer tightens the rope for the final time, when the canisters of napalm slowly tumble toward the pagoda filled with children, always happen while other people are going about their daily routines, in the many unremembered details of ordinary life. All that link the two worlds are memory and imagination, but even they can't really bridge the chasm.

While marines died in Hue and while villagers were huddling in their bunkers at My Lai, I was breakfasting on smoked kippers and studying for my exams in the green elegance of Oxford. Throughout the war hundreds of American pilots lay inside the cells of the Hanoi Hilton and the Zoo, their bodies covered with sores, while outside children played on the small playground in the shadow of the walls. Kim Phuuc was fleeing down Route 1, her body smoldering from napalm, on a day when I was back in Texas, working with happy intensity to begin my own magazine.

That sudden shock—how could this be happening to me?—is what transforms our fearful fantasies—the endless sleepless imaginings of walking into an ambush, of stepping on a booby trap, of being shot down over North Vietnam—into intense reality. It is that first flash of the AK-47, before you even hear the sound, that first tug of the trip wire on your ankle, that terrible moment when the footfall on a creaky stairs late at night turns out to be real, and worse even than your fears. How could this —this terrible thing—be happening, here, now, to me?

6

THE TARGETS OF
NAM DINH

Early the next morning we were to leave Hanoi for the Red River Delta, the agricultural heart of the North, a densely populated area south of Hanoi that was heavily bombed during the war. In the hotel restaurant I pondered what to have for breakfast. The waitresses all wore white cotton shirts, black silk trousers, and what seemed to be standard-issue platform shoes with extremely high heels. As a result, orders were taken and delivered in a sort of slow-motion ballet, made more dramatic by the fact that three of the five women were in advanced stages of pregnancy, and their balance aboard these clunky shoes was problematic at best.

Phuong, the most phlegmatic of the waitresses, gave me a small example of how a Vietnamese with authority views the principle of consumer choice.

"Today, *pho*," she said, *pho* being noodle soup.

"Okay," I say, "I'll have *pho* and maybe an omelette."

"No omelette. *Pho*."

"Okay, I'll have *pho* and toast."

"No toast. *Pho*," she said.

"Okay, I think I'll just have *pho*."

"You want *pho*, then?"

"Uh, yeah, *pho* sounds great."

After a big bowl of *pho* we were on our way out of Hanoi,

past the railroad yards with their museum-piece engines and railroad cars and down the dusty, pitted surface of Route 1, the national highway. As we drove, Minh told me the story of the Lake of the Returned Sword. "In the fifteenth century our country was oppressed by the Chinese aggressors. A young man named Le Loi was sitting by the lake, saddened by our loss of freedom and independence, when a giant turtle appeared. The turtle gave him a magic sword, and with that sword he drove out the Chinese aggressors and united the country."

I kept my eyes on Minh. I could not bear to look out the windshield as the car roared through the dense thicket of humanity. Minh shouted to make himself heard above the constant blaring of the horn.

"And then, when we were free, Le Loi went back to the lake and returned the sword to the turtle. So we call it the Lake of the Returned Sword."

I asked him if everyone knew this story.

"Of course. Any child could tell it to you."

After a few moments, Minh spoke again. "You know," he said, "in September of 1969, when Uncle Ho died, we were all filled with gloom. But then we had heavy rains, and a giant turtle came out of the lake. Many people saw it as an omen—that in spite of Ho's death we would prevail."

America is a nation of immigrants, of starting over, of moving on. We are built on the future. Vietnam is anchored in the past. Its people share a history that goes back thousands of years, a continuing drama in which they all play a part and in which the stories of the American war, and its heroes, are woven into the fabric, told by grandmothers to their grandchildren in the huts at night. The century is immaterial: time does not diminish the immediacy of the stories. Le Loi is recalled almost as vividly as Ho Chi Minh. I had always wondered why the Vietnamese we fought were so determined. I had found one answer: they are intoxicated by their history and its heroes. They have a sense of destiny.

The recounting of these stories is like an Apostles' Creed, an affirmation of faith in something beyond the individual. By contrast, not once did I hear a Vietnamese quote Marx. In Vietnam it has always been difficult to tell where the nationalist ends and the Communist begins, or which is the tail and which is the dog. I tried to imagine a dedicated Communist—which Minh clearly is—telling me such a story in, say, East Germany, and simply could not.

I don't mean to suggest that Vietnam is free of ideology; on the contrary, it is ruled by it in the most narrow, mind-dulling way. Ministers and peasants mouth the same phrases, trot out the same jargon. If it is decided that the Chinese are waging a "multifaceted war of aggression," then everyone who refers to the Chinese, anywhere in Vietnam, condemns their "multifaceted war of aggression."

Language, as the tool of thought, is controlled by the state. And this uniformity of thought, from common legends to common phrases, was crucial to beating the French and outlasting the Americans. Few societies have been so tightly organized. To an American, this uniformity is frightening. But like patience, which has also served the Vietnamese well, it has the virtue of success.

The day before, I had met with Do Xuan Oanh, one of Vietnam's leading experts on America. Xuan Oanh was born in a reed boat off the coast of Haiphong and grew up working in a coal mine. Without formal education, he became a witty and cultivated poet and translator. He also became a dedicated revolutionary and the escort for visiting Americans like Tom Hayden and Susan Sontag, who found him charming and sympathetic. While he was stationed at the North Vietnamese embassy in Paris he dealt with the wives of American POWs, who found him cold and merciless, the very symbol of the enemy.

Xuan Oanh and I had a long, meandering discussion in English about Marxism and Vietnamese culture. "I became a Communist in 1941," he said, "when I was sixteen. We believed then that we had to proceed in stages. We had to develop very detailed, very concrete knowledge about the people, then carry out our propaganda, then organize the masses. We learned that we first had to appeal to the great spirit of nationalism among our people. Then we could teach our ideology. We taught the people that they were being exploited by the French—that was an easy matter. Then we taught them they were being exploited by their landlords—that was more difficult.

"We built upon the people's belief in the extended family. Ho Chi Minh became 'Bac Ho'—Uncle Ho. He had no children of his own—we were all his nieces and nephews. The country was united by that sense of family. Our fighting units were organized in cells of three. They all pledged to care for each other's wife and children. They lived and died together—like brothers.

"This country is very hard to understand. The French were here a hundred years and they never understood. One clue is that every Vietnamese is a poet. We are very cautious on the outside, very romantic on the inside. The secret to Vietnam is in the songs of the buffalo boys."

I asked him what those songs were like. He thought for a minute.

"They are like," he said, "Bob Dylan's 'Subterranean Homesick Blues.' "

That stopped me.

"Do you read many American writers?" I asked him.

"Of course. I translated *Huckleberry Finn* while American bombs were falling on Hanoi. American writers are very popular with us."

"Which ones are your favorites?"

"Oh, I have several," he said. "Ernest Hemingway, Jack London, Mark Twain, Sidney Sheldon."

"Sidney Sheldon?" I asked.

"Yes, he is very good on the excesses of capitalism."

• • •

For almost two hours the car had been bouncing, swaying, swerving, lurching. Minh began to feel carsick. In my toilet bag I had a supply of medicines comparable to the stock of an average Vietnamese district hospital. I offered Minh a Dramamine. We stopped at a little roadside stand for some tea to wash down the pill. Outside of Hanoi, dysentery and diarrhea are endemic. The driver performed a ritual before we ate or drank anything: he would order tea, then take the kettle of hot water and rinse off all the dishes, the glasses, and the chopsticks; only then would we have our tea or our food. The driver bought each of us one local cigarette. We sat on tiny stools, smoking and sipping tea. I hadn't smoked cigarettes since I had fought here; now that I was back, I had started again.

"Was there any bombing here?" I asked the old woman who ran the stand. Several children came up, one with sores in his scalp. She began to talk rapidly. Minh was looking quite green, but, gamely doing his duty, he translated.

"Sure, a lot. There"—she pointed to a small bridge—"and there and there. A pellet bomb fell behind this hut. Many people were injured."

The woman smiled at me through teeth stained with betel nut. Her eyes never left my face. The children crowded around, staring at me with such intensity that I finally locked eyes with one of them, a boy of about twelve, and stared back. To my surprise, he didn't even blink. I was looking right into his eyes, but he obviously did not believe I saw him. I was not another human being looking back at him, but a different creature. They were as unaware of my watching them as they would be of a monkey looking back at them in a zoo.

We paid the old woman a few dong for the tea and cigarettes. I asked if she or the children had ever seen an American before.

"No, never," they said, all speaking at once. As we left, the children reached out to touch me.

• • •

Nam Dinh, a provincial capital in the Red River Delta, is a textile town of about 200,000 people. During the war it was an obligatory stop for American visitors like Harrison Salisbury and Tom Hayden, who were brought here to see the effects of American bombing. I was to meet with members of the People's Committee, which runs the city out of the old French administrative offices.

I was escorted to a room with red walls and a large chrome bust of Ho Chi Minh. The table was neatly set with a white tablecloth and red flowers, along with a bowl of fruit and teacups at each place. The vice-president of the People's Committee and two of his assistants, one man and one woman, took their seats opposite me, and the meeting began with the customary formalities of exchanging cigarettes. They offered Dien Bien Phu and Flying A from Laos. I had bought Salems in Bangkok, since they had been the favorite cigarette of the South Vietnamese soldiers. The Salems were accepted only out of politeness. The cigarette of choice in the North is 555, a British make popularly believed to have been Uncle Ho's favorite cigarette.

The vice-president began by saying he wished to discuss "U.S. war crimes," which they have methodically divided into two files—"the crimes of the LBJ period" and "the crimes of the Nixon period." The files looked worn, and for good reason. The reports of the early bombings were, word for word, the same reports Harrison Salisbury had heard when he visited Nam Dinh for the *New York Times* in December 1966.

Under the benign smile of the vice-president, the male assistant began reading from the LBJ file. "During this period Nam Dinh was bombed one hundred seventy-eight times, including seventy-two night raids. Sixty percent of the houses were destroyed."

Then he went on to describe particular raids, of which I give one example. "On April 14, 1966, there was a raid against Hang Thao Street at six-thirty in the morning. The children were getting ready for school. Many of them were among the forty-nine people killed; two hundred forty homes were destroyed."

Then they showed me photographs of victims of the bombings. As I looked at the pictures I was conscious that they were expecting me to say something. I put the photographs down, looked up, and said the only thing I could think to say: "I'm sorry this happened. I really am."

The woman began to discuss the Nixon file: "This was worse than before. On June 12, 1972, we had the largest raid on Nam Dinh—twenty-four planes attacked at three p.m. They dropped one hundred and two bombs. Many people died."

I asked how she knew it was precisely 102 bombs; weren't they hard to count?

"We kept precise records," she said. "Also, our spotters had to mark each bomb as it fell. If it did not explode, we would dig it up, defuse it, and put it to the service of the fatherland."

I asked her opinion of why we had bombed here.

"The Americans would bomb whenever they saw lights or crowds or any sign of life. There were no military targets. It was just psychological. They destroyed dormitories, schools, kindergartens, hospitals. The children had to go to school underground. They wore hats and coats of thickly woven rice straw for protection against the pellet bombs and the shrapnel. We used to say that some people were killed twice—they were wounded in one raid, carried to a hospital, and then killed when the hospital was bombed."

The vice-president, who had very delicate features and graying hair, interrupted. "You know, we were bombed so much people began to be bored with it. The siren would go off and we wouldn't want to get out of bed or leave the table and go into the shelter. Not again, we'd think, not down into that hole again."

The woman resumed her litany of bombings, of families killed, of children mutilated. Finally I asked her if she felt any hatred for the Americans.

"How could we not feel hatred?" she said, but her voice stayed calm. "Many of us lost our whole families, our whole happiness."

The vice-president interrupted again. "When you fight you

must have hatred. Whenever we needed someone for a dangerous mission, or if in the South we needed a suicide fighter, so
many people wanted to sacrifice for the fatherland that we had
to hold elections to see who would get to do it. When we were
bombed, the best time to shoot down the planes was when they
dived, but it was also the most dangerous. It took hatred to keep
us out there, our fingers on the trigger, as the jets came in with
their guns blazing."

By this point his dark eyes were flashing and his nostrils
were flared. But then he paused, took a breath, and returned to
the Party line. "Of course, we did not feel hatred for the American people, or even for the pilots. We saw them as victims. Our
hatred was for the imperialists who forced this war on all of us."

I asked to see the street that had been bombed, so we piled
into the Volga and drove to a residential street near the river.
On one side was a warren of houses, on the other a Catholic
church. An old man described the morning of the bombing, in
almost the same words I had heard earlier, while the usual
crowds of curious children surrounded us. As he gestured to
show the flight of the bombs, I looked around and could see
nothing but a city at peace. There was no evidence of destruction. The children were too young to have witnessed it. The past
had been swallowed up. Only the memories remained.

That night we had a lavish ceremonial meal, with a dozen or
more dishes, countless toasts, and many stories. I asked my
hosts why they had fought so long. The two men had both joined
the Viet Minh to fight the French in the 1940s, when they were
teenagers.

"The French laughed at us," the vice-president said. "They
saw us only as little people with primitive weapons. You made
the same mistake. That's why your strategy of strategic hamlets
failed. You didn't understand why the people would hate you for
making them leave their native village, for destroying that core
of themselves. Every street corner of his village, every rice
paddy, is almost holy to a Vietnamese. He holds them in his heart

through years of absence, he writes poems about them at the front, he sings his comrades songs about them. I was away from my home fighting for more than ten years. I know this to be true."

As it happens, Nam Dinh was not exactly the helpless provincial town inexplicably attacked by American bombers as my hosts would have had me believe. In Nam Dinh were gasoline-storage tanks, textile plants, heavy equipment, and some of the most powerful antiaircraft batteries outside of Hanoi and Haiphong. And the Vietnamese were fighting total war; they were not naïve or burdened with scruples. Among the American pilots the stories were legend of the bombing run that missed its target by mistake, struck a school or a dormitory, and then the school or dormitory blew up with huge secondary explosions. The Vietnamese had kept their ammunition there.

Colonel Jack Broughton described the dilemma of "a war that pits high-speed fighters against small, hard-to-see targets in the middle of politically sensitive areas." According to Broughton, "The first time [the American pilot] goes to Viet Tri, he will be shot at from the 'hospital,' but this is of no import. He must be accurate." Broughton recalled several pilots who should have jettisoned their bombs "but did not because the bombs would not have gone on their target. They got killed for their trouble." Not one to mince words, Broughton referred to the whole system as "sick." That the bombing campaign worked at all, he said, was only because of "the guts and dedication of the drivers."

I would not be surprised if an American pilot with some bombs left over, after long periods of being shot at from prohibited targets, would just decide that he was tired of seeing his buddies shot down by antiaircraft guns on the roof of a hospital or from SAM sites parked next to a church. And the bombs—understandably, in the pilot's view, this being a war—would fall, just as they fell on the monastery at Monte Cassino during World War II, when the Germans put a gun emplacement in its shadow.

My hosts brushed these points aside. "We would not have had antiaircraft sites if you had not been bombing us," one of them said. "We were not attacking your planes on their carriers. You were attacking us. We had to protect ourselves."

I kept asking what it was like to be out in the open, firing at the diving planes. I was invariably told that it was terrible but necessary. But I came to believe that the men and women who did it in truth loved it—it was a great sport, like skeet shooting, but better, since the target shot back. They talked about shooting down American planes with a sort of childlike wonder. Why, they kept asking, would those pilots keep flying into the flak and the SAMs? There was admiration in their voices, but pity too.

That night the power went out, and I stood on the balcony looking over a city wreathed in the smoke from countless tiny fires. In the park below, thousands of people strolled in the darkness, past dozens of women selling rice cakes, fruit, cigarettes, dried squid, and nuts from little baskets lit by candles, each candle winking along the path. Inside each home a kerosene lantern burned. Food was being cooked over fires of charcoal, wood chips, or even sugarcane husks and buffalo dung.

I tried to imagine what it would have been like here when the bombers came in from the *Enterprise* or the *Constellation*— the air-raid siren, the frantic search for children, the agonizing wait in the shelters, the terror as the bombs hit. And then I realized that if the bombs had struck the power plant the night would have been no different than it was as I stood there in darkness. In America the loss of electricity would bring chaos. Everything would stop, as it did in New York City in 1965. In Vietnam the power went out everywhere I went, and nothing, absolutely nothing, changed.

It was as if the incredible technology of our air power, with its smart bombs and guidance systems and supersonic aircraft, required a comparable technology to attack. Against an enemy whose only technology was his antiaircraft batteries and SAM missiles, our power was nullified. We could inflict suffering, but not damage.

A rooster crowed all night, and I tossed and turned under my mosquito netting. My room had a tub, a bidet, a toilet, and a sink —but no running water. I had the same experience in government buildings all over the North. Plumbing fixtures were like mute relics of a lost civilization. In a way it was a humbling experience—the nation which put men on the moon was defeated by a nation where deputy ministers use outdoor privies.

I washed from a pitcher of water left in the bidet. In the morning I discovered that the pomegranate on my bedside table had been eaten by rats. I was ushered into the banquet room, where I had a breakfast of fried eggs, cold bread, coffee: what they think Americans like. In the next room, Minh, the driver, and the young women who worked in the hotel were all eating bowls of *pho*. I could hear them laughing.

7

PHAT DIEM:
"EVERYONE DID IT"

After breakfast we drove to Phat Diem, one of the bishoprics of North Vietnam and the site of its most famous church. A scene from Graham Greene's *The Quiet American* takes place there. Fowler, the British journalist, is trapped in Phat Diem during a Viet Minh raid in the early 1950s. Pyle, the quiet American, comes down from Nam Dinh in a boat, through the Viet Minh lines, to tell Fowler, man to man, that he is in love with Fowler's mistress.

"I never knew a man," Fowler muses, in a line that would describe America's entire history in Vietnam, "who had better motives for all the trouble he caused."

As we drove we passed long lines of women working on the railroad bed. Their faces were wreathed in checked scarves. They worked two to a shovel. One held the handle and filled the shovel; the other lifted it with a rope tied to the blade. Up and down, up and down they dug, like metronomes. They were still at it, holding the same rhythm, when we returned eight hours later.

Down the road we encountered a long line of bicycles, each loaded with five large sacks of rice. The bicycles had a bamboo pole attached to the seat and another to the handlebars, so that a man walking alongside the loaded bicycle could maneuver it. The men were moving their huge loads at a rolling, steady gait; their eyes seemed focused on some distant point on the horizon.

This is how they built the Ho Chi Minh Trail, I thought, this is how they repaired the bombing damage, and this is how they moved all those supplies south—shovel by shovel, bag by bag, little by little.

On the way Minh talked about growing up farther south along the coast, in Thanh Hoa. Minh's village was next to the Ham Rong Bridge, the Dragon's Jaw, probably the most fiercely attacked target of the entire war. When the war began, Minh moved to Hanoi to live with his father, but in 1967, like most schoolchildren in the city, he was evacuated back to his native village to avoid the bombing. "It was much worse in my village than in Hanoi," Minh said, laughing. "I couldn't win."

At the Dragon's Jaw, on April 4, 1965, four MiG-17s burst through the clouds and shot down two F-105s—the first attack by MiGs on American planes in the war. Between 1965 and 1968 this bridge withstood everything American air power threw against it; to the North Vietnamese, it became a symbol of their nation's toughness and determination. When the bombing of the North resumed in 1972, Air Force F-4s using newly developed laser-guided bombs dropped the western span and then Navy F-4s from the carrier *America* sent the center span into the river.

"I remember when the bridge was finally destroyed," Minh said. "It was for all of us like losing an old friend, a valiant fighter."

"So the bombing finally was a success, after all?" I asked him.

"Not exactly," he said with a smile. "You lost so many planes, so many brave pilots against that one bridge. And we had already built a pontoon bridge. When you destroyed the Dragon's Jaw, we simply went around it. No problem."

At Phat Diem I was introduced to the vice-chairman of the People's Committee, Madame Yu Thi Que. She was dressed in the traditional black trousers and white shirt, and her hair was pulled back with a ribbon. She was a beautiful woman in her forties, formal and earnest, but with a trace of a smile that did not hide a toughness underneath. While an older man brought out tea, rice wine, and grapefruit I asked Madame Que about herself. During the war her husband was away, fighting in the South, for nine years.

"How often was he able to return home on leave?" I asked her.

She smiled at me. "Never," she replied, "not until the war was over."

"So did you hear from him? Did he send you many letters?"

"I received one letter," she said. "I remember it well. It was in 1969."

I tried to absorb what I had just been told. Her husband was away, at war, for nine years, more than twice as long as American soldiers who fought in World War II from Pearl Harbor to V-J Day. And she received one letter!

All I could think to say was "That seems like a long, long time."

"Everyone did it," she replied with a shrug.

I asked Madame Que to tell me about Phat Diem during the war.

"We were bombed fiercely from 1965 to 1968," she said, "and again in 1972. We didn't have a siren, the way they did in Nam Dinh. We only had a bell in a tower. I can still hear it ringing, ringing, ringing. They tried to hit the transportation systems at first, but never did. Instead they bombed the marketplace, pagodas, schools, neighborhoods. They wanted to destroy our morale, but they only made us stronger. And then in 1972 they bombed the church and the monastery. Many people were killed. And they also used the priests here."

"They did what?"

"They used the priests. They made the priests work for the CIA. It was just like in 1954, when the CIA had the priests tell all the people that Catholics would be killed. They said God had gone South. A million people fled—many from this district. And they used them again during the American war."

"You mean the priests were spies?" I asked.

"Most were Vietnamese first and Catholics second. But we knew that some were working for the United States."

"What happened to them?" I asked.

She smiled and offered me another grapefruit.

Phat Diem is the heart of Catholicism in North Vietnam. Driving from Nam Dinh, I was never out of sight of a church. I had the driver stop the car at one point, and when I got out and looked around I could see no fewer than four church steeples rising out of the paddies. But many of the churches were boarded shut, and others were in ruins. In some of the Catholic cemeteries weeds covered the gravestones.

The regime rigidly limits the ordination of priests. No new bishops can be named without its approval. The cardinal of Vietnam is under virtual house arrest in Hanoi. In the area of Phat Diem today, for some 70,000 Catholics, there are only five priests. But Madame Que is a Catholic herself, and was quick to say that "patriotic Catholics" had no difficulty with their worship. "We have regular mass," she assured me, "and on feast days the churches are overflowing."

We walked to the cathedral compound, a group of many buildings that covered about fifteen acres. The cathedral doors were locked, so Madame Que sent an assistant to find a key. While we waited, we walked around the grounds and she pointed out the damaged areas: "The cathedral was bombed August 15, 1972. The entire west wall was destroyed. So were three of the convents and two of the schools."

I would not have thought, except for some slight change in shade of the stones around the church, that it had ever been bombed. The nearby chapels were a different story. They stood roofless, the steel skeletons of their rafters exposed to the sky. Walls were reduced to rubble. It looked like Coventry. In my four weeks in Vietnam, this was the only place where I could actually see the effects of bombing.

At last the key appeared, and we returned to the cathedral, a striking building almost as long as a football field. Its architecture is whimsically eclectic, as if pagodas had been dropped onto the towers of a Gothic church. French missionaries built the cathedral in the nineteenth century from local wood, and it has a handmade, crafted feeling. The pillars were carved from massive trees; above the altar hung the portraits of some thirty missionaries and priests—most of them European.

The cathedral stands in the paddies of Phat Diem like a spaceship from another planet. Its religion is Western, but the Catholics of Phat Diem have been baptized for generations; their faith belongs to them as much as it does to the Italians or the Irish or the Poles. Silent, the cathedral echoed with their voices. Empty, it seemed filled with their humanity. Faith is not an easy matter here. As in early Rome, as in Eastern Europe, to be a Christian in Vietnam today is an act of courage. Inside the cathedral I felt, for the first time in my trip, at home.

Lunch was another ceremonial meal. Spread across the table were pork heart, roast chicken, bacon, beef, meatball soup, pickles, rice, fish sauce, and a huge carp. After dinner the night before in Nam Dinh, I had asked Minh if there was a tactful way to let it be known I did not require such treatment. He smiled. "Do not be embarrassed," he said. "They want to do it. You are an excuse for us all to eat well for a change."

Madame Que told me that during the war, with so many men gone, the women took over the running of the district. Then she went on to echo the same theme of the power of place that I heard in Nam Dinh. "We drew our strength from our neighbors, from our village. You have to understand our love of ancestors and our village to know how we fought so well."

But the South Vietnamese forces loved their villages too, I said.

"They were corrupted," she replied. "You corrupted them with your money and your values."

Having spent the day asking them questions, I paused during the meal and asked if there was anything they would like to know about the United States. There was a long moment of silence.

"We know about unemployment," Madame Que said, finally, "and of course every Vietnamese knows about the hero Morrison."* Her voice faded, and she reached for some more carp. I wondered what I could tell them. Should I say that in America people are constantly moving, that few stay near where they were born, that freedom means you go looking for opportunity and happiness wherever you can find it? Should I say that in America even poor people have refrigerators and televisions and cars, items not one person in the entire district of Phat Diem possesses? Should I say that Vietnamese who came to America after the war with nothing now own fishing boats, stores, homes, and cars; that their children attend Stanford and Harvard?

I was beginning to feel that nostalgia for a simpler life that is a disease of the West. Those who have much yearn for the purity of having little. The thought keeps nagging away: is less really more? When my grandparents talked of the hardships of the Depression there was always nostalgia in their voices, a longing for days when no one had much of anything, when life was simpler, purer. In the countryside of Vietnam I was seeing a way of life rooted in the land and in the harvest of rice. The tasks of survival required everyone, from children to old people, to help his neighbor, for without common effort the village would not survive.

*On November 9, 1965, Norman Morrison, a Quaker, went to the Pentagon with his baby daughter, Emily. As workers streamed out of the entrance, he put the baby down, doused himself with gasoline, and burned himself to death. Now almost no one in America knows his name, but in Vietnam it is on everyone's lips. Morrison and Nguyen Van Troi, who was shot after an unsuccessful attempt to assassinate Secretary of Defense Robert McNamara in 1966, are the two most revered heroes of the war. Xuan Oanh's most famous poem is titled "Emily."

When I returned from this trip to Vietnam, I met Emily, who is now a student at New York University and wants to be an actress. At first, she resented what her father did. "I couldn't understand why he would leave us," she said. "For a long time I didn't want to know about Vietnam, since it had taken my father away. But now I understand that he did what he did because he loved me, because he loved everyone. I want to know more about Vietnam and about the war now—because it changed me forever."

At the same time, I knew that no one was more entrepreneurial than a peasant. The studies of Vietnamese villages
by Gerald Hickey and Samuel Popkin confirm the point: even
though he is tied to a community, the peasant constantly
seeks to better his own position. During the war there were
few rewards for such effort. But today that was changing. The
countryside was better off than the cities because peasants
were allowed to produce for themselves and to sell to others.
And some peasants were earning enough to begin to buy
things.

What would happen, I asked Madame Que, if someone in the
village made enough money to buy a television? She replied
without hesitation: "Everyone in the village would go to their
home to watch it."

I wasn't so sure about that, or if the village sense of community could survive material progress. And I knew I was being
shown the idealized village life. But even so, life in these villages
stood in such contrast to what I knew in American cities that I
could not help but feel a silent rebuke: to my selfishness, to my
materialism, to my ambitions, to my rootlessness. But I was no
longer a part of the land, of the cycle of the harvest. The seasons
no longer measured my life. I had eaten of the forbidden fruit,
and I could never go back.

As we were about to leave Phat Diem, I spoke to the older man
who had fetched the key to the cathedral. "I was in the war," he
said. "I was wounded twice at Dong Ha." He pulled up his
trouser leg to show me the scar on his leg, and then pulled up
his shirt to exhibit a long scar on his back.

"How were the American soldiers?" I asked, expecting
the usual answer, that we fought bravely but in the wrong
cause.

He looked at me, knowing I had fought near where he had
been wounded. "Not good. Not good," he said. "They were

afraid to leave their bases, their helicopters, their artillery. They weren't brave."

Only the night before I had felt guilt about the bombing of Nam Dinh, had in fact apologized, for all the good it would do. But at this moment I felt something entirely different.

"Got you, though, didn't we?" I thought to myself.

8

MARCHING OFF TO WAR

On the way back to Hanoi I kept thinking of Madame Que, whose separation of nine years from her husband barely merited a mention. I heard similar stories many times on this trip. The war was everything. Nothing, absolutely nothing, was more important. Still, I imagine that a young man leaving the rice fields of Phat Diem to fight the terrible Americans would have been as apprehensive as I was when I was sent to Vietnam to fight a mysterious enemy. But I doubt that he would have gone to war feeling as alone and as confused about why he was going as I had. In his world, everyone did it.

In my world, it seemed that no one was doing it. When I flew to Los Angeles on the way to Vietnam in 1969, I was the only passenger in uniform. I had been taken from my family and my career. I had been taught a set of values at odds with the values of civilized society: I had been taught to kill, and to lead other men in killing. And I was being sent to kill, and possibly be killed, in the name of a society which seemed not to care why or even that I was going.

I knew, from books, that once in battle a man fought for his comrades. That powerful emotion, writ large, is patriotism. It makes war intelligible for the citizen soldier: he is killing and risking being killed for his country, for ancestors long dead and for children yet born. To be a patriot is to believe that there are values greater than one's own life, values worth dying for.

But in Vietnam patriotism rang hollow. What was at stake, if anything? And if great values were at stake, why did everyone on the plane, why did all my parents' friends, why did all *my* friends, want of the war only to forget it? To those in power, Vietnam was not a war; it was a policy. It was an item on the agenda. It was not even, technically, a war. But the young men who were dying in Vietnam were, technically and every other way, dead.

On the plane to Los Angeles I read Robert Graves's World War I memoir, *Goodbye to All That*. Another English poet, Siegfried Sassoon, denounced the war and refused to return to the front. But for Graves the war had its own morality, and it was too strong for him to break. He kept going back to the horrors of the trenches to be with his battalion, even though almost everyone he knew had long since been killed.

"The only moral thing," Graves wrote, "was to keep going back until we were killed there."

But what good was that? In *The Warriors*, J. Glenn Gray recounts the story of a German patrol ordered to shoot some Dutch civilians in reprisal for an attack on a German unit. The soldiers lined their captives up against a wall. Then one soldier told the sergeant it was wrong to kill the civilians, and he refused to do so. The soldier was promptly stripped of his weapon. His comrades lined him up with the Dutch captives, shot them all, and threw their bodies in a ditch. A minute or two after his great moral decision, the German soldier was dead.

How many other such decisions go unnoticed, trees falling unheard in the forest? What if Robert Graves had been killed on his return to the trenches, as two million of his British and French comrades were? What of his morality then? Yes, he would have kept faith with his comrades, but he would also, like most of them, be dead. And his book would have been unwritten, his story forgotten.

As I flew to California, I began to find my own moral scales oscillating. I thought the war was wrong but my going was right. It was a contradiction. Since I was against the war, why should I participate in it? I had decided that it was worse to manipulate the system so that another man would fill my shoes. But the higher their price, the harder moral decisions are to make. The price of this particular decision was, quite possibly, my life. Was it worth that?

That thought grew in me even after I arrived at Norton Air Force Base outside Los Angeles, my first stop on the way to Vietnam. At drinks in the Officers' Club I kept encountering lieutenants who had just returned from the war. Their eyes seemed to look right through me. They told each other stories in which their friends always "got wasted" or "bought the farm." Dead, dead, dead, I kept thinking. My imagination began to fail me. I simply could not see myself doing it.

And so an idea began to build in my mind. I would do what Sassoon had done. I would refuse to go. A Marine lieutenant refusing to board the plane to Vietnam because he was against the war—it would be a great gesture. Unlike my going to Vietnam, which was a moral gesture that would most likely go unnoticed and which could leave me dead, this gesture would definitely be noticed—and I would live.

I grabbed my bags and headed for the Los Angeles airport. In the taxi I took off my uniform and put on some jeans and a sweater. I stuffed my uniform into the bag without even bothering to fold it. I spent the rest of the ride composing the announcement of my refusal to go to Vietnam. I wrote it in the form of a letter to my children not yet born, explaining to them why I had decided to take dramatic action against this war.

When I got to the airport, I called my wife and read her the letter I had written in the taxi. It said that I wasn't a pacifist, that I believed there were things worth fighting for, but that this war wasn't one of them. I concluded by saying I was refusing to go in the hopes that my children would not have to face my choice. It wasn't at the level of Sassoon's manifesto, but for a statement written in a California taxi, it wasn't bad.

On the other end of the line there was only silence.

"Where are you?" she asked.

"The airport. I missed the last flight, but I'll be home sometime tomorrow morning."

"Just give me the number of your pay phone, and don't go anywhere just yet."

Her voice was tense. I was taken aback. This was the most dramatic decision of my life. I was certain it would make the network news. I began to polish the prose in the letter. And then the phone rang.

It was Jan Lodal, a friend who had tried to get me a direct commission at the Pentagon, where he worked.

"Broyles!" he said, in his command voice. "Read me the letter."

I did, although it didn't sound quite so powerful reading it to him as it did before.

"Can't do it. Out of the question. Impossible."

"Why not?"

"Cost-benefit. Costs too great. Benefits too little. Costs: A. Ruin your life. B. Ruin your wife's life. C. Ruin your parents' lives. Benefits: None. The war goes on."

"But I don't believe in the war."

"Not relevant. That decision window has closed. Too late now."

"Jan, I'm serious about this."

"No. Timing's all wrong. No one's going to believe this is principle. They'll just think you were afraid."

"Jan, it *is* principle."

"Facts aren't the issue. Get on the plane to Nam. Get a safe job when you're there. It will look good someday. Potential benefits are great."

"Yeah, but the cost is I could die."

"Low probability, very low probability."

"Easy for you to say."

"Look, just do it. If you go, the chances are you'll be fine. If you don't go, there's no doubt what will happen: you'll screw up your life."

I didn't have anything more to say.

"Thanks, Jan."

"Well? Well? You getting on the plane?"

I hung up. My moral gesture had been tarnished by logic and realism. I sat in the coffee shop the rest of the night. At dawn I put my bags in a locker and took a cab to Santa Monica and went walking on the beach. I walked for hours, down to Venice, up to Pacific Palisades, the sound of the surf always in my ears.

Jan was right about one thing. I did compose that statement to conceal a simple fact: I was afraid. Worse, I had tried to hide my fear behind morality and principle. If I were going to take a stand against the war, I should have done it long before. And I knew what I had to do now.

I caught a cab to the airport, picked up my bags, and headed back to the base. On the way I dug out my crumpled uniform and put it on. I went straight to the terminal at Norton. They were checking in another flight. I gave the sergeant my orders.

"Holy Christ, Lieutenant," he said. "You were supposed to leave last night! How did that happen?"

"I don't know," I said. "I think I must have overslept."

"I've got to report this to the officer of the day," he said.

"Look, I met this girl," I said, fumbling for a plausible excuse. "It was my last night, we lost track of the time . . . But I'm here now. Couldn't you just mark me off yesterday and write me in today? It's not like I'm deserting or anything."

He thought for a minute.

"Sure, why the hell not. What can they do, anyway? Shave your head and send you to Vietnam?"

We both laughed about that.

The plane was filled with young Americans headed for the third American war in Asia in twenty-five years. We talked nervously to each other about everything but the war, and we cast envious eyes at the Army officer who had brought his wife and children along for a holiday in Hawaii. I tried to read, to talk, to daydream, to sleep. Nothing helped. And then a thought struck me with such cold clarity that it sent a shiver of fear down my spine. I was not coming back.

At that moment, I knew I was going to die in Vietnam. When I think back on that flight, now more than fifteen years ago, I still remember that shiver, and I still feel that fear. It was in a way more frightening than the real danger, when it came.

The Army captain and his family got off in Honolulu. I watched them make their way through the arrival lounge. Two smiling Hawaiian women draped leis around their necks. The smell of gardenias filled the terminal. Men wore Hawaiian shirts. Women had on bikini tops and shorts, their hair wet as if they had just come from a swim. Their legs were brown, their smiles flashed white across the room. I was in my winter uniform, heavy with scratchy wool. My shirt was buttoned at the wrists and my tie was tight around my neck. Even my clothes made me feel like a prisoner being transported under guard, through a world where everyone else was having a grand time.

The plane was very quiet after Hawaii. And then the pilot came on the speaker: "Men, that island off your starboard side is Iwo Jima. Since you're marines, I thought you just might be interested."

Iwo! We came up out of our seats and crowded around the windows. I was a reluctant marine, bound for a war in which I did not believe, but I was still a marine. Never mind that all those marines had died on Iwo so that a few pilots could have a place to land if they ran out of fuel. It was not the result, but the courage, that mattered.

To be a marine was a matter of style. If you were a real marine, you didn't care that you had it the roughest, that you always got the short end of the stick, that you might fight and die for a fuck-up. That was part of the mystique. If things were easy, if you had all you needed, if your mission made sense, you might as well be in the Army or be a civilian—not that the two were all that different.

We spent three days in Okinawa, filling out forms, getting

our shots, and storing our gear. We scrounged up some camouflage fatigues and some jungle boots and stood in front of the
mirror, trying our best not to look like imposters. Okinawa was
the last stop in World War II on the bloody path toward the
invasion of Japan. Thousands of marines had died here, fighting
the Japanese on their own homeland. I walked by many of the
old Japanese bunkers. They were neatly kept, and lined with
flowers.

On my first night in Okinawa eight of us went into Koza City.
We all piled into a single cab, over the protests of the driver.

"Hey!" one of the marines said, after the door handle had
come off in his hand. "What kind of car is this?"

"It's a Toyota," I said. "It's made in Japan."

"This car is made in Japan!" My friend was amazed. "The
Japs are making cars! Can you believe that!"

We went into Koza each night. There were bars everywhere,
wedged in among short-time hotels and massage parlors. American music roared out of every bar, and so did bar girls, who came
running after us, grabbing our arms and trying to bring us
inside. We were seeing for the first time the seductive side of
war—a whole city built for us, catering to our fantasies, designed to free us from our inhibitions and, of course, from our
money. The first night most of the marines went compulsively
from bar to bar, massage parlor to massage parlor. By the third
night everyone was fairly subdued. We bought drinks for a few
bar girls, talked awhile, and then went back to the base. There
was nothing else to do.

The next morning we left for Da Nang. We lined up on a ramp
leading to the plane, which had just arrived from Vietnam full
of marines coming home from the war. We were in our fresh
uniforms, all pale and clean and nervous, not knowing what to
expect of the war or of ourselves, not knowing if we would ever
see home again.

The men who came off the plane were tanned and hard, laden

with captured weapons and other souvenirs, their uniforms worn and tattered, a dull light in their eyes. We looked at them as if they were gods. Not a word was exchanged. They walked by us as if we did not exist.

Their war was over. It belonged to us now—to us and to those young men from Phat Diem waiting for us. Our enemies had gone to war down the Ho Chi Minh Trail, sleeping in caves, shivering from malaria, hiding from our bombs. And they weren't going home in a year. Until it was over, the war was their home.

9

TALKING WITH GENERALS

When a war ends, the winners write a military history; the losers pen apologies, or contrive to blame defeat on everyone but themselves. In America the finger-pointing began long before the fall of Saigon. The soldiers blamed the generals, the generals blamed the politicians, the politicians blamed the protesters, and everyone blamed the press.

While I was in Hanoi, I set out to see this long defeat from a different perspective—the winner's. I planned to spend as much time as I could in the South talking to the soldiers who had fought, as I had, in the paddies and mountains. But first I wanted to talk to the Vietnamese generals, to find out why, in their view, they won and we lost.

During the war the Communist generals didn't live in air-conditioned houses, as the American generals did. They didn't have one-year tours of the war and then return home. They didn't hover above the battlefield in helicopters and then return to civilized life each night to dine on white tablecloths with settings of silver and china. And they were often out of contact with Hanoi for long periods, so they had to exercise considerable tactical independence, beyond that expected or desired of American generals, whose superiors in Washington dictated everything from patrol coordinates to ordnance on jets. They saw a very different war, and, of course, they won, which gives their views a certain authority.

I began at the Foreign Ministry, perhaps the most beautiful of the old French colonial buildings. It sits in the shadow of the

Ho Chi Minh mausoleum, a massive, forbidding piece of funereal Gothic completely out of character with the austere man it honors. Normally Uncle Ho lies inside in eternal slumber, but unfortunately for me he had been shipped off to Moscow, the world capital of embalming, for his annual refurbishing, and I was unable to view him.

At the Foreign Ministry I met Hoang Anh Tuan, now the Vice-Minister for Foreign Affairs but for many years a Viet Cong general in the South. General Tuan is a southerner from Hue. He joined the Viet Minh in 1945, when he was twenty.

General Tuan had commanded the Viet Cong 2nd Division from headquarters in the Que Son Mountains southwest of Da Nang. His forces were among the major enemy units in my division's area, which made him the first real "enemy" of mine I met.

As with most matters in Vietnam, the visitor interested in opinions about the war with the Americans must first endure the Communist party line. My questions about the reasons for North Vietnamese victory and American defeat inevitably evoked the reply that they had fought *with* the people while we had fought *against* them, that their cause was just and ours was not, and that imperialism was destined to be banished from the globe. This was followed by the obligatory litany of Vietnam's long history of repelling foreign invasions, including eleven invasions by the Chinese.

But after this standard overture—more or less like grace before a meal—was completed, it was usually possible to discuss the war on its own terms; in fact, several of the generals seemed eager to talk about the war with an American who had fought there. We had, after all, shared an experience of considerable importance to us both, and, like old soldiers anywhere, we were grateful for a fresh and appreciative audience.

General Tuan slapped me on the knee and told me about the war. He took my hand and put it to his face.

"Feel that," he said.

Near his eye I could feel some grainy lumps under the skin. "Japanese shrapnel," he said. "I lost an eye fighting them in 1945. And look at this." He pulled up the leg on his perfectly tailored tan trousers. His shirt was a matching tan and neatly pressed. He was, by far, the best-dressed Communist I met, a formidable man, tall, with bushy hair, a high forehead, and a forceful presence. He leaned into me and his good eye flashed as he talked. I was reminded, perversely, of Lyndon Johnson.

"I took a French bullet in this leg," he continued. "It's still there. Fortunately you gave me no such souvenirs. When the Americans entered the war, we spent all our time trying to figure out how to fight you. The incredible density of your firepower and your mobility were our biggest concerns. I myself saw the first B-52 raid, on Highway 13 on June 18, 1965. I will never forget it. Twenty-six B-52s dropped their bombs four kilometers from me. It was horrible. Two or three hectares of land were simply blown away. Our losses were huge.

"And then after several battles—near Chu Lai south of Da Nang, in the Ia Drang Valley in the Central Highlands—it came to us. The way to fight the American was to grab him by his belt"—at which point General Tuan, by way of illustration, reached out and grabbed my belt—"to get so close that your artillery and air power were useless. The result was interesting—our logistical forces, which were farther from the Americans, took greater losses than the combat units."

I asked him about the Tet Offensive of 1968, when the Communists launched attacks on cities and towns throughout South Vietnam in an enormous surprise attack that was the turning point of the war.

"In the spring of 1967 [General William] Westmoreland began his second campaign. It was very fierce. Certain of our people were very discouraged. There was much discussion on the course of the war—should we continue main-force efforts, or should we pull back into a more local strategy? But by the middle of 1967 we concluded that you had not reversed the balance of forces on the battlefield. So we decided to carry out one decisive battle to force LBJ to de-escalate the war."

In other words, the Tet Offensive was the Vietnam War's equivalent of the Battle of the Bulge in 1944 or Lee's invasion of Pennsylvania in 1863—a desperate attempt to break the will of a stronger enemy. In World War II and in the Civil War, the tactic failed; in Vietnam it was a spectacular success. No matter that the offensive was crushed and the Communist political and military forces in the South so crippled it took them years to recover; the battle had been won where it counted—in America.

I asked General Tuan if they knew they had won the war in 1968.

"Yes and no. Nixon began the withdrawal, but Vietnamization was a difficult period for us, at least in the beginning. Your years here, 1969 and 1970, were very hard for us. The fighting was very fierce. We were often hungry. I was the division commander, and I had no rice to eat for days."

The Communists divide the war into four periods, beginning with "special warfare," or insurgency, from 1959 to 1965. The second period, from 1965 until Tet in 1968, they refer to as "local warfare" with larger units, the search-and-destroy era when we Americans dominated the war. The period from Tet to the Paris peace agreement in 1973 they call "fight and talk," followed by the "final offensive" that ended with the fall of Saigon in 1975. In 1969 they were on the defensive, as General Tuan admitted. But by then the true battlefield was in the United States, for American opinion, and for that battle the talk was more important than the fight.

I met General Tran Cong Man, who is now the editor of the Army's newspaper, in his office. He is a studious, professorial sort who seems very unmilitary, as if he had borrowed his uniform from someone else.

"Our regular forces, compared to yours, were small," he

said. "You were near Da Nang. There were tens of thousands
of American and puppet troops there. But we seldom had more
than one regiment in regular forces. Why couldn't you defeat
us? Because we had tens of thousands of others—scouts, mine
layers, spies, political cadres."

I said that I agreed up to a point: I was sure it made no
difference to American soldiers whether a North Vietnamese
general or a nine-year-old boy laid the booby trap that killed
them. These "self-defense" guerrilla forces did not win the war;
it took regular North Vietnamese troops in corps- and army-
sized units, fighting a mobile blitzkrieg, to win the final victory.

"You are right," he told me. "But that was only possible after
you had left. Without the self-defense forces, we would never
have gotten you out. If you were told to attack the Da Nang air
base and destroy the planes there, how many troops would you
need? Several divisions, right? Well, we did precisely that with
thirty men—thirty! It was a new kind of war, and you never
understood this source of our strength."

In the early years of the war, the American commanders—
with the exception of the Marines—concentrated on fighting the
major enemy units: the North Vietnamese Army and the main-
force Viet Cong divisions. The Marines wanted to expand their
beachheads in the northern part of South Vietnam by clearing
out the local guerrilla units—the tactic of pacification. As Marine
General Victor Krulak said, "It is our conviction that if we destroy the guerrilla fabric among the people we will deny the
larger units the . . . support they need. There was no virtue in
seeking out the NVA in the mountains and jungle; so long as
they stayed there they were a threat to nobody . . . our efforts
belonged where the people were, not where they weren't."

General Westmoreland's view, however, was that the Marines, like the Army, should "find the enemy's main forces and
bring them to battle, thereby putting them on the run, and reducing the threat they pose to the population." The Westmoreland
view prevailed, and the identification of the North Vietnamese

as the major enemy produced the tactic of "search and destroy," with its objective of seeking out the NVA units wherever they could be found and bringing all the weight of our firepower and mobility against them. And it led directly to the reinforcement of Khe Sanh on the Laotian border just south of the DMZ, as the precursor of a major battle with the NVA. It was to be the decisive encounter we Americans yearned for—a Dien Bien Phu with a new ending: we win.

I asked General Man about the siege of Khe Sanh. "Westmoreland thought Khe Sanh was Dien Bien Phu. But Dien Bien Phu was the strategic battle for us. We mobilized everything for it. At last we had a chance to have a favorable balance of forces against the French. We never had that at Khe Sanh; the situation would not allow it. Our true aim was to lure your forces away from the cities, to decoy them to the frontiers, to prepare for our great Tet Offensive."

Some American generals and historians agree with him; General Westmoreland, among others, believes the NVA wanted to take Khe Sanh, but could not. "They put too much into their siege of Khe Sanh for it to simply have been a feint," he told me. "They abandoned their attack because we made it impossible for them to win."

And Khe Sanh, for Westmoreland, was not simply bait for the NVA, or a blocking position to prevent them from attacking Hue and cutting off the two northern provinces of South Vietnam. It could have been the base for the campaign that had been crucial to Westmoreland's own strategy since early in the war: a major operation down Route 9 and into Laos, with the purpose of cutting the NVA's single most important strategic asset—the Ho Chi Minh Trail.

Without Khe Sanh, the attack would have been impossible. With Khe Sanh secure, Westmoreland could continue to hope President Johnson would change his mind and allow him to strike the NVA at their most vulnerable point. But Johnson never did, and Khe Sanh proved useless as a defensive position;

during the Tet Offensive the Communists seized Hue anyway.
The marines who had held Khe Sanh through the most dramatic
siege of the war had to abandon it, with as much dignity as they
could muster under the circumstances.

I asked General Man why the people hadn't risen up to join
the Viet Cong during the Tet Offensive, and if that didn't show
the Viet Cong lacked the popular support they were always
claiming.

"Not at all," he said. "Uprisings were very successful in the
early years of the war. But it would have been suicide to ask the
people to rise up unarmed against American soldiers."

"Why, then, did you call the Tet Offensive 'the general offen-
sive/general uprising'?" I asked him. "Isn't an uprising what
you expected? Didn't 'the people' reject you?"

He looked at me, his eyes harder. "We expected to win, and
we did."

Bui Tin is the Kilroy of Vietnam, who seemed always to have
been wherever history was being made—from Dien Bien Phu,
where he was a regular soldier, to Saigon, where in 1975 he was
present at General Duong Van Minh's surrender. Today he is the
military correspondent for *Nhan Dan,* the Communist Party
newspaper. In his opinion, the Americans lost for three reasons:
"One weak point was your rotation of soldiers. You were strangers here anyway, and as soon as someone began to learn the
country you sent him home. Your second weak point was to try
to win the hearts and minds of the people while you were using
bombs to kill them. And finally, you had a very bad ally; ninety
percent of the puppet army was corrupt, and the ten percent that
were good soldiers were not enough."

Bui Tin saw the best the Americans had—the astonishing
mobility of helicopters, the terrifying power of artillery and
B-52s, and the huge losses such a modern army could inflict.

"Of course we had heavy losses," Bui Tin said, "but we

learned. We learned to build special shelters, to decoy your artillery and planes with sham positions, to tie you to your fire bases
and helicopters so that they worked against you."

They learned these lessons at a terrible cost in dead and
wounded. To the Americans, who were measuring progress in
the war by counting bodies, those losses meant we were winning. Our logic was the logic of the trenches of World War I: if
you kill enough of your enemy's troops, sooner or later he will
have to realize that the price is too high and give up. But while
that logic might hold true in the rational world of game theory,
it had no appreciable effect on our enemy in this war. In fact, it
proved to be true, but only for *us*—we got to the point where
our losses were too high, and we quit. The war was the equivalent of Muhammad Ali's "Rope a Dope" tactics; they let us
pound them until we gave up.

The Communist leaders were ruthless and insulated from
suffering. Death did not deter them. And the soldiers they kept
sending down the trail were prepared to die, and their families
prepared to mourn. Whatever the reason—ideology, romanti-
cism, patriotism, brainwashing, or the herd instinct—they saw
death not primarily as tragedy but as part of a higher purpose.
Like the Texans who fought to the death at the Alamo, they
were ready to sacrifice themselves.

With our firepower our best weapon, we Americans did our
best to limit our own losses. Our enemies steeled themselves to
use men as we used bombs. And we Americans had grown distant from death. We never saw someone wring the neck of a
chicken; our relatives died in hospitals. We were brave, and we
fought well. And despite what I was being told, I knew from
experience that many Communist soldiers had been afraid and
had fled from death. But in the end they were willing to keep on
killing and dying, and we were not.

I asked Bui Tin about the losses the Viet Cong suffered in the
Tet Offensive.

"Some companies were wiped out," he said, "and in Saigon

and Hue we suffered terrible losses. But we did not lose even one-third of all the Viet Cong forces."

I said that seemed like a lot to me, the equivalent of the Americans losing 180,000 men in one battle. Bui Tin brushed this aside, as every Vietnamese did whenever I mentioned the terrible losses they had taken; it was the best evidence as to why the strategy of attrition was doomed to failure.

"We had hundreds of thousands killed in this war," he said. "We would have sacrificed one or two million more if necessary. Every family had relatives killed. I myself have closed the eyes on hundreds of my comrades. Many of my closest friends sacrificed their lives. But we had no choice!"

Late one afternoon, as the light was fading, I met with General Nguyen Xuan Hoang, the principal Army historian of the war. His biography was like that of so many others of his generation I had met. He joined the fight against the French in Hanoi in 1945. He fought at Dien Bien Phu and in 1965 was the aide to the general commanding the North Vietnamese forces at the first big battle with the Americans, the battle of the Ia Drang in the Central Highlands on the Cambodian border.

"I look back on that time with sadness," he told me. "By the end of 1964 our forces in the South had defeated the puppet troops. The war could have ended then, without so much bloodshed and suffering."*

I asked General Hoang about the battle of the Ia Drang, which had done so much to shape the future tactics of both sides.

"We could not indulge in wishful thinking," he said. "We were facing a modern army, very mobile, never short of fire-

---

*Later, in Saigon, a veteran of the Viet Cong told me the same thing, with an added barb. "If you had not come in," he said, "we southerners could have won the war and set up our own government. Thanks to you, the northerners had to come to our aid. They took over the war, and now they have taken over the country. And you are to blame."

power. When you sent the First Cavalry Division to attack us at the Ia Drang, it gave us headaches trying to figure out what to do. I was very close to the front, and several times the American troops came very near me. With your helicopters you could strike deep into our rear without warning. It was very effective. But the First Cavalry came out to fight us with only one day's food, a week's ammunition, their water in cans. We were amazed at how dependent you were on helicopters.

"Our mobility was only our feet, so we had to lure your troops into areas where helicopters and artillery would be of little use. And we tried to turn those advantages against you, to make you so dependent on them that you would never develop the ability to meet us on our terms—on foot, lightly armed, in the jungle.

"Also, you seldom knew where we were, and so you spent so much of your firepower against empty jungle. Our guerrillas served to keep you divided. You could not concentrate your forces on our regular troops, so your advantages were dissipated. You fell into our trap."

I replied that we had been much more effective than that. The Viet Cong had been virtually destroyed after Tet, and by 1969 pacification was working. The Communists were unable to mount a single major offensive in 1969, and much of the countryside was secure. Also, whenever American troops faced Communist regular forces in major battles, either we were clearly victorious or the outcome was a draw.

He smiled indulgently at me. "Of course we had many losses, made many mistakes, suffered many defeats. But a victory by your brave soldiers meant nothing, did nothing to change the balance of forces or to bring you any closer to victory. Time was on our side. We did not have to defeat you; we had only to avoid losing.

"And don't forget," he said, "that although after Tet we had to turn to North Vietnamese troops to bear the brunt of the fighting, you had to turn to the puppet army. From the beginning of your invasion in 1965 we knew your weak point was your ally. We could win if we could separate you from them. But we were still afraid you would come back if it appeared the puppets were in mortal danger. That's why before the final offensive in 1975 we took Phuoc Long [a province northwest of Saigon] and then waited. We wanted to be sure you would not send troops back in, or begin a bombing campaign as you had in 1972. Once it was clear you would do nothing, we knew victory was near."

Some of the criticisms by the North Vietnamese generals were self-serving, such as suggesting that we should have forgone our great advantages of mobility and firepower and fought as they fought. They did not drive us from the battlefield; we left, not by force of arms, but because we decided the war was not worth the costs. But much of what these generals said was right on the mark. For the past thirteen years Edwin Simmons, a retired Marine brigadier general, has been in charge of writing the official Marine Corps history of the war. During my last few months in Vietnam I was his aide.

When I told him what the North Vietnamese generals had said about the war, he replied, "It's true we violated many of the basic principles of war. We had no clear objective. We had no unity of command. We never had the initiative. The most common phrase was 'reaction force'—we were reacting to them. Our forces were divided and diffused. Since we didn't have a clear objective, we had to measure our performance by statistics. My favorite was Battalion Days in the Field; every day we'd get a call—'How many battalions you got out there today?'

"And the war was so political, so attuned to the media. In our very first operation, Operation Starlite, in 1965, we had President Johnson asking us about the loss of an amtrac squadron. So we had to stop the war and explain to the White House what had happened.

"I came back in 1970, and everything was just as I had left

it. The same hamlets were giving us trouble, the same units were in the same place. The only difference was that macadam and plywood had replaced mud and canvas. Our base camps and fire-support bases had become fortified islands. Our helicopter mobility worked against us. The rule of thumb was, if it was more than four kilometers, you went by helicopter. This gave the illusion of controlling ground we didn't really control."

As I spent more and more time talking to Vietnamese who had fought for twenty years and more, I began to believe that the one-year rotation policy was even more damaging than I had thought at the time. When I was commanding a platoon of marines my men were always departing and new ones taking their places. I seldom knew where they came from, or where they went. Since a man's performance in combat depends above all on his feeling tightly bound to his comrades, the effect of this rotation policy was devastating.

In Vietnam, getting home meant surviving for 365 days. It didn't matter if the war was going badly or if your unit was in trouble. When your time was up, your war was over. What would have happened in World War II if the most experienced troops fighting at Iwo Jima or the Battle of the Bulge had gone home in the middle of the battle? The Vietnam soldier's feelings of patriotism and self-sacrifice were pitted against his instincts for self-preservation. The result was moral confusion, and it crippled them as surely as a jammed rifle.

John Paul Vann, a legendary American adviser who was killed in Vietnam, used to tell young officers that "America doesn't have ten years' experience in Vietnam—we have one year's experience ten times." For each new soldier the war began the day he arrived. The ordinary infantryman reasonably thought that the war wouldn't be won in a year, so why try? The ambitious officer, on the other hand, realizing that he would have a combat command for only six months, naturally became powerfully aggressive, a hard charger whose goal was not winning the war but rather a good fitness report in his files. And our allies could simply wait out any American who asked them to do such unpleasant things as to think about the people and to stop making money on the black market; after all, that American would soon be gone.

On the Communist side, a sixteen-year-old messenger might rise to be a squad leader, a platoon commander, a battalion commander. His experience grew, and his goal stayed the same. Ho Chi Minh said it: nothing is more important than independence and freedom. A propaganda slogan, but it set, clearly and succinctly, the enemy's goal. That goal burned deep into their hearts and minds, and let none of them rest until it was achieved —no matter how long it took.

Against that single, transcendent goal, we had our short-timer's calendars. Each night we marked off another day. That was our goal, no matter what we or our leaders said. The war was like a vast parody of the American preoccupation with quick results, from instant gratification in love to instant success on quarterly earnings reports. There was no single goal in Vietnam; there were 2.8 million goals, one for every American who served there.

And in the end the nation's goal became what each soldier's goal had been all along: to get out of Vietnam.

Much of the American military history of the war focuses on what might have been. The Confederate veterans of the Lost Cause did the same thing. For decades they would refight the battles, looking for those moments when it might have turned out differently. Was Lee or Longstreet to blame at Gettysburg, and why had Stuart ridden off just when he was needed? Couldn't they have crumpled Grant's right at the Wilderness the way Jackson had the year before in the same place? Normally these discussions center on tactics. Slavery is almost never mentioned, or the principle of Union. Our goals in Vietnam, likewise, don't often come up in comparable discussions. That we fought is sufficient reason to assume that we should have, could have, won.

Still, some American strategists believe we could have won, on the battlefield at least, if only we had had a clear strategy, if only we had not had so many political constraints, if only we had used our great strength and gone for the jugular with massive force and not piecemeal escalation, if only . . .

The most articulate proponent of this view is Harry G. Summers, Jr., a retired colonel and the author of *On Strategy*, an application of the principles of Clausewitz to the Vietnam War. Summers insists that Westmoreland paid too much attention to pacification, which in Summers's view was confusing the cape, the Viet Cong, with the bullfighter, the North Vietnamese. He contends that we should have left the pacification to the South Vietnamese and concentrated on the invading North Vietnamese army—our strategy in Korea.

Summers suggests, for example, that we should have focused American troops on cutting the Ho Chi Minh Trail. Westmoreland had, in fact, wanted to do just that as early as 1964; he also suggested an amphibious landing in North Vietnam like General MacArthur's landing at Inchon in Korea. But President Johnson would never agree to widen the war.

I asked General Hoang whether this strategy might have worked.

"There were three things we thought the Americans might do that they didn't," he said. "One was to land north of the DMZ, as at Inchon, another was to attack the Ho Chi Minh Trail, and the third was to use tactical nuclear weapons at Khe Sanh. The landing would have been the most foolhardy. We knew we could easily defeat as many as a hundred thousand men there. As for cutting the trail, we kept our best army corps there, waiting for you. Those strategies would have caused us difficulties, we would have suffered losses, but you would have had to pay a far more terrible price, and it would never have worked.

"You know," he said, as the light faded in the room and a

shadow fell across the portrait of Ho Chi Minh, "your mistake was not in your tactics or even in your strategy. You simply should not have gotten into this war in the first place. It is far easier to start a war than to end one—that is a valuable lesson."

There was much tragedy in these bland words. The origins of John Kennedy's and Lyndon Johnson's war at least were understandable. For President Kennedy, memories of the Korean War and Fidel Castro's guerrilla success in Cuba were fresh; in Vietnam the Communist tide could be turned. President Johnson was obsessed with the thought that if he wavered in Vietnam his political enemies on the Right would gut his Great Society domestic programs. And throughout the government there was a buoyant belief that we could do anything we set our minds to—weren't we going to the moon?

But certain things were beyond our power—or at least our will—to accomplish, and victory in Vietnam was one of them. We were tied to an unreliable ally in a country we did not understand. We had tried to help them be independent even as we made them dependent upon us. The very foundation of our policy, the idea that South Vietnam was a viable nation, was so shaky that it would have required a massive commitment of men and money for years—perhaps permanently—and all in a region where we had few long-range interests. The Tet Offensive did succeed in separating the American people from the war. Lyndon Johnson, whose political antennae were second to none, realized that, and at the price of his presidency admitted defeat.

But the Nixon years of the war are much harder to accept, both in the larger arena of strategy and in the dirty corners where the war was fought. After 1968 the war had lost its idealism. We could no longer realistically believe we were fighting and dying to save South Vietnam or to preserve democracy or even to stop the spread of Communism as we had in Korea. We were fighting, as Henry Kissinger put it, "for negotiating objectives," and to preserve our supposedly fragile credibility as an ally in the major arena of our interests, Western Europe. And we were there because it was easier to continue than to take the hard steps to admit failure, and deal with the consequences.

Before Richard Nixon was inaugurated, Clark Clifford, LBJ's Secretary of Defense, told Henry Kissinger that Nixon had a rare opportunity to end the war at once, to put it behind us before it became his war too, as it had been Johnson's. But Clifford's plea fell on deaf ears. Virtually half of the American deaths were still to come, along with the deaths of hundreds of thousands of Vietnamese. In 1969 we could have negotiated a departure not unlike that of the French. We had many cards to play, many ways to protect those who had depended on us. But we chose instead to fight for four more years, so that Richard Nixon's share of the war lasted longer than America's role in World War II.

And despite all the negotiations and all those men who died long after not a shred of purpose remained, we left in ignominy anyway, the Marine helicopters churning on the roof of the American embassy, the people who had depended on us abandoned to the mercy of the victors. We had fought all those years under Richard Nixon largely to show that our commitments meant something. Our enemy knew those commitments were worthless, and as the helicopters departed, our allies and the rest of the world knew it too.

"In the first analysis," John Kennedy said in 1963, "it is their war. They are the ones who have to win it or lose it."

That was the point, clearly drawn—and at the beginning of our longest war, not at the end. We knew the dangers going in, but we went in anyway. In Vietnam our reach exceeded our grasp. We were seduced by the spectacle of our overwhelming military strength. We could have imposed military domination of Vietnam, as the Russians are showing they can do in Afghanistan. But what we could not do was create a country. President

Thieu was no different than any of the dreary list of dictators we have supported around the world. The millions of South Vietnamese who could have been inspired by a more democratic government were embittered and betrayed. The final defeat revealed what a sham the South Vietnamese government really was: the generals deserted, the leaders fled, and the people who had counted on them—and on us—were abandoned to their fate.

In the end, it *was* their war, and all our dead and wounded young men, all our billions of dollars, all our resourcefulness and energy, only made worse what would have happened in 1964 if we had never sent combat troops. What changed, of course, is that Southeast Asia was permanently destabilized. In Vietnam, the heart and strength of the southern guerrillas was destroyed, giving the North, our original enemy, far more influence than it would have had. Cambodia was brought into the war, and became first a charnel house and now a Vietnamese colony.

And the fear that started it all, the fear of Chinese expansion? Well, we are now China's most important ally, while China's most bitter enemy, and the staunchest foe of its expansion into Southeast Asia, is of course Vietnam.

10

TAN TRAO—
WHERE IT ALL BEGAN

There was one place in the North I wanted to see more than any other: a tiny village called Tan Trao in Ha Tuyen province, a mountainous region on the Chinese border. Tan Trao was Ho Chi Minh's headquarters in the summer of 1945. From August 13th to August 17th he and his small group of revolutionaries designed their new flag, gathered their tiny army, declared war on the French, and first proclaimed the independence of Vietnam. The thirty-year war in Indochina, the war that ended with the fall of Saigon in 1975, began in Tan Trao.

I was searching for clues to the character of Vietnam, for the sources of its tenacious resistance, for the reasons we lost. Tan Trao seemed a likely spot to look. So far as my hosts in Hanoi knew, no American had been there since August 1945, when a group of OSS officers known as the Deer Team parachuted into Ho's headquarters to deliver some crucial supplies and to train his ragged men to fight the Japanese.

Once again we left Hanoi early in the morning, but on this trip we crossed the venerable steel spans and massive concrete piers of the Paul Doumer Bridge, which stretches more than a mile across the Red River. The Doumer Bridge is Hanoi's link by road and rail to the north and east and to its port at Haiphong. It was one of the most famous bombing targets of the war.*

The bridge and all other targets near Hanoi were off limits to American bombers until 1967. More than 300 antiaircraft gun positions and at least 84 SAM sites guarded the bridge. The American pilots headed for the bridge often made a point of approaching over Hanoi at supersonic speeds, so that their comrades down in the Hanoi Hilton would know from the sonic boom that they weren't forgotten. The bridge was knocked out several times in 1967–68, but was always repaired in a few weeks. After President Johnson halted the bombing on March 31, 1968, the bridge was not bombed again until 1972.

We inched over the bridge behind bicycles and pedestrians. A steady stream of old women and teenagers passed us, heading into Hanoi with fifty or a hundred pounds of banana leaves, vegetables, or charcoal on the poles over their shoulders. They moved with a constant, rhythmic lope, one arm steadying the pole, the other beating the air, elbows high, like Olympic walkers. I told Minh that I had always marveled at how much these women could carry.

"When I was a boy," he said, "my job was to bring water from the well. I would carry forty or fifty kilos in buckets on one of those poles."

"Every day?" I asked, thinking again of the remarkable strength and endurance which was assumed to be a normal part of peasant life—the sort of strength and endurance which would translate so directly into the qualities needed to fight a long war.

"Yes, of course. How else would we get water?" Certainly not by casually turning on a tap, I thought. "During the war," he continued, "there was a very famous girl near my native village. She served on the antiaircraft crew at Ham Rong Bridge

---

*American pilots sang a song about it called "The Doumer Bridge Blues": "They got a little place just south of the Ridge/ Name of the place is the Paul Doumer Bridge."

—the Dragon's Jaw. Her name was Ngo Thi Tuyen. She weighed forty-two kilograms, but she could carry ninety kilos of ammunition on her back—with a pole just like those. When the bombs were falling and everyone was in their shelters she would run out with those ninety kilos and deliver it to the batteries."

Another bridge is being built downriver. It was started years ago with Chinese assistance. When the Chinese invaded Vietnam in 1979, the Russians took over. The bridge is years behind schedule.

"It will be finished this year," Minh said proudly.

There were no workers to be seen anywhere. The bridge looked like an ancient ruin. Not in our lifetime, I thought to myself. We Americans could build this bridge in two years. We can do so many things, but we could not defeat a people who carried ammunition on poles and who build bridges by hand.

We drove past Phuc Yen, where the MiG-21s had been based during the war, then Viet Tri on the Red River, another primary target of the bombing campaign. Beyond Viet Tri we began climbing into the mountains and soon passed the Swedish paper mill. Begun in 1974 as a showcase aid project, the mill is a bureaucratic mess and first beginning now to produce paper. Neatly terraced paddies of mountain rice lay scalloped into the hillsides. As we climbed they gave way to rows and rows of tea plants. Spring floods had washed out the bridges, so we had to ford several streams. The roads were lined with dark-skinned tribesmen bringing trees down from the mountains, one log at a time.

We stopped in Tuyen Quang, the provincial capital, and changed our Volga for a Russian version of a Jeep Cherokee with four-wheel drive. We picked up our guides, two local officials, one a Tay tribesman, the other a Muong. We drove north along dirt roads. The huts of the lowlands gave way to large wooden houses built on stilts with thatched roofs, surrounded by fences of woven bamboo and stands of banana and other fruit trees. Along the road everyone, even children, carried machetes.

"Uncle Ho came to Tan Trao in May 1945," one of the tribesmen said. "Since the spring of 1944 we had a revolutionary
administration here—the very first in the whole country. He
lived with Nguyen Tien Su, the president of the Viet Minh there.
In August, after the Soviets had defeated the fascists, he called
a meeting for all the Viet Minh leaders. They came to Tan Trao,
announced a general uprising, and then Uncle Ho left for Hanoi.
For a while that summer, he was very, very sick. General Giap
thought he would die. They brought in a traditional healer from
Dai Tu—he gave Uncle Ho special herbs and potions of ground
turtle shell. But he did not become well until some Russian
friends gave him modern medicine."

Considering that the Soviet Union did not declare war on
Japan until early August 1945, his account of who defeated the
fascists in World War II left out a bit. And in fact Ho was saved
not by Russian friends but by the Americans of the OSS, the
forerunner of the CIA.

Allison Thomas, now a lawyer in Ann Arbor, parachuted into
Tan Trao with the Deer Team in the summer of 1945. "Our medic
gave Ho antibiotics," Thomas told me. "He was very sick, but
I'm not sure he would have died without us. He was a remarkable man—slight, stooped, but with the most penetrating eyes
I have ever seen. There were only about a hundred Viet Minh
troops there. They had very primitive weapons and no military
skills to speak of. They were led by Giap, an unremarkable
young man—who would have thought he would become a military genius!

"When we got the news of the atom bomb attack on Hiroshima, Ho recognized it was his golden opportunity and began
all the meetings and organization that led to his taking over
Hanoi later that month. The night before he left for Hanoi we
had a farewell dinner They gave us what food they had, even
though people were starving—there was a terrible famine. At
the dinner I asked Ho if he was a Communist. He said, 'Yes, but
we can still be friends, can't we?'

"I always felt Ho was as much a nationalist as a Communist. If we had supported him back then, instead of backing the French, I believe he would have become an Asian Tito, Communist but independent. He told me he would welcome a million American troops in Vietnam to fight the Japanese and help win their independence. And he meant it. We were the first nation to win our independence from colonialism. He admired us. That's why he used our Declaration of Independence as a model for Vietnam's. We never really understood just how strong their nationalism was—how persistent and tenacious they were, how determined to fight as long as it might take. Giap wrote me several letters. He would always close by saying, 'Vietnam will be independent!' "

I asked Thomas why the men who made American policy in those three decades after 1945 hadn't taken the advice of the few Americans who actually had worked with Ho Chi Minh.

"Oh, that's simple," he said. "No one ever contacted any of us."

"Excuse me?" I said, thinking for a moment I had misunderstood.

"Oh, no. To my knowledge none of us who were there was ever contacted. We made full reports, of course. But I don't believe they were ever read."

We stopped at the Lo River and waited for the ferry, an antique steam-powered hulk filled with people, livestock, and a few trucks. Its gunwales barely cleared the water. The jungle came down to both banks of the river, which was about a half-mile across. After we left the ferry we climbed higher into the mountains. The road narrowed as we approached Tan Trao and became not much more than a cattle track through the thick jungle.

At intervals I saw neat piles of rocks. At each pile, two or three boys were patiently pounding the rocks with a hammer. Those piles had begun as large rocks in Tuyen Quang. Each large rock was broken by hand into smaller rocks, which were then carried here by truck and, when the road became impassable, by oxcart. Each small rock was then pounded laboriously into dust, which was spread over tar melted with charcoal fires to make a road surface. To make a one-lane road could take five, ten, even twenty years. The sons of the young boys I saw pounding rocks could one day be pounding rocks, just as patiently, for the same road their fathers had begun. Nothing, in Vietnam, is easy; everything takes years, whether building a road or fighting a war.

Two hours after we left the ferry, we arrived in Tan Trao, which consisted of a large clearing in the jungle, a handful of long wooden huts, and two huge banyan trees with hundreds of exposed roots—under which a woman and some children were weaving bamboo mats. In 1945, a frail and sickly Ho Chi Minh stood beneath the larger banyan tree and proclaimed, to a small gathering of Viet Minh, tribespeople, and American soldiers, the independence of Vietnam. And beneath that banyan tree General Giap read the first military order to the Viet Minh army.

We drove down to the old communal house where the Viet Minh had met. It was a beautiful structure, made of polished logs. The rafters were carved with dragons and Chinese characters. Outside were a few stone tables where in the spring the tribespeople bring food and other offerings in hopes of receiving a good crop.

"The Viet Minh all slept on one side and used the other side for their meetings," my guide said. "The people of the village gave them one cow, one pig, and two chickens for their food."

For some reason, the thought of the founding fathers of Vietnam meeting in this tiny log house made me want to laugh. This is where it all began, all that determination, all that long war, all those deaths: with a few men meeting in the jungle, fed with a cow, a pig, and two chickens. We Americans were here at the beginning, I thought, and then we fought so long to prevent the end.

And then, right on cue, appeared Mr. Su himself, the old Tay tribesman who had taken care of Ho while he was here. He was dressed in a tattered fatigue jacket and shorts. He was barefoot and carried a machete on his back. A rag was wrapped around his head, and there was only one tooth left in his mouth. I offered him a cigarette and he told me about Ho.

"I was the president of the Viet Minh here," he said, gazing over my shoulder as if he were looking into the past. "I was told I would have a guest, and a few days later an old man* appeared, alone, carrying a walking stick. He looked up at the sunshine and said, 'Ah, Mr. President, you have brought me good weather. For many days I have walked through the rain.'

"For a few days he stayed in my house. Then one morning he got up and said, 'Mr. President, I can no longer impose on your hospitality. Today I will build myself a house. Find me a place with trees and water and a good path to retreat on if we are attacked.' I showed him three places. The first had no escape route, the second not enough trees."

Mr. Su seemed to lose his train of thought. Three young girls in brightly colored dresses were sitting by the path, watching us and picking their teeth with a knife they passed back and forth. One of the girls said something to Mr. Su, and at once his face cleared.

"Oh, yes," he continued. "The third had trees and a good escape route, but not much water." The girls giggled. They had heard this story before.

"So Uncle Ho said, 'This one will do. I only drink two glasses of water a day anyway.' He immediately began to cut down trees, and he sent me to the market to buy some palm fronds for the roof. And he made sure I paid and didn't use credit. When I returned, we put on the roof. And that was where he lived, until he left for Hanoi."

I asked him what the tribespeople thought of Ho.

---

*Ho Chi Minh was then in his early fifties.

"He was very busy—and then he was very sick for a while. I brought him food, and my wife washed and mended his clothes. He would have us bring the children to him, even when he was sick, and he would tell them to go to school and to learn. 'There is no emperor and no mandarins anymore,' he would tell them. 'In a democracy we are all equal, and you must prepare yourself.' And then he worked a miracle."

"A miracle?" I turned to Minh and asked him to translate again. Minh spoke to Mr. Su for a few moments, then turned back to me.

"Yes, a miracle," Minh said. "That's what he said."

"What kind of miracle?" Mr. Su's cigarette had burned down to the tip, but he held it in his fingers without seeming to notice. I gave him another one.

"One day," Mr. Su continued, "Uncle Ho told me to take some villagers and go to a clearing and wait. He told us that men—men like you"—he pointed at me—"would fall from the sky. We were very doubtful, but we had faith in Uncle Ho, so we went. We waited most of the day and nothing happened. And then we looked up and there was an airplane, and from the airplane men came floating down. Everyone had to say that Uncle Ho was a genius. How could he have known such a thing would happen?"

Mr. Su then invited us for tea, but it was late, so I gave him my pack of cigarettes and we headed for the ferry landing. By the time we arrived it was dark, the darkness of the jungle on a cloudy night. We honked the horn and in a few minutes we could hear voices across the river. For almost an hour they tried to start the engine on the ferry. We could hear it cough to life, then choke and die. The only other sound was the river flowing by.

Finally the engine caught, and in a few minutes the ferry appeared. It was almost eleven o'clock when we returned to Tuyen Quang, but even at that hour yet another ceremonial meal awaited us. Beef with onions, fried pork, meat rolls, roast chicken, scrambled eggs, soups, rice, relishes, and fish sauce filled the table. The province vice-president, Vu Ke, a Muong tribesman, had been waiting for us since eight and had already drunk enough rice wine to be in an expansive mood. We excused ourselves to wash in the cistern. When we returned the toasts began.

"Many Americans came here with bombs, in planes," Ke began after we had all filled our glasses with yellow lemon wine. "You are the first to come as a friend. To peace!"

He drank his wine in one gulp and slammed his glass down. He then began a long speech. Minh listened intently. When Ke paused, Minh turned to me and began to translate.

"He says that he pledges you great friendship, I think. But you know"—Minh continued to speak as if he were translating—"he doesn't speak Vietnamese very well and I can't really understand a word he says. But drinking is very important to these tribesmen, so you should do your very best to keep drinking with them. And now perhaps you could just smile and say something I could translate back to him?"

This was not my first adventure in translation. On one memorable occasion, when Minh translated while a Swiss journalist and I jointly interviewed a planning minister about the economy of Vietnam, we had the following exchange:

"I have it on good authority," the Swiss said, "that Vietnam is exporting mice to the Soviet Union at cheaper prices than you sell mice in Haiphong."

"Mice?" Minh asked him.

"Yes, mice."

"Okay," Minh said, and translated the question.

The minister became incensed; his face reddened, and his response was long and irate.

"He says that Vietnam does not export mice," Minh translated, "and that it is an insult to our country to say that it does."

But the Swiss would have none of that. "I have the clippings," he said. "I know it's true. Tell him I know it for a fact."

There followed several exchanges, with the journalist and

the minister all but pounding the table and the hapless Minh translating back and forth. Suddenly it came to me what the problem was.

"Minh," I said, "I think he means maize—corn."

"Of course I mean mice," the Swiss said. "What did you think?"

When Minh turned to me and confessed he was not understanding a single word Ke was saying, I felt deep sympathy for him. So, with appropriate gestures, I raised my glass in a toast to Bruce Springsteen. Minh translated with great formality. Whatever he said, the tribesmen liked it, for they smiled and laughed and the one nearest me patted me on the back. Then we drank another glass of lemon wine. At that point the power went out. We all pulled out our cigarette lighters and continued eating and toasting in their glow until one of the young women serving the meal brought a kerosene lantern.

After several more glasses of lemon wine, either Ke's Vietnamese improved or Minh rose to new heights of creative translation. At any rate, we had a long, increasingly slurred argument about politics culminating in emotional pleas for peace for all our children. We then tailed off into the telling of war stories. Ke had been a bearer at Dien Bien Phu, carrying supplies and ammunition over the trackless mountains to the Viet Minh soldiers tightening the noose on the French. We talked about courage, about fear, and about comrades who had died, and by the end we were all shedding boozy, honest tears.

It was after two in the morning when we finished dinner. I lay awake under the mosquito netting, looking out the window into the black night, listening to the hum of crickets and the cries of strange birds. At dawn I woke to the sound of women laughing as they washed clothes by hand at the cistern. After a quick bowl of *pho*, we drove back to Hanoi. Minh listened to Bruce Springsteen all the way.

11

DIPLOMATIC
MISUNDERSTANDINGS

The night after I returned from Tan Trao, Michael Flaks and I went to the other restaurant in Hanoi—Cha Ca, literally, Fried Fish. Cha Ca occupies the second floor of a house on Cha Ca Street, in the old market neighborhood where the streets bear the names of the goods which were traditionally sold there: Silk Street, Cotton Street, and so on. Cha Ca serves, predictably, fried fish, prepared with considerable flair by a woman who cooked the fish with noodles and scallions at the table in a charcoal brazier. The walls were decorated with travel posters donated by various embassies: the snow-covered mountains and suntanned skiers sporting hundred-dollar sunglasses were like a fantasy from a different universe.

After dinner we went to the Thang Loi, a modern hotel built with Cuban help that is already sinking into socialist decay. The hotel is in the northwest part of Hanoi, on the banks of the "Big Lake." During the war, Navy Commander John McCain was shot down in a raid against the generating station, bailed out, and landed in the middle of the lake. There is a monument commemorating his capture on the bank.

The ritual at the Thang Loi is drinks on the roof overlooking the lake, and the drink of choice is a "Saigon cocktail," made with cognac, cream, eggs, and sugar. When we arrived the five tables along the railing were full. Michael described the occupants: "That's the Cuban table. The next one is Russian. Then comes the PLO-Arab table, and on the end is the Non-Aligned table—those are Malaysians, Indians, and, yes, an Indonesian."

"What about that table?" I asked, pointing to where a man and a woman sat in intimate conversation.

"That's the table for lovers—no politics allowed."

The social life of the diplomatic community is not a trivial matter, and it follows a fixed schedule. On Mondays at five-thirty there is jogging in Lenin Park. On Tuesdays, movies at the French embassy. On Fridays there's the Billabong Bar behind the Australian embassy. On Saturdays it's International House, where local bands play bad Abba imitations and there's a rare opportunity to mingle with some Vietnamese. And every third Saturday is the pinnacle of social life in Hanoi, the Swedish disco.

The foreigners in Hanoi live a sort of cruise-ship life, with the Vietnamese the surrounding, opaque, and occasionally hostile ocean. Their movements are restricted, their contacts with Vietnamese limited. They are constantly under surveillance. They fight a maddening bureaucracy to do their jobs, and they have almost no idea of what is going on. Naturally, under such conditions two things happen: they all become instantly close, and they all pass on the most outrageously inaccurate rumors.

The three most common topics of conversation are the black-market exchange rate, sexual mores, and the inner politics of the Politburo. It is not uncommon for all three to appear in a single conversation.

"I got two hundred and thirty dong today."

"Where?"

"At the Swedish bank."

"Helmut got two-forty in Haiphong."

"Too bad about poor Patel."

"Poor Patel?"

"He got sent home. Bribed the Vietnamese guard at the embassy to look the other way while he brought a girl in, but another policeman came along and he didn't think to bribe him too. So he got reported. Bad luck."

"I hear Giap [the former Defense Minister and the hero of Dien Bien Phu] is on the outs. Too close to the Chinese."

"Oh, no, I hear Dung [the current Defense Minister and the hero of the final offensive against Saigon] is going to be dumped. And Giap will be brought back in."

"Rubbish. Giap will never be back. He's too close to the Chinese. He'll be in charge of family planning until he kicks—"

"The ———— lost their driver yesterday."

"What happened?"

"I don't know. Either he got reported or his reports weren't good enough. Off to reeducation somewhere. The new guy's a real cop."

"Too bad. He was a good fellow. What was his name again?"

One night I had dinner at the British embassy with Mike and Wendy Wood. After we ate we watched a videotape of the Badminton horse trials. Unfortunately, the embassy was short on electrical power, so whenever the refrigerator compressor would come on the television would go off. Mike went around the apartment and turned off all the lights and every other appliance, but to no avail. Just as the horses attempted a jump the screen would go black. By the time the compressor turned off and the television came on, we had missed whatever it is that makes watching horse trials so worthwhile. So we talked instead.

"The Vietnamese never throw anything away," Mike said. "So they've simply placed each new bureaucracy on top of the one before. The French bureaucracy was laid over the Confucian bureaucracy, and the Communist bureaucracy over that. It's impossible to figure out. Even the Vietnamese don't understand how it works."

After hearing, day in and day out, the litany of complaints

about inefficiency, corruption, and mismanagement, I began to find my sympathies going out to the Vietnamese. Weren't most of these complaints true of all developing countries? I asked a tableful of UN aid workers.

"Yes," said one. "All the problems of developing countries you see here; but you also see so many that are unique. It is like a museum of problems. They are their own worst enemy."

"The worst thing is what happens to your employees," one aid official told me. "They have to fill out reports on us. He talked to this person, he met with that one, he changed money at so-and-so's. They know everything about us. And they have to report on each other. And that produces real tragedies. If they don't like someone, they'll just say he or she is getting too close to the foreigners, give a few vague examples, and before you know it, that person is gone."

Another UN official interrupted. "We have been trying to do a project for three years. We were getting nowhere. Last month I discovered that all this time we had been arguing with the wrong agency—which no one bothered to tell us."

"Nothing is ever decided," said another. "You go out of a meeting and you feel you've accomplished something. Then the next day they start right back where you started the day before, as if it never happened. No one can approve anything. Everyone is afraid to take responsibility. So the smallest decisions get kicked all the way to the top."

"One agency brought in a special computer," a Western diplomat told me. "It was a gift for the Vietnamese government. But they impounded it in Saigon and insisted the agency pay twenty-eight thousand dollars to transport it to Hanoi—and it was for them!"

The director of a European voluntary agency, who was in Vietnam checking on its projects, shook his head and told me of a trip he made to a provincial health official. "He spent an hour attacking the capitalists, and then presented me with a list of what they wanted: a hundred thousand dollars' worth of audiovisual equipment for remote villages—where there's no electricity!"

The stories went on and on. Not one foreign diplomat or aid official could name a single success story.

At another lunch, a European diplomat listened to a long discussion about the inefficiency and the police state and, looking out the window, said in a flat voice, "All this is just bureaucracy. What matters is that they are truly evil."

He said it softly, but with such passion that the whole table became quiet. When the conversation picked up again, it centered on how to smuggle antiques out in diplomatic pouches.

This disillusionment is not simply the disgruntlement of a bored diplomatic community. It's a symptom of Vietnam's most serious problem. Like Israel, Vietnam was much more popular as a victim than it is as a regional power. Despite its martial success —or perhaps because of it—Vietnam is a terribly poor country. It has the fourth-largest army in the world and a per capita income lower than India's. Its people suffer from malnutrition and curable diseases. These problems are compounded by a postwar baby boom of monumental proportions: from some 38 million in the early 1970s the population has exploded to more than 60 million today.

Vietnam desperately needs aid of all kinds, from medical supplies to developmental assistance, but its continued occupation of Cambodia has made Vietnam virtually an international pariah. Almost every country outside the Soviet bloc has canceled direct aid. The United Nations projects continue, but even Sweden, Vietnam's staunchest friend in the West, is considering reducing its commitment.

The occupation of Cambodia has been more than a diplomatic and military problem. It was a thorny metaphysical dilemma as well, and in a Communist state problems of logic carry more than casual significance. I talked about Cambodia with Bui

Tin, the military correspondent for the Communist Party newspaper.

"It was very hard for us at first to accept what was happening there," he told me. "I interviewed hundreds of refugees in 1978, but it still didn't sink in how deep the horror ran. The regime was our fellow Communists. We could understand their making mistakes, as we have done. But to practice genocide against their own people? How could a Communist Party do that? We Communists are the people—how could we try to exterminate ourselves?

"I had known Pol Pot and Ieng Sary. They were educated in Paris. They were very intelligent, very cultivated. You wouldn't think they were madmen. But they wanted the flame of revolution to extinguish everything that wasn't pure. If you knew how to drive you weren't pure. If you wore glasses. If you had a toothbrush. If you could read. And if you weren't pure, you died. It was a horror. And these monsters were our allies. We had helped them, trusted them.

"That's why we can't leave there. We can't allow Pol Pot to come back. We have to protect the Cambodians."

Wherever I went I heard some version of this story. Even when I didn't ask about Cambodia I was told how the Vietnamese Army stayed there for humanitarian reasons. And in 1979 I might have believed it. Even in 1982. But this was 1984, and the Vietnamese occupation was entering its sixth year. If they had gone into Cambodia for humanitarian reasons, they were staying for other ones.

General Tran Cong Man, the editor of the Army newspaper, did not beat around the bush: "Yes, of course we are there to help the people of Kampuchea.* But basically we are there to protect our own independence. Our southwestern flank is vulnerable. The Chinese could threaten us from Kampuchea. We are there to protect the fatherland from attack, and we will stay there until the threat no longer exists."

*Cambodia's post-revolutionary name.

Some American critics of the war blame the Cambodian Holocaust on the American bombing of Cambodia. They insist that the bombing and the invasion of Cambodia in 1970 led to —perhaps even directly caused—the subsequent massacres by the Cambodian Communists. That sort of thinking is based on the tyranny of opposites: if we are bad, our enemies must be good. The same reasoning excuses the police state the Communists imposed on the South after their victory: if it hadn't been for us, so the logic goes, they would never have done such things.

The Vietnamese Communists themselves, who presumably would have a great interest in advancing the idea that the United States was at the bottom of all the problems of Southeast Asia, believe that such theories are junk. Whenever I would suggest that the horrors of the Khmer Rouge might be related to the American bombing, they would look at me in amazement: it was a preposterous idea. To the Vietnamese, the Khmer Rouge committed genocide for a concrete, specific reason—they succumbed to bad ideology.

We Americans had nothing to do with it. Just as we couldn't "save" Vietnam from the Communists, so we didn't "cause" them to imprison hundreds of thousands of people in reeducation camps, institute a police state, and, in Cambodia, kill two million people. We didn't do those things. They did. The Vietnamese consistently told me that their ideology—good in the case of Vietnam, bad in the case of the Khmer Rouge—was the basis for such actions. Americans are pragmatists; we tend to believe that people respond to circumstances. We underestimate the power of ideology. The Vietnamese Communists, ideologues themselves, do not.

Having been part of a foreign army in Southeast Asia whose presence was considered an outrage by much of the world, I have to confess to feeling a certain satisfying irony at my old enemy being hoist with its own petard. Still, none of this pressure seems to have swayed the determination of the Vietnamese to stay in Cambodia. They have learned throughout their history that if they are stubborn enough, if they suffer long enough, they will get what they want.

At the Thong Nhat there lived a Russian diplomat who was actually friendly, an oddity of such magnitude that all the other foreigners assumed he must be KGB. One evening he invited me to his room for a chat. The Russians import everything: food, drink, even Russian television by satellite. We drank Stolichnaya vodka and Moldavashii wine, which is very sweet, like Tokay. His wife brought out Russian sausage, boiled carrots, and chocolates wrapped in gold foil. I asked them why everyone thought I was Russian.

She considered my face for a moment. "Because you look Russian," she said.

"I look Russian?"

"Yes, but you have American eyes—very intense, very innocent."

The diplomat's main interest seemed to be how to get an assignment to an English-speaking country—America preferred. "Everyone should see America, don't you agree?" he asked me.

I asked him about relations between Vietnam and the Soviet Union.

"The Vietnamese are very independent people," he replied. "We will always support them."

"Any chance of better relations between you and the Chinese?" I asked.

"The Chinese are, well, very Chinese. You will learn."

"If the price of cooperation with the Chinese was dumping the Vietnamese, the way we had to dump Taiwan, would you do it?"

Thanks to the Vietnamese occupation of Cambodia, Russia is not only Vietnam's only ally, it is virtually its only friend. Vietnam lives on Russian gasoline and, to a lesser degree, Russian grain. It rides to battle on Russian tanks, fires Russian weapons, flies Russian planes. Its shabby manufactured goods could be sold only to the captive markets of the Eastern bloc. And China, China is very large, and it knows the way into Vietnam, having been there many times before. To have the Russians and the Chinese back together would make the Vietnamese very nervous; to have it happen at their expense, as it did with Taiwan, is their deepest fear.

The Russian smiled. "More wine?"

The Siberian workers left the day after they had plied me with *obshchestvo* and vodka, and were replaced at the Thong Nhat by a Russian women's volleyball team, which had come to play the Vietnamese. I couldn't, myself, imagine less of an exercise in socialist friendship, since the Russian women ranged in height from six feet way on up, and I have never seen a Vietnamese woman over five feet four. And then I learned they were going to play the Vietnamese men, but that sounded even worse somehow.

The Russians were big, rawboned girls who walked like football players. I talked to them for a while one morning *("Obshchestvo!"—"Obshchestvo!")*, and when they left a few days later one of them stopped at my table and, without a word, gave me a small wooden doll she had brought from Moscow. I opened it and there was another doll inside, and another inside that. It seemed a particularly appropriate gift.

12

GHOSTS IN THE ZOO

From the moment I arrived at the airport in Hanoi I felt helpless. The last time I had been in Vietnam I was one of half a million armed Americans; now I was alone in the country of my former enemy, which my comrades had bombed unmercifully, and where I had fought with all the weapons I could muster. My passport was of no use—we have no diplomatic relations with Vietnam. I spoke only a few words of the language, and I was a foot taller than almost everyone I met. I was, so far as I knew, the first combat veteran to visit North Vietnam alone, with the exception of the American pilots shot down during the war, who were somewhat more unwilling guests.

I expected at best a mixture of curiosity and hostility. Instead I was met with an eerily perfect hospitality. It was as if some giant switch had been thrown and everyone, from government ministers to peasants, suddenly stopped fighting Americans and began courting them. War? What war? We are friends, friends, friends . . .

I was a guest in a country which had fought for thirty years to rid itself of Western control and influence, a country whose anti-colonial passions sustained it for generations. I was one of the soldiers they had defeated, yet I was being given the respect, deference, and special handling the French had once expected as their right. It was a jarring experience, like living a mixed metaphor.

I wasn't sure why I was being treated this way. Perhaps there is nothing less egalitarian than a Communist society, where privilege determines everything. Or perhaps long years as a colonial people had taught the Vietnamese how to manipulate Westerners with deference. Or perhaps the very structure of their society, with its respect for elders and its passion for appearances, enforced a superficial politeness. Or perhaps, for reasons cynical and/or genuine, they wanted better relations with the United States. After a week or two of such hospitality I found myself responding in kind: I wanted, almost against my will, to be as pleasing and polite in return.

After a time, I began to assume the simple language of the Vietnamese. I began referring to the fall of South Vietnam as the Liberation, as in "Were you in the South before the Liberation?" I began to call the million or so Vietnamese who served in the South Vietnamese Army the puppet troops, as in "Were you in the Liberation forces or the puppet army?" It was overwhelming, this constancy of language. It wore down subtleties and nuances, forcing complex reality into neat building blocks. Language and, through it, perceptions exist to serve the state. After a couple of weeks I gave up fighting. If I wanted to be understood, I had to use language, I had to approach reality, as they did. The more I spoke in this way, the more a certain peace of mind began to envelop me: it was the clarity of childhood, of simple concepts, simply put. And it made me feel as if I were a child dealing with children.

I don't mean this in a condescending way, because some of the values the Vietnamese exhibited with almost childlike purity I found very appealing: hard work, fidelity, thrift, patriotism, respect for elders, devotion to community and place. The cycle of harvest imposes a stern discipline—work, hard, physical, exhausting work, is a constant in the lives of most Vietnamese. But they never seem to indulge in self-pity for having to work harder than I have ever seen Americans work or for having suffered through thirty years of war, with destruction, death, wounding, and long separations of ten and twenty years or more.

The word "sacrifice" is used only to mean death, as in "Many of my comrades sacrificed." No other hardship is considered worthy of mention. Many Vietnamese saw their own wives and children and mothers and fathers killed, saw their own plans for careers permanently altered, suffered for years, for something larger than themselves. And I saw not one who was sorry.

Not long after I arrived my desire to please my hosts had been mixed with another emotion—fear. For the first few nights after I changed money on the black market I lay awake, my mind besieged with images of being led away into the Hanoi Hilton, to the old cells of the Americans, to the interrogations, the isolation, the tortures of the rope trick. Virtually everyone I spoke with mentioned matter-of-factly that the regime knew everything, that their informers were everywhere, that they kept dossiers on everyone, that knowledge was power. I began to feel that sense of fear that is the daily ration of life in a police state: *They know,* I was convinced, and they are just waiting before they come to arrest me. I thought of burying the money, or of sinking it with a stone in the Lake of the Returned Sword, to rest with the turtles and the sword of Le Loi.

I was nagged with guilt. I dreaded every summons to meet with the press office. I even went so far as to change money at the national bank. It took five giggling young women thirty minutes to change my $100 into 1,200 dong. When I changed money on the black market I was given 24,000 dong for the same amount, and the whole transaction took less than a minute. But even though I had to respect the capitalist efficiency of the black market, I became convinced that I had sold my freedom for 22,800 dong, a currency with which I could buy almost nothing I really wanted. I felt materialistic and greedy, as if I had succumbed to the very temptations that my hosts were constantly claiming had so crippled the South. I would not talk to other foreigners in my room, for fear it was bugged. I began to listen for the knock on the door in the middle of the night.

But after a week or so I began to realize that the Vietnamese expected decadent Westerners to do such things, and that even if they knew—and I began to suspect they were less sophisticated in gathering intelligence than the legends implied—they would look the other way. I was, in short, adapting.

One night I asked a European about the dangers of changing money on the black market. He laughed.

"Listen," he said. "Not too long ago one of our new diplomats complained to the Foreign Ministry about how expensive everything was at the official exchange rate. He was told to ask some of his more experienced colleagues and they would explain to him how to solve that problem. There's only one solution: the black market."

The black market is everywhere in Hanoi; it is, in fact, the dominant economy of Vietnam. Several high officials attempted to tell me that the black market is a problem only in the South, but they had trouble keeping a straight face as they did so. While the leadership retains the austere lifestyle of Ho Chi Minh and seems to have little of the cynicism of the ruling class in the Soviet Union, even they cannot avoid the black market—which sets the price of everything from blue jeans and gasoline to currency and chickens, and manages with considerable efficiency the basic buying and selling of these and hundreds of other commodities.

From clerks to ministers, every government worker must put his rationed food, cigarettes, and clothing into the black-market economy in order to survive. In a month an interpreter makes 280 dong, or about $1.25 at the black-market exchange rate; a doctor about 400 dong, or $1.70. A bowl of soup costs 30 dong, a grapefruit 20 dong, a pack of cheap cigarettes 30 dong. If he buys one of each of these a day, as most workers seem to do, he will have spent his entire month's salary in less than four days. And so everyone holds several jobs, sweeping out pagodas, teaching English, weaving mats, stringing beads.

My other problem with money was also coming to a head.

Before I left for Da Nang I would have to pay for my car rental, my airplane tickets, my hotel bill, and my guide's services for the entire month. And then in Da Nang I would have still more car rental fees and more airplane tickets and more hotel bills—all in cash. I sent a cable through a foreign news agency to a friend who was a journalist in Bangkok, asking for film, notebooks, and, above all, money. I made arrangements for him to send the package with the pouch that came regularly to one of my new friends in Hanoi. Unfortunately, the pouch left early and he missed it.

The next night I went down to dinner, with visions of reeducation camp dancing in my head. Michael Flaks joined me. We talked in a desultory fashion for a while.

"Oh," he said, "I almost forgot. A friend of mine brought in a package for you last night. It's in my room."

As quickly as was seemly I got the package, retired to my room, and ripped it open. Inside were ten rolls of film, five reporter's notebooks, and . . . nothing else.

What to do?

I paced up and down the room. No answers. I was being reminded that money is the passport of the West. Money bought freedom, and in Vietnam freedom wasn't cheap. Then I picked up one of the notebooks as I tried to figure out my next step. I flipped through a few pages. Five one-hundred-dollar bills fell out. I was saved! I had money. I was myself again!

Whenever I met with my escorts, I would stress how interested I was in the MIA issue. Finally they took me to meet Cuu Dinh Ba, who is in charge of North American affairs at the Foreign Ministry. The MIA issue is his responsibility. Not surprisingly, he dismissed the possibility that some American POWs might still be held in Southeast Asia.

"They have all been released," he said. "There may be a handful who chose to stay here, but no one is being held against their will. Finding information about the remains of dead MIAs is very difficult. More than seventy-eight thousand Americans missing in World War II were never found. That's more than twenty-two percent of all the American dead. In Vietnam, you say you have twenty-five hundred MIAs. That's only five percent of your dead. Still, we want to help. It is the humanitarian thing to do."

I asked why there had been so little cooperation on the MIA issue in the South.

"The fighting was very fierce there," he replied. "The people are still bitter. And, listen, you see all those cemeteries of our heroes, all over Vietnam? Most of the bodies aren't buried there. Many thousands of our own dead were never found. Do we tell the people that the bodies of Americans are more important than the bodies of their own husbands and sons who died because of the Americans? We will keep looking, but frankly, it would help if we had better relations, if the people did not believe you were helping the Chinese in their—"

"Multifaceted war of aggression?" I said.

"Exactly," he replied, with the air of a man congratulating a good pupil.

I continued my inquiries wherever I went. The Swedes have the most freedom of any Westerners, and there are rumors that while riding around on their motorcycles, they have seen Americans on work brigades. I could not pin down any of those rumors. It was just as Paul Mather had told me back in Bangkok: you hear lots of stories, but you can never find the person who will say he saw them with his own eyes and here's where it was. It is very unlikely that any Americans remain, but it is possible. That's what makes giving up impossible.

One afternoon in Hanoi we drove into the suburbs along the Street of Victory over the B-52s. We were headed for the offices of FaFim, the agency that markets Vietnamese newsreels and documentaries. Its compound is tucked back away from the street and surrounded by a wall about ten feet high. Inside were graceful one-story buildings of blue-green stucco and red tile roofs. In the courtyard, a large pool was surrounded by well-kept rose bushes. In one doorway, a chicken strutted back and forth; in another, two men in shorts were squatting and smoking a bamboo pipe, quietly passing it back and forth.

We were met by a young woman in high heels and jeans, who took us into a large room where I was shown movies about the bombing of Hanoi and Haiphong, including some brief clips of American POWs looking well fed and unrepentant. The films were extraordinary. Searchlights scanned the night. Antiaircraft guns spun back and forth, their muzzles spitting fire. Missiles blazed off launching pads. From horizon to horizon the sky was exploding. The flashes came with staccato swiftness; the sound was deafening.

Every now and then I could make out a lone figure racing through the explosions, or a gunner silhouetted against the sky. I was fascinated by this glimpse of what the war looked like to the other side, but even so, I found my gaze wandering from the films to the room in which I was seeing them. It was a large, nondescript room with stucco walls. Its very banality almost overwhelmed me. I was watching films of the war against the American pilots in the headquarters of one of the main prisons where captured American pilots had been kept—what the POWs called "the Zoo."

Whenever I brought up the treatment of the POWs, I was invariably told they were well treated. Bui Tin told me that on Christmas he would take over a turkey and a guitar and sit around singing folk songs. Pham Tuan, the jet pilot/cosmonaut, said that he had visited the POWs and shared informal talk about flying. Cuu Dinh Ba insisted that they got better rations than their guards and that they were treated humanely and well.

"Go and ask them yourself," said Pham Tuan. "They will tell you they were treated fairly."

Well, not exactly. The POWs themselves have given eloquent and depressing accounts of their treatment—the isolation, the interrogations, the torture, the forced confessions, the prisoners beaten to death. It is not a record that makes one feel comfortable about the fate of any Americans who might still be there.

Two weeks after I arrived Hanoi celebrated the thirtieth anniversary of its liberation from the French. There were performances of traditional and popular music, speeches, a parade (at which the French ambassador, rather sportingly, I thought, stood at attention, wearing a special medal issued for the occasion), fireworks, and a concert in Lenin Park.

Most of the singers at the concert were tentative and wooden, but the last group came out sporting long hair and sharp outfits. The lead singer had down a modest version of Mick Jagger's moves. I went backstage after the concert and discovered what I should have known—the first groups were from Hanoi; the last one from Saigon. At another concert, when the rock music was over, a band began to play patriotic music. The young people in the crowd got up and left. It reminded me of what must surely be the worst of the Politburo's fears: it reminded me of America. Of such events are Moral Majorities and Cultural Revolutions made.

Hundreds of thousands of people crowded around the Lake of the Returned Sword for the fireworks. The regime had spared no expense: the display was spectacular. The boom of mortars was continuous. The sky came alive. Only a few hours before, I had been watching the films of the air battles over Hanoi. As I made my way through the crowds around the lake, I kept thinking this was how it must have looked during the Christmas bombing of 1972, when waves of B-52s bombed Hanoi and the city responded with the fiercest antiaircraft barrages in history. But the people around me were curiously silent. As the mock battles raged above them they simply stared, transfixed.

The next morning I asked Minh about the fireworks display. "The fireworks were a powerful experience," he said. "I could see everything again. All the fear and pride came back. I know it was like that for many, no matter how subdued they appeared. But the bombing ended twelve years ago. Perhaps half the country is too young even to remember. For them the war with the Americans is a story, like the battles of Le Loi. They don't know how hard we had to fight to win our freedom, to unite the country. They have other things on their minds."

When I discussed my visit to Da Nang, Duong Minh had told me that he had not mentioned I had been a marine there during the war. "Better not to give them an excuse to find your visit inconvenient. You can explain it when you arrive. But I wouldn't tell anyone in the South you fought there. The officials should be no problem, but some of the ordinary people might still have some bitterness."

We left the hotel at five-thirty in the morning. No cars were allowed into the airport without the appropriate documentation, which we produced for the guard. Vietnamese traveling to Da Nang had to have special permits, which were carefully checked at the counter, a process so laborious that although we arrived more than an hour and a half before the flight was to depart, long lines had already formed. After a cursory check we were waved upstairs to a special lounge for foreigners. Two Russian-made planes waited on the runway—a shiny new jet and an old AH-24 turboprop.

We were loaded onto the turboprop. Half the passengers were European—a mixture of Soviet-bloc functionaries and German tourists; the other half were Vietnamese, an even odder mixture of officials and old women with betel-stained teeth, who, I assumed, were the relatives of Party members. The plane hummed and vibrated at a deafening pitch and was insufferably hot until about halfway into the flight, when the air conditioners came on, sending clouds of vapor into the cabin and obliterating one's view of the person across the aisle.

Mercifully, we had smooth flying until we approached Da Nang. Just north of the city a spur of the Truong Son mountain range that runs down the spine of Vietnam bulges out to the sea —dividing the North and the South neatly in two about sixty miles south of the old Demilitarized Zone. The passage over those mountains is called Hai Van Pass, and flying over it we hit heavy turbulence. Our little plane was tossed up and down— dropping suddenly like a stone, then struggling back to stability, only to drop and pitch again. I clutched my armrest, closed my eyes, and tried, by sheer force of will, to blot away the cold sweat on my body and my rising nausea.

It was as if nature itself was reminding us that despite the political unification of the two Vietnams, there was still a barrier between them that could not be crossed lightly. After what seemed like hours the clouds suddenly parted to reveal the airport directly beneath us. At once I felt better. I was coming home.

13

AMERICAN BOYS

I first came to Da Nang on November 3, 1969, on board a Continental Airlines jet from Okinawa. The stewardesses wore tan dresses cut several provocative inches above the knee. They went up and down the aisle serving breakfast, under the silent stares of a hundred or so men, each of whom believed somewhere in his heart that those stewardesses might be the last American women he would ever see. I thought of my father's generation, going to war in the cramped and foul bowels of slow-moving troopships, playing cards and shooting craps on blankets. No one wanted the flight to end, but we had hardly finished our coffee when we landed in Da Nang. One of the stewardesses stood at the door and told each of us, in a soft Texas drawl, "Be careful, now, you hear?"

The monsoon winds were sweeping rain across the airport, which in 1969 was one of the busiest in the world. Jets heavy with bombs and rockets took off with metronome regularity. Passenger planes from shiny chartered jets to battered CIA C-46s and Vietnamese DC-3s waited to take off. Helicopters of every description buzzed like swarms of dragonflies. The noise was deafening. The runways and parking lots were snarled with vehicles, the waiting rooms filled with American soldiers and marines waiting for flights or sleeping on their duffel bags.

We lined up to fill out the inevitable forms and show our orders, and an old Marine gunnery sergeant gave us the first of many briefings. He said nothing about freedom, liberty, or the wickedness of our enemy, or about American interests, our patriotic duty, or why we were there to fulfill a citizen's ultimate responsibility to his country, to risk our lives in battle in its name.

"How many of you boot peckerwoods want to go back to the world in a year?" he barked. "Raise your hands."

A few hands went up. The rest of us looked around nervously. We were new, but we knew enough about the military to know that raising your hand was never a good idea. The sergeant then proceeded to tell us, not about how to survive ambushes and booby traps, but about dangers far more real— the black market, drugs, and, above all, women. The last he described in graphic detail.

"Now, men," he said, "I know it's going to be hard for you to keep your pecker in your pants for a whole year, but there's a new strain of syphilis here. Can't be cured! You go and get it, ain't no way we can let you go back to the world, give that horrible disease to a civilian. Nope. You get it and they gonna ship you out to a special island off the coast here till they find a cure. So the first time one of these little skivvy girls comes up to you with something to sell, just ask yourself—are those few seconds of pleasure worth never seeing your momma, your daddy, your girlfriend, not ever again?"

The man next to me turned and said, "I wonder if they get the Viet Cong fired up like this?"

The lecture drew on one of the most durable myths about the war—the existence of an incurable strain of VD. And it may have frightened some of the younger men—for a few days. But beneath the myth was this reality: for most Americans in Vietnam, catching VD was the greatest danger they faced—unless they also exposed themselves to the risks of becoming a junkie or an alcoholic. Bad dope. VD. Too much alcohol. Those were the big enemies.

We were constantly told that Vietnam was a war without front lines, that the enemy could strike anywhere. It was a lie. By 1969 the great majority of Americans in Vietnam were in about as much danger from the enemy as they might have been from a mugger or a drunk driver at Fort Benning or Camp Pendleton back in the United States. The line between the men who fought and the rest of the country began not in America but in Vietnam, a fact painfully clear to the small minority of American soldiers who did any fighting. It was not a privilege to be able to fight; it was instead evidence that one had failed to understand how to manipulate the system, as if anyone not smart enough to get a deferment or at least to get a job in the rear was too dumb to do anything but carry a rifle.

My first week in Vietnam was spent in briefings at the headquarters of the 1st Marine Division, a large, self-contained American base on the outskirts of Da Nang known as Freedom Hill. Life was good on Freedom Hill. There were movies and a library and handball courts and clubs with live entertainment; and there were many women, including some American Red Cross volunteers known as Donut Dollies. The food was excellent—steaks, shrimp cocktails, fresh strawberries, and ice cream: nothing was too good for our fighting men!

Officers lived in neat huts with cots or even real beds. Their uniforms were washed and pressed, and their beds made, by Vietnamese women who worked on the base and who were handy conduits to the black market and other pleasures. My first night in Vietnam I had dinner, a few drinks at the Officers' Club, and then watched *The Graduate*. If it had not been for the occasional rumble of artillery breaking through the sound track like distant thunder, I could have been back in America.

After a few days, I realized that this was the place for me. I harbored hopes of hiding myself in the rear, which would have been more or less like being stationed at Club Med. Instead, I was loaded into the back of a deuce-and-a-half truck with three other new lieutenants and driven through the gate and into the war. We drove along dirt roads and through rice paddies on the way to Hill 10. The boys guiding water buffalo as they plowed the paddies, the old men in black pajamas slowly poling sampans beside the flooded dikes, the old women picking lice out of their daughters' hair by the side of the road—the sheer tumult of rural life—laid out before a background of mist-covered mountains rising to the sky. It was so beautiful and so captivating that I almost forgot none of us had a weapon, not even a pocketknife.

Hill 10 was like any other American combat base. Its name came from its elevation—ten meters above sea level. There was a mess hall, clubs for enlisted men, noncommissioned officers, and officers, a small PX, an infirmary, offices for the various administrative components (which were labeled S-1 to S-5 and consisted of administration, intelligence, operations, logistics, and civil affairs), and living quarters known as "hootches" scattered throughout. Showers and privies were outdoors. Support groups such as the engineers, artillery, and transport had their own areas. We had a battery of 105 howitzers, some 4.2 mortars, and a landing zone for helicopters.

The entire base was surrounded by thick doughnuts of barbed wire, interspersed at regular intervals with bunkers and watchtowers. All the buildings were built the same way—with two-by-four skeletons, a row of plywood topped with screening for the sides, plywood floors, and tin or canvas roofs. Each building had its own bunker in case of mortar or rocket attack, and the bunkers were crowded with spiders and rats and four years' worth of garbage. Sandbags were everywhere, and the filling of sandbags was, like the painting of the Golden Gate Bridge, a constant activity. In the dry season the red dust coated everything and turned sweat into a thick soup. When the rains came the base was a sea of mud. Nothing grew there.

Hill 10 was built on a promontory of rocky ground southwest of Da Nang that rose out of the last rice paddies before the mountains. To the north was the Tuy Loan River, to the south a long finger of hills called Charlie Ridge. East of Hill 10 was an intricate pattern of hamlets and villages, then a circle of hills, then Da Nang and the shore of the South China Sea. To the west were the foothills and, beyond, the great Truong Son mountain range. A few miles in one direction was the second-largest city in South Vietnam—more than a million people and a vast American complex of airfields, bases, movie theaters, ice-cream parlors, round-eyed Red Cross girls, and GIs drawing combat pay as lifeguards. There were dedicated Americans working twenty-hour days in air-conditioned offices, computer programmers, miles of supplies, and at the main airport a desk where you could check in, after a year, for your flight back to America, to college or the mill, to Woodstock, the Moon Landings, rock and roll, red Camaros and miniskirts and the GI Bill.

A few miles in the opposite direction was what we called the Yellow Brick Road, the spur of the Ho Chi Minh Trail that led into Da Nang. I could stand on Hill 10 at night and watch the illumination flares drift down on their little parachutes, reflecting for a moment the distant mountains on the flooded paddies, and imagine following that trail back, back to the vast armies of men and women who were fighting us and had fought the French, back even, to Hanoi, the capital of that war, to the nameless people dressed in black and white who floated through Hanoi's streets on bicycles like silent clouds. Back up that trail were steaming bowls of *pho* in the morning, air-raid shelters and antiaircraft batteries, and the timeless cycle of the rice harvest. Back up that trail, in those mountains, was the enemy.

I thought about the enemy almost every waking minute in the two days I spent preparing to join my new platoon. The night I arrived there was a firefight not far from Hill 10. Five NVA soldiers were killed. The colonel commanding the battalion insisted they be brought to his door. As I went back to my company's office after breakfast, I was greeted by the sight of five bodies being driven by on a mechanical mule. They were wrapped in ponchos, but I could see the faces, the skin gray like clay, the eyes glazed and dull like fish eyes in a market. The colonel looked at the bodies, smiled, then waved them away. The young marine driving the mechanical mule saw me staring and flashed me the two-fingered "peace" sign as he drove by with his war booty.

Dressed in newly starched fatigues and feeling painfully clean and innocent, I flew out to the platoon's position in a helicopter. We circled a blasted hilltop still smoldering from enemy mortars, where tanned men in ragged combat fatigues moved slowly about in their morning rituals, fixing breakfast and collecting their gear. The platoon was the usual collection of rednecks, ethnics, blacks, Chicanos, and an Indian called Chief. I had spent the morning going over the records of my platoon. I wrote at the time: "I have fifty-eight men. Only twenty have high school diplomas. About ten of them are over twenty-one. Reading through their record books almost made me cry. Over and over they read—address of father: unknown; education: one or two years of high school; occupation: laborer, pecan sheller, gas station attendant, Job Corps. Kids with no place to go. No place but here."

They had enlisted because where they came from that was what you did when there was a war on. Or they had been told to join the Marines or go to jail. Or a few of them had been drafted. They did not care that I had been to college or studied at Oxford. They only cared that I keep them alive. As for me, I got off that helicopter with that exquisitely embarrassing feeling of a young officer sent to command men, every one of whom knows more about war than he does.

My platoon was a graphic illustration of what determined who went to war: age and class. At the core of the experience of the war was a matter of simple arithmetic—few of the men who fought it had counted to their twenty-first birthday. The average age of the infantryman in World War II was twenty-six; in Vietnam it was nineteen. "He was only twenty-four," Norman Mailer wrote of Gallagher in *The Naked and the Dead.* In another platoon there was a lance corporal who was twenty-four. He was called Pops.

What happens to a man at nineteen affects him differently than what happens at twenty-six. At nineteen, the Vietnam soldier or marine had just graduated from high school. By and large he was away from home for the first time in his life. He was impressionable, immature, uncertain of himself, eager for approval from his peers, as yet unformed by experience. And what an experience he was going to get! A war of exceptional brutality, waged at times by old men, women, and children, who would treat him with exaggerated kindness during the day and try to kill him at night; a war without front or purpose, or even a reason; a war where he saw friends who meant more to him than any other friends he had ever had get shot, ripped by shrapnel, or torn to pieces by booby traps. They died in his arms. Their blood and guts stayed on his clothes for days.

When they came back, their contemporaries who went to college were still in the first semester of their sophomore year, worrying about political science tests and getting a date for homecoming. The veterans returned utterly changed to an unchanged world—no wonder it was hard to adjust.

"On the night of my class's senior prom," my radioman Jeff Hiers recalled years later, "I was out on Go Noi Island calling in artillery and medevacs. I was telling pilots where to land and gunners where to fire. I was only eighteen, but everyone was depending on me to do my job fast and to do it right. I had so much power—and then I came home and went to college and everyone thought I was still a kid."

My men grew up in Vietnam. There are many better ways to do it—but few faster. College, in stark contrast, was a means of prolonged adolescence. Even those students who took the occasional risk at an antiwar demonstration did so with the indulgence of the university which sheltered them from the world. In 1968 John Gregory Dunne wrote about an early-morning antiwar demonstration outside the induction center in Oakland. At 7:45 a.m. the marchers suddenly dispersed. They were students at Berkeley, and didn't want to miss their eight o'clock class.

I was hardly surprised to discover that most of my men were high school dropouts, since no one I knew from Rice or Oxford went to Vietnam. The critic Leslie Fiedler wrote that he "had never known a single family that had lost a son in Vietnam, or indeed, one with a son wounded, missing in action, or held prisoner of war. And this despite the fact that American casualties in Vietnam are already almost equal to those in World War I. Nor am I alone in this strange plight; in talking to friends about a subject they seem not eager to discuss, I discover they can, must, all say the same."

A survey conducted by Notre Dame found that "men from disadvantaged backgrounds were about twice as likely as their better-off peers to serve in the military, go to Vietnam, and see combat." Congressman Alvin O'Konski took a personal survey of a hundred inductees from his northern Wisconsin district. Not one of them came from a family with an annual income of over $5,000.

James Fallows tallied his twelve hundred classmates in the Harvard class of 1970 and counted only fifty-six who entered the military, just two of whom went to Vietnam. One of his non-Harvard friends, a Rhodes Scholar who became a corporate lawyer, told Fallows that "there are certain people who can do more good in a lifetime in politics or academics or medicine than by getting killed in a trench." "I got a good steady job," a Delaware defense worker said. "I'm making good money and having a ball every weekend. Why the hell should I want to go?" It's little wonder, then, that in a 1971 Harris Survey the majority of Americans agreed with the proposition that the men who went to Vietnam were "suckers, having to risk their lives in the wrong war, in the wrong place, at the wrong time."

The same thought crossed the minds of my men more than once. A few weeks after I joined my platoon I was on radio watch late one night. Suddenly I received a frantic message from a major in the battalion operations: Da Nang was being rocketed. We were ordered to move across the river and attempt to intercept the NVA rocket team. To me, this was serious. Da Nang—

rocketed! It sounded like London being bombed or Pearl Harbor being attacked.

"What is it, Lieutenant?" Hiers asked. My talking on the radio had woken him up.

"It's Da Nang. They're hitting it with rockets."

"No shit?"

"Yeah, they just told me."

"All fucking right!" Hiers said. "Hey, listen up!" he yelled as loud as he could into the silence of the night. "They're rocketing Da Nang!"

The response was not what I expected. The response was—cheers. All around the perimeter my fellow marines, the descendants of the heroes of Guadalcanal and Iwo Jima, were shouting with joy.

"Get those REMFs!"* was the gist of what they said. For the first time I realized that in the eyes of my men the enemy was not simply the NVA—that was a mere accident of politics. The NVA soldiers, after all, were out in the jungle too. They were wet and tired and scared, just like us. They were grunts, just like us. The Americans back in Da Nang, however, were the handiest of the other enemies—everyone who wasn't out there with us. *We* were here because *they* had sent us. And if a few rockets were falling on them, then so much the better. Let them have a taste of the war.

I called my squad leaders in and told them we had to move across the river.

"No way, Lieutenant," they said.

"What?" I couldn't believe what I was hearing.

One of my squad leaders answered. "Ain't no way we gonna move this platoon, at night, off this hill, cross that river, and go diddy-bopping through that jungle trying to find some gook rocketmen. We gonna get our asses kicked—and you know it. And all for some REMFs."

*Rear-echelon motherfuckers.

"But we've got orders," I said, without much conviction.

"No sweat, Lieutenant," Hiers said. "We just do it all on the radio. We'll show you."

I thought for a minute. This was the Marine Corps. We were supposed to charge up any hill, anytime. The merely difficult we do at once, the impossible takes a little longer. But then I realized that the major on the radio was drunk,* that we would never find the men who shot the rockets, and that it would expose my platoon to great danger if we went. I decided to hell with the major and the war. I was going to protect my men.

"Okay," I said.

And so for the next few hours we simulated the radio traffic of packing up, moving out, crossing the river, and setting up new positions—all without ever leaving our foxholes. And at first light, we did it for real. We may have been suckers, but we weren't stupid.

The first two days I was with the platoon I watched my predecessor, Staff Sergeant Mackie, expertly send out patrols and ambushes and set up the position for the night. At dusk we would station two- and four-man listening posts along the most likely avenues by which our position could be attacked. Every fifteen minutes they would click the handsets of their radios to let us know everything was secure. The platoon command post (two sergeants, two radiomen, two corpsmen, and I) would take turns monitoring the radio.

Those first two nights no one had to wake me for my watch. I was lying on the ground, my eyes wide open, my ears tuned to the slightest sound. Shadows took on strange shapes and moved, every rustle became an NVA commando. All night the sound of artillery and mortars played on my nerves like a finger-

---

*The most dangerous drug problem in Vietnam wasn't enlisted men using too much dope; it was officers and noncoms drinking too much alcohol.

nail scratching down a blackboard. The sunrise had a special meaning.

On the third day I took charge of our return to Hill 10. I did everything I had learned in training at Quantico—I sent out flanking units, I moved forward, consolidated, moved forward again, protecting my rear, securing my point, communicating by hand signals with my squad leaders. It was a real textbook operation—but it happened to be through an area just outside the battalion perimeter, an area so secure the supply clerks played football there during the day. A good deal of the battalion watched my efforts with glee. It became known as the day Broyles took the football field.

During those first few weeks my men were weighing whether to let me stay as their platoon commander or shoot me themselves—the modern version of the way soldiers once elected their own officers. My textbook operation on the football field was not a point in my favor.

While we were back on Hill 10 I kept passing Hiers. He'd wave casually and say something like "Howdy, Lieutenant, how's it hanging?"

I was fresh from Quantico, where enlisted men saluted their officers. I gave Hiers a friendly lecture along those lines, but he still just waved. And then I told him that each time he didn't salute he'd have to fill a hundred sandbags.

In three days we'd reached several thousand sandbags. Finally Hiers took me aside and said, "Look, Lieutenant, I'll be happy to salute you, really I would. But if I get in the habit of saluting you back here in the rear where it's safe, I just might salute you out in the bush. And those gook snipers are just waiting for us to salute and tell 'em who the officer is. You'd be the first one blown away."

We forgot the salutes—and the sandbags.

The war had its own brand of humor. Much of it was post-combat euphoria, the laughter of survivors. One of my men, Robertson, was convinced he was invincible. Whenever he could get away with it, he neglected to carry a rifle. One day his squad took fire from a tree line and everyone hit the dirt. Robertson pulled his Ka-Bar knife out of its scabbard, waved it over his head, and charged the tree line, yelling at the top of his lungs. That should have been it for Robertson. But for whatever reason —shock, mystification, admiration, or wit—the NVA didn't shoot him. Instead, they retreated, so Robertson made it to the tree line, then turned and beat his chest in triumph and yelled like Tarzan.

"Well, Lieutenant," Hiers said as Robertson waved for us to move up. "John Wayne lives."

Another young marine, March, was profoundly dense. He kept falling asleep at the worst times—on watch or on an ambush. I woke him up once by holding an M-16 next to his head and letting off a magazine on full automatic. It did no good. On one ambush he dozed off, rolled over in his sleep, and fell into the river. On another ambush he was gently awakened by the sound of his comrades firing at three NVA soldiers who had been standing above him with their AK-47s pointed at his head.

Such behavior put the whole platoon in jeopardy; in combat everyone is totally dependent on everyone else. March was in imminent danger of being conveniently shot during our next contact with the enemy, so I sent him back to the rear to do some punishment work.

At Hill 10 the plywood privies contained oil drums filled with diesel fuel. Every day the barrels were pulled out and the diesel fuel burned, producing a distinctive odor that even now, along with the sound of helicopters, is one of my enduring memories of Vietnam. This process was known as "burning the shitters."

"March," the company sergeant said one day, "I want you to burn the shitters."

"Burn the shitters?" March replied.

"Don't I speak English, you maggot?" was more or less the response.

So March went out, took a big can of diesel fuel, soaked down the entire privy, and set it on fire.

Great billows of black smoke rose up over the hill. Bucket

brigades were formed. Commotion reigned. Our platoon had just come in, and Hiers and I were sitting in the company area playing cards. Someone ran by, headed for the smoke.

"What happened?" I yelled at him. We didn't bother to get up. We had been two weeks in the bush. Nothing at battalion headquarters short of a full-scale ground attack by an NVA division was of any concern to us.

"Some idiot burned down the shitters," he shouted. "The EM Club is about to go up!"

Hiers looked up from his cards.

"March," he said.

"March," I replied. Had to be.

Many games were played with grenades. There was something comforting about a grenade, even though when it exploded it would most likely kill or wound anyone within a fifteen-meter radius. It was deceptively harmless, like a steel baseball that felt good in your hand, practically begged you to throw it. And a grenade didn't impose the same sense of personal responsibility that a rifle did. A bullet, after all, traced a line between you and your target, tied you to your enemy by logic and action. A grenade was different. It was the closest thing an ordinary soldier had to the impersonal killing practiced by jet pilots and artillerymen, who seldom saw the consequences of the deadly projectiles they launched. They weren't killing people; they were firing cannons or flying jets. Technology shielded them. They merely set it in motion.

Such forms of death on the battlefield are expressed in the passive voice: "He was killed by artillery fire/napalm/a bomb." The man who pulled the lanyard or dropped the bomb isn't even part of the language. It's a matter between the victim and the object. "I shot him," on the other hand, is unambiguous. Two human beings are linked, and the essence of war is revealed in stark honesty. There wasn't even a word in the language for killing someone with a grenade until "fragging" came into use, and it was specifically meant to describe the deliberate assault on one of our own men, most often an unpopular officer or noncom.

But for all that, grenades were simply too ubiquitous and too seductive not to have been constantly in use. Up on Hai Van Pass my platoon amused itself by a contest in which two men would stand on a ledge overlooking the ocean, pull the pins on their grenades at the same time, and then see who would be the last one to drop the grenade. The most skillful at this game could hold the grenade so that it exploded just after it passed their feet.

One day Hiers emptied the charge out of a grenade and staged a brief but compelling scene of post-traumatic stress syndrome outside a tent where four of his friends were playing cards. The scene concluded with "I can't take this anymore! I'm gonna end this for all of us!"

He then yanked the pin on the grenade and rolled it into the tent, sending everyone flying. "Just kidding, guys," Hiers said as they picked themselves up out of the mud.

Since war offers great intensity of experience, superlatives tend to become devalued and understatement then comes into its own. One afternoon a single rocket the size of one artillery round was fired into Da Nang from the opposite bank of the river near Hill 10. The hapless NVA gunner was then hit with every piece of ordnance in the American repertoire. The big guns of the artillery, the 155s and 175s, boomed, their huge rounds roaring overhead like freight trains in the sky. Then the naval gunfire came in, twice as big, shaking the earth. All the while our smaller pieces, the mortars and the 105s, were firing away.

After the artillery, jets swooped in, dragging load after load of napalm across the earth. Black clouds billowed up. Then gunships strafed the escape routes with hails of machine-gun fire. I watched the whole display with Lieutenant Bill Aue, the company intelligence officer. Neither of us said a word. After about an hour, things began to quiet down.

"You know," Aue said, "sometimes I think we overreact to rocket attacks."

Through one two-week stretch my platoon never stayed more than a night in the same position. We couldn't bathe or change clothes. Each day we chopped our way through elephant grass and spent the few short breaks picking off leeches. We were wet and hot during the day, wet and cold at night. Each morning it took two men to lift up each man's pack and set it on his shoulders. When the wet straps bit into your flesh and the weight settled on you, you couldn't believe you could take a single step. And then we would go for miles. The NVA were all around us. The days faded into one another.

"Hey, what day is it?" someone asked as we were digging our foxholes on still another hill.

"I don't know. Thursday?"

"Nah, Thursday was days ago."

"Saturday?"

"Yeah, that sounds right. Saturday the, must be, the twenty-ninth."

For a moment there was silence. Then, from the next foxhole, Meyers, the corpsman, said, "Hey, guys, we better get on the stick. There's only twenty-one more shopping days till Christmas."

The men read each other's mail, as if they had had so little experience with women that they had to share whatever tenderness and intimacy they had. They wrote off and became ordained ministers by mail order, and would go around marrying everyone. On one day I witnessed the marriage of various of my men to an old mama san with stained teeth, to a prostitute, and to a water buffalo. After we set up our position they would spend hours writing letters designed to play on the heartstrings of the people back home, primarily to entice the sending of cookies and other foodstuffs. One letter Hiers wrote to his church began: "As I fight the lonely battle against Communism, I have no fear, because God is my point man."

I said, "Hiers, you can't send that."

"C'mon, Lieutenant, it's worth three or four dozen chocolate-chip cookies."

And it was.

Mail was everything. Every night in the violet hour before dusk, the men would pull out their pens and write letters—to their parents, to their girlfriends, to girls whose addresses they had got from *Stars and Stripes*, the armed forces newspaper. It was the one connection they had between who they had been and who they had become. Some days we were so wet that it was almost impossible to write—the pen went right through the paper. Other days we ran out of paper and had to write on the back of old letters or even on C-ration boxes.

Every three or four days we would get resupplied by helicopter. With our rations and our ammunition and our medical supplies would come a large red sack of mail, which each squad leader passed out with a running commentary, much of it obscene. But every now and then someone got a Dear John, which was almost as bad as stepping on a mine. Then all the laughter stopped and everyone moved away, leaving the victim to read and reread his letter alone. After a while, some close buddy would come up with a deck of cards and maybe a C-ration delicacy like peaches and pound cake with melted chocolate. The two of them would talk quietly and everyone else would clean their rifles or dry their socks in silence. A Dear John was a calamity for the whole platoon. It took days to recover.

After a couple of weeks I was sleeping through all the friendly artillery. It came to seem part of the natural order of things, like sleeping in the mud and eating C rations. And then, on a dark night when the clouds hid the moon, I got my first taste of combat.

As usual, I had sent an ambush patrol out along a trail by the river. Often I would go on such ambushes, but this night I stayed at the platoon position on a nearby hill. Down the trail came a North Vietnamese unit, escorted by some local Viet Cong. The marines opened fire, and a firefight developed. I could see flashes and could hear, above the roar of small arms and the explosions of grenades, a high-pitched chorus of screams. The patrol leader radioed in, frantic, saying they were running out of ammunition. I sent out a relief unit, but it was ambushed. By then we were stretched very thin at the platoon position, so when the enemy began to probe our perimeter we realized we had got more than we bargained for. Soon the fire was coming in from all directions, the green AK-47 tracer bullets crossing our red M-16 rounds in the darkness.

After a long night of pushing back probes and calling in illumination rounds, artillery fire, and gunships, I finally got the platoon back together. It was a typical encounter in Vietnam—confused and chaotic, against a mysterious, all-but-invisible enemy. I described the scene in my journal: "We've all been under fire now, heavy fire, and we worked well together. A man never knows how he is going to act until it happens, and when it happens there is so much to do you don't worry about it. It's only afterwards that you remember yourself playing John Wayne and you get scared. You ask yourself: Did I do that? And then it becomes funny, somehow, and you stay up all night rehashing it, making the terror into humor.

"The best men were the shy, skinny, frail ones you'd laugh to think were marines and not stamp collectors or clerks. The man who led the reaction force said, 'The path just opened up before me. I didn't even have to look for it. It was just there.' The man who first saw the enemy patrol said, 'They came across the paddy like ghosts, two or three feet above the ground.' "

Afterwards I kept asking myself the question: Why do men fight? Why did they keep coming out of those trenches at Passchendaele and the Somme, walking in rows into machine guns? Why did they keep charging up Mount Suribachi or Hamburger Hill? Why did the North Vietnamese and the Viet Cong keep coming into our wire, keep pushing forward through the terrible hail of fire we rained on them? Every instinct would seem to be saying: Flee, flee. But there always seem to be reasons why men don't.

Many men in battle are more afraid of being a coward than of being killed. They would rather risk their lives than forfeit the respect of their comrades. Other men fight for theoretical motivations, such as religion or ideology, or for concrete ones, such as knowing they will be executed if they retreat.

But sometimes there don't seem to be any reasons. There is only action. A squad is trapped by machine-gun fire. Without being ordered, two men risk their lives to attack the guns. Often they don't know that they did it, much less why they did it. Something made them, that's all. Something beyond knowing. Something ingrained in the species.

The fighting around our position was heavy, but, miraculously, none of my men was killed. And although we found many blood trails in the morning, we recovered only one enemy body. As I read back through my journal years later, I was disappointed that I recorded no sense of remorse for the Vietnamese who were killed or wounded. I was concerned only for my men, and for myself. I was still armed with the soldier's most lethal weapon—the ability to see the man on the other side not as a human being but as the enemy.

14

ALL QUIET AT THE DMZ

When I landed in Da Nang in October 1984 our plane was the only aircraft visible in the entire airport, and my fellow passengers, and an equal number of people waiting at the gate to board the plane to fly on to Saigon, were the only people. Instead of the whirlwind of energy and activity that surrounded the Da Nang airport in 1969, there was only silence, a strange, pre-modern silence, the silence of the paddies. It was as if history had passed on, leaving behind a few people, the mountains wreathed in mist, and the clear sky.

For the first time I was on familiar ground. The streets were well paved and crowded with cars, trucks, tiny vans, three-wheeled tri-Lambrettas, motorcycles, and big Dodge and De Soto buses overflowing with passengers and piled high with goods. There were garages and tire repair shops, lumberyards, and hundreds of little stores that actually had things for sale. I saw tractors and heavy equipment. The houses were larger, the shops bigger, the streets wider. I had at once the feeling of space. It looked much as I remembered it, which meant that it looked like a different country from what I had just left.

During the war Da Nang was like a mini-Saigon—loud and raucous, teeming with refugees, mutilated beggars, hustlers. Now it was subdued and obviously less crowded, as if some bizarre party had ended and everyone had gone home. (It was, in fact, back to its prewar population of 350,000, its size before refugees from the war swelled its population to more than one million people in 1970.)

At the airport I turned over my papers to various officials and began talking to my guides in Da Nang. The man in charge was Tran Hien, a softspoken, formal man my age. His assistant, Dinh Mien, was of the younger, postwar generation: he had the beginnings of a wispy goatee on his chin and was dressed in tailored trousers and platform shoes.

"Is this your first time in Da Nang?" Mien asked in careful, formal English.

"No, I was here during the war," I said.

"You were a journalist?"

I decided to ignore Duong Minh's advice and tell the truth; that, after all, was why I had returned. "No, I was in the Marines."

Hien looked up, surprised.

"But you were forced to join, isn't that right?" Mien asked me.

"No, I wasn't forced to join," I replied.

"They made you come, right?"

"No."

"You wanted to come and fight us?" he asked.

"No, not really."

"So you were forced to come?" he asked, determined to put the best possible face on this troubling matter.

"No, it was just"—I couldn't quite decide how to put it—"it was just my duty."

Minh had been translating this exchange for Hien. At my last comment he gave a slight nod. To shift the conversation off myself, I asked Hien what he had done in the war.

"I was in the Liberation forces," he said.

"Where?"

"Here. Da Nang."

"When?"

"The whole war," he said.

Hien had been a company commander just south of where I had been, but at times had fought into my battalion's area. He was the man I had fought. Finally, I was face to face with my old enemy, and he was a slight, polite man with brown eyes as gentle as a deer's. I had dozens of questions for him, but he simply smiled.

"You are late," he said. "They are expecting you in Hue. We will talk when you get back. The war is over. It is past. None of it will change in two days."

We left the two guides at the airport and climbed into a new Toyota. We drove north with Laura Branigan playing on the driver's stereo. Along Red Beach, where the highway runs near the ocean, there had been a long stretch of American bases, including an Air Force base with its own massage parlor. As we drove by, I saw only sand, some cemeteries, and rusty wire. We crossed the Nam O Bridge and began the climb up to Hai Van Pass, high above the sea. Halfway up, I asked the driver to stop. I got out, the wet sea air in my face, and looked back on Da Nang. I could see almost the entire area of the 1st Marine Division—Elephant Valley, Ba Na Mountain, Charlie Ridge, the Arizona Territory, Marble Mountain, and the Que Son Mountains, visible only as a dim smudge on the horizon.

Beyond the narrow stretch of coastal plain, where the Tuy Loan and other rivers flowed out in a wide delta, were the mountains hidden in clouds, thousands of square kilometers of them to Laos and beyond. It reminded me of the narrow coastal valleys of California. Da Nang Bay is like a mirror image of Monterey Bay, and off the coast, floating in the South China Sea like Santa Cruz Island off Santa Barbara, is Cham Island.

So much had happened in that small stretch of coast that I was seeing again, so much war, so many people killed. But now it lay beneath me, bucolic and peaceful. Even the mountains, which had been etched in my mind as a land of mystery and danger, the domain of the enemy, were only scenery. Behind me waterfalls coursed down through tropical foliage; hundreds of feet below gentle swells broke on deserted beaches scalloped from the rocks. It is one of the most beautiful places I have ever seen.

It seemed unthinkable that so much war had been here.

We drove on, through low clouds and patches of rain, past waterfalls and rockslides, to the summit. The old Marine position that had guarded the pass was gone. We descended into the plain through a beautiful landscape of sea and lagoon. Compared with North Vietnam, this area between Hai Van Pass and the city of Hue was virtually unpopulated. The houses were spread out, not concentrated like jumbled blocks in hamlets. They seemed larger, more substantial. Some were made of well-carpentered wood; tin roofs were everywhere. We passed a sign that said: HANOI 690 KILOMETERS.

From the car the only clue to the presence of an old American base was a sudden increase in scrap metal for sale at the houses along the road. We passed Phu Bai, the first American enclave between the DMZ and Da Nang, and then Camp Eagle, the headquarters of the 101st Airborne. All that remained were some rubble, a lonely abandoned watchtower, and a few strands of rusty barbed wire. The huge supply staging areas, the movie theaters, the Dairy Queens, the Officers' Clubs—all are gone.

At none of the old bases does anything grow. The bare red dirt lies on the earth like a scar, as if the land itself is cursed. It is like what the Romans did to Carthage—plowed the city under and sowed the furrows with salt. The names we gave the country—Charlie Ridge, the Arizona Territory, Dodge City, Mortar Valley, China Beach—names that made this alien land familiar, a metaphor of what we knew, they too are gone. Of all the millions of Americans who passed through here, of their fears, joys, sufferings, victories, and defeats, nothing remains.

In Hue we picked up a new guide, Nguyen Van Mai, an intense and studious young man with a distracted look who had spent six years studying in Moscow to be a teacher. Instead he had ended up in the foreign relations department of the province, a job he clearly regarded as less than fascinating. In 1972, when he was still a schoolboy in what they call the "liberated zone," he was wounded by American artillery near Quang Tri.

We drove north from Hue toward the DMZ, into the heart of the beast, where names now faded into obscurity then told of the war's most brutal fighting: Hill 881, Con Thien, the Rockpile, Dong Ha, Quang Tri, the A Shau Valley, Hamburger Hill, Lang Vei, Khe Sanh.

Stacks of old shells were everywhere, ready for recycling into tools. Rows of newly planted eucalyptus and *falao* pine lined the road and marked the boundaries of fields and paddies. Throughout the war virtually the entire region had been a free-fire zone. The people had been evacuated, the fields abandoned, and the trees and houses blasted into the mud. Quang Tri, the one town of any size, had been obliterated in 1972, during the 138 days the Communists had held it against some of the heaviest bombing of the war.

Now the people were back, and rice was being harvested and brought in from the fields. Women with pitchforks threshed the rice by tossing the straw under our speeding car, just as they had in the North. But in the North the road would be lined for miles with rice, and we would run an unbroken gantlet of flashing pitchforks and flying straw; here the women were few and far between. The central coast is very different country from the Red River Delta: the land is wilder, more open, and windswept —like the California coast around Morro Bay.

Past Quang Tri the land rose into high meadows, and the paddies were tucked into small valleys. On top of one of the hills was a large sign announcing the failure of the "Mac Na Mar lin." The McNamara line was a scheme by Defense Secretary Robert McNamara to create an electronic barrier just below the DMZ, a sort of high-tech Hadrian's Wall, that would detect Communist troops trying to infiltrate into the South. Like most of the high-tech gear we tried in Vietnam, the sensors and other equipment that made up the line malfunctioned constantly.

They were no better than the people sniffers that were

dropped from airplanes to detect movement along the Ho Chi Minh Trail. At one stage these sniffers worked by detecting the presence of urine. The Communists foiled this sophisticated system by suspending bags of buffalo urine from trees, an example of how time and again our efforts to substitute technology for will and courage were doomed to fail.

We thought that our great edge in technology could take the place of basic soldiering and common sense. From the creative brains in our military laboratories poured hundreds of ideas in a never-ending flow, all designed to solve, by magic, a problem that could only be solved in the age-old way—by one soldier defeating another, in close combat, on the ground. Throughout the war we tried to find the secret—through firepower, helicopters, bombing, technology—that would let us avoid this unpleasant fact, but we never did.

For the ordinary soldier or marine, these electronic brainstorms were a menace. We had to set out and painstakingly monitor electronic sensors along infiltration routes, which then would be set into hyperactivity by passing animals or by the wind rustling the leaves of the trees. But when the sensors were triggered, we had to go "check it out," which usually meant we had to undertake complicated and dangerous night patrols, normally to discover that a water buffalo had walked by or a tree limb had fallen.

In one memorable episode, a Marine unit had to secure and reinforce a hill astride a suspected infiltration route southwest of Da Nang. For weeks we laid sandbags and strung barbed wire, while in a separate tent a special, top secret team worked with the latest technological breakthrough. Finally, it was unveiled. The idea seemed good. A special scope, illuminated by concentrated starlight, was focused on a target. A button was pushed, and a laser beam shot out to the target and bounced back into a computer, which fed the precise coordinates to the artillery battery.

The classic problem with artillery is that it is blind; the only way to determine the precise location of a target of opportunity is by firing a round, then adjusting the next round to the target. For a highly mobile target, this first shot is the cue to disperse and depart, so that when the battery fires its next rounds they tend to land on recently vacated real estate.

The laser scope changed all that. The full battery could fire at once, and catch the target by surprise. On its first night in operation, the scope worked brilliantly. A dozen or so North Vietnamese were spotted on a path. The laser bounced off them and into the computer, and the battery fired—with lethal effect. The top secret detachment cheered and passed around whiskey.

The next night, and every night after that, the NVA soldiers simply used trails on the opposite side of the hill. The scope was useless. The high-tech specialists went back to the safety of Saigon. Then, on the first overcast night, which was only a few nights later, rain being common in Vietnam, NVA sappers crawled through the wire with satchel charges and attacked the position. The ordinary marines, who had been guarding the laser scope instead of attending to more sensible pursuits, took heavy casualties—from naked men throwing homemade bombs.

We passed Route 9, which led west past Camp Carroll and the Rockpile to Khe Sanh.

"Hey," I said, "I thought we were going to Khe Sanh."

We stopped the car. Minh had a brief discussion with Mai.

"He said that we are too late to go to Khe Sanh today. The road is very bad. We will go there tomorrow. Today we see the DMZ."

Long before we should have arrived at the old Demilitarized Zone—my mind being attuned to the old travel times in military vehicles along less than secure roads—we were there. Some sampans floated idly in the Ben Hai River, for twenty-one years the boundary between the two Vietnams. Without ceremony we crossed the Gio Linh Bridge. I walked onto the bridge, from their side. On the south side—our side—were rice paddies, a few houses, a boy on a water buffalo. Three women were wading slowly in the river, gathering water potatoes and oysters. I stood on the bridge, on the only road connecting Hanoi and Saigon, for half an hour. Not a single car or truck came by. Finally an old Dodge van, converted to a bus, lumbered across the bridge from the south and stopped by our car. Five or six children poured out and ran off down a narrow trail, chattering and carrying their satchels from school. The wind made patterns in the yellowing rice. To the west the gray mountains blurred into the sky. From the sea, clouds were blowing in.

In this place of combat with no quarter, where we waited for human waves to pour across the border as in Korea, the head-on, fair-fight invasion which never quite came—in this blasted moonscape where we waited and fought and died while the war rotted away behind our backs—today there is only normal life. It is like the quiet fields of the Marne, or the green hills of Gettysburg—a landscape now, where only those with memory know that history happened. The guns, the voices, the terrible energy that makes war, all are stilled. There was a reason men fought so fiercely here for so long, but the gentle river, the paddies, and the sky yield no secrets.

There was nothing to do but get into the car and go back. The driver was playing "Gloria" as loud as the stereo would go. During the war we were the ones who filled Vietnam with rock-and-roll; the Viet Cong and NVA read each other poems from the poetry notebooks most of them carried. Ho Chi Minh announced the Tet Offensive with a poem. Le Duc Tho, who shared the Nobel Peace Prize with Henry Kissinger shortly before departing for South Vietnam to help direct the North Vietnamese Army's final offensive, wrote a poem commemorating the Final Victory which is inscribed on a monument in Quang Tri. I tried to imagine Lyndon Johnson and Henry Kissinger penning verse during the siege of Khe Sanh or after the Christmas bombing, but I simply couldn't conceive it.

So instead I put on the tape of Vietnam combat which Jeff Hiers had sent me, plugged in my earphones, and as we drove through lengthening shadows, past the silent fields and mountains, I was surrounded by the sounds of ambushes and medevacs, the booming of artillery, the roar of jets, the whirring of helicopters. I listened to an ambush, and there, after fifteen years, were all the sounds again—the crack of AK-47s, the sharp pop of M-16s, and the voices of men yelling—frightened, confused, and brave.

The voices were in my ears, but the men were all gone. Only I, of the almost three million Americans who fought in Vietnam, was here now. I felt intensely, totally, alone.

That night the driver, the two guides, and I ate at a small café deep in the heart of Hue, where foreigners never go. It was called, simply, Kitchen. At several tables bleary-eyed young men lingered over cigarettes and stacks of dirty dishes. Each group had arranged dozens of empty bottles of Saigon Export beer on the table into different patterns and designs—here a star, there a spiral, here concentric circles. Mangy dogs wandered in and out. From the darkened streets children would occasionally emerge, stand in the doorway and stare silently at me, then depart. Foreign cigarettes were sold openly, not clandestinely, as in Hanoi. In the South, Capstan cigarettes are as prized as the ubiquitous 555s. I bought several packs and simply laid them on the table for everyone to smoke.

Hue was the old Imperial capital, and at the Emperor's court Vietnamese cuisine reached its highest levels. Hue is still known throughout Vietnam for its food, and this dinner was superb. We had steamed fish, duck with garlic, beef with mushrooms, and a plate of the huge crabs for which Hue is famous. The owner of the café apologized profusely; if he had known we were coming, he said, he would have prepared something special. I asked Minh if we could eat the crab with our fingers.

"Of course," he said. "We have a saying: to use a fork to

eat crab is like using a translator to, uh, to talk to your girl-friend."

Through the first courses we carried on a desultory discussion about politics, dampened by Mai's recounting of the party line on every subject. The long years at the University of Moscow, and the burden of being an anointed member of the Communist Party elite, seemed to have turned his mind into a Marxist catechism. Finally I lost interest and asked him if he had any questions for me.

"As a matter of fact, yes," he said. "Who is this Michael Jackson?"

I laughed. "Hey, why don't you listen to Russian music?"

"Are you kidding?" he replied.

After that exchange, by mutual agreement, we didn't discuss politics for the rest of the meal. We talked about music and women instead. Minh, the northerner, said his favorite singers were Abba and Karen Carpenter. Mai and the driver, both southerners, looked at him with pity: they preferred U2 and the Eagles.

The more Saigon Export beer we drank, the more difficult it was to translate the conversation. The beer came in the same bottles as had 33, the *ba muoi ba* beer we had drunk constantly during the war. Even in the most remote villages we seemed always to be able to find *ba muoi ba* on ice, a tribute to the entrepreneurial skills of the Vietnamese peasant. During the dry season we were so hot after long patrols that even the distinctly formaldehyde taste of the beer was a welcome relief. The 33 name is gone now; the brewery has been nationalized. But the formaldehyde bouquet still lingers in the brew.

Mai and the driver began to talk in Vietnamese. Even as they ate they kept a cigarette lit, and would take long puffs between bites. Minh and I began to discuss women. Minh is thirty-five, and his long years of working in embassies abroad had left him single and without prospects—a situation that in his infrequent idle moments left him depressed.

"What about the two at the hotel?" I asked him. "They were beautiful."

"Yes, they were," he said. "But I could never approach them."

"Why not?"

"Because I do not know them," he said, with a sad, resigned firmness. "I don't know their families. I don't know their values."

"But couldn't you just ask them out and get to know them that way?" I asked him.

"Oh, no. It has to be arranged. I have to know their families."

"But, Minh," I said, "why can't you just spend some time with a woman you meet at the movies or in the park, and get to know her yourself?"

"I just could not do it."

"But aren't you limiting your chances?"

He finished his beer. "That is how we do things," he said stiffly. I marveled again at what a strange and interesting man he was: a dedicated Marxist, but a Victorian in social matters; an atheist, but a scrupulous observer of his family's religious practices; a sophisticated traveler, but a man of village values; a romantic and a poet, but a disciplined bureaucrat.

The bill was 1,240 dong: about a hundred dollars at the official rate, or five dollars at the black-market rate, and the equivalent of more than four months' salary for any of my companions. I paid.

After dinner, we went for a drive around the darkened streets of Hue. A mass was in progress at the Hue Cathedral, a strikingly modern structure grafted onto the Gothic architecture of the Hue seminary. The church was half full. As in Phat Diem, I felt I was in a sanctuary of the West, a place which I understood, even if I was unable to follow the mass. Minh, Mai, and the driver sat in the car. I wandered out into a field behind the church.

In this field, during the Tet Offensive of 1968, the Communists executed a young U.S. Information Service employee named Stephen Miller. I am sure they killed him as brutally and as matter-of-factly as General Loan of the Saigon police executed the Viet Cong terrorist in the streets of Saigon the same week. That execution, so dramatically captured on film—the captive brought up, the pistol being raised to his head and fired, the man falling over, blood spurting on the pavement—became a visual metaphor for the brutality of the whole war. (What American viewers didn't know was that the Viet Cong terrorist had just finished massacring the wife and children of a friend of General Loan's, a fact that while not excusing the summary execution, at least makes it a less casually callous act.)

Stephen Miller died no less brutally than the Viet Cong terrorist, and so did the several thousand civilians the Viet Cong executed in Hue while they controlled the city. But their deaths —and the deaths of the family the executed terrorist had just murdered—weren't televised and therefore, in the practical terms of politics, might as well never have happened.

I never knew Stephen Miller, but at that moment he seemed a symbol of everyone who had died unremembered and unnoticed in Vietnam. I stood in the field and thought of all the people who had died such anonymous, pointless deaths here. My guides, the victors, sat in the car, smoking, their cigarettes red dots in the blackness.

15

AN ARGUMENT IN HUE

That night a typhoon blew in from the South China Sea. The wind beat against the windows of my room, the power, of course, went out, and the Perfume River rose steadily, churning with debris. Route 9 was impassable, so my trips to Khe Sanh and to My Lai, south of Da Nang, were canceled. As the rains fell, we toured the Imperial museum. There was all manner of furniture, inlaid with landscapes in elaborately carved mother-of-pearl. The Emperor's clothes were on display, richly embroidered with gold thread. One golden jacket and a pair of black slippers were worn only when the Emperor was carried to the fields to plow the first furrow of the new season. The Emperor's traveling chair was carved in the shape of a dragon; it took sixteen servants to carry it. There was a game called *do ho*, in which the object was to bounce twelve wooden sticks in such a way that they each landed in a narrow wooden vase.

"It looks impossible," I said.

"Oh, no," the guide replied. "The Emperor Bao Dai was expert at it. Of course, he had nothing else to do."

A tea set made of intricately carved ivory nestled in a golden case.

"Out of these cups," the guide said, "the Emperor would drink only tea brewed with the dew gathered from the lotus blossom."

It was my favorite item in the museum.

My Vietnamese escorts seemed to take an almost prurient interest in the most outrageous excesses, as if the Emperor's decadence both scandalized and titillated them. They were, after all, a new breed of man, proud to be Communists, and the Emperor represented everything they were against. It was a museum of the forbidden life, a relic from the trash heap of history preserved to remind them of the evils of inequality. But like Russian Communists eager to show off the treasures of the Czars, they seemed proud that the trappings of their former royalty were so indulgent and so elegant.

From my trip to Hue in 1970 I remembered that Hue craftsmen made special conical hats. The bridge over the Perfume River, the Imperial tombs, and other scenes of Hue were woven into the straw, so that they appeared in silhouette when the hat was held up to the light. From the museum we drove to the market, but it was flooded and closed. The hat would have to wait. We did pass several stores displaying rack after rack of blue jeans. On the wall of one hung a—very large—green raincoat. At last!

We stopped the car and I dashed through the rain to the store. The owner wanted 300 dong. I paid without haggling and donned the raincoat, which was still several sizes too small. When I returned to the car Minh asked how much I had paid for it. When I told him, the car erupted in an uproar. I had been robbed! I should have paid only 250 dong—at the most! Everyone wanted to go back and get my money. I said no, never mind. I didn't want to haggle in the rain over a few pennies that meant nothing to me and everything to the store owner. There was much grumbling as we drove through the flooded streets. I had clearly slipped a few notches in their eyes. Why would I willingly be taken? How could a people who paid the asking price in the market accomplish anything?

Our next stop was the headquarters of the People's Committee, which was in the French colonial compound that had been used by the American advisory command. We were met by Nguyen Minh Ky, the vice-president of the province's People's Committee and an assistant. The assistant looked like a profes-

sor on leave from his university doing a bit of government service. I kept expecting him to pull out a pipe. Ky, on the other
hand, had the wavy hair and good looks of a movie star. It was
impossible for me to imagine that they spent more than fifteen
years living in the jungle—but they had. The Viet Cong we
captured or who defected to us during the war were tough,
dedicated people, but they had the look of peasants who had just
come from the fields. These men looked as if they had just come
from discussing a movie deal.

The hurricane was still raging, and they were preoccupied
with the flooding. Last year this province lost 70,000 acres of rice
after a similar hurricane, and for Vietnam, where malnutrition
is endemic and the average consumption of rice is beneath the
usually accepted minimum level of basic nutrition, such a loss is
a national disaster. I asked about the effects of the war, which
was as fierce here as anywhere in the country.

"We had six hundred thousand refugees at Liberation," Ky
told me. "They went back to the land bare-handed; their homes
had been leveled, their fields destroyed. There were unexploded
mines and bombs everywhere. So far we have found nine million
—one girl in Dong Ha found three thousand by herself—at the
cost of four thousand people killed and injured, including two
children killed by a pellet bomb last week."

"Nine million?" I asked, doing some quick calculations in my
head. "That's nine hundred thousand a year, or, let's see, about
twenty-five hundred a day—that seems like a lot."

"Nine million," he repeated, undeterred. "Nine million is correct. And all the trees were destroyed. We planted fifty thousand
trees last year. After Liberation we had to import rice; now we
are almost self-sufficient. There were no industries here at all;
we have begun many new cooperative ventures. We have built
hospitals and secondary schools in each district, we are restoring
the old Imperial district, we . . . "

Ky was rolling off programs and statistics like a politician
running for reelection, pausing only to receive messages about

the progress in fighting the flood and to offer me fruit and tea and cigarettes. And I had to agree that since the war they had achieved a great deal. What I couldn't see was the price they had paid.

"You know," he said, "in war everything is simple—you fight for what you believe in, and you risk your blood and even your life. In the jungle we didn't have time to think about floods and cooperatives and running a province. Life is much more complicated now."

We ate lunch on the roof of the hotel, overlooking the river, which by now was roiled and angry. The old city and the market across the river were barely visible through the storm. In the center of the flood sampans balanced precariously amid the howling winds, the children on board searching for anything of value in the debris being swept by. Two young women in yellow *ao dais* laid out the most lavish meal of my entire trip, beginning with plates filled with artfully arranged giant prawns.

I asked Ky if he had been in Hue during the Tet Offensive in 1968. He beamed. "Oh, yes. I was here for twenty-four days and nights. I was in the Citadel; I was everywhere in the city. The Americans and the puppets bombed us with everything they had, but we made them fight for every street. It was very fierce. The people had been living under oppression for fourteen years; many of our fighters had not seen their families since 1954. They hugged each other and wept. It was glorious."

The fighting at Hue was house by house, street by street, block by block. It was some of the most bitter fighting of the war, and it produced some of the best television. For once, the combat was concentrated, with an objective—the squat stone tower of the Citadel, from which defiantly flew the Viet Cong flag. Night after night, as I sat transfixed in the Middle Common Room at Worcester College in Oxford, I watched young Americans fighting and dying in the shadow of the enemy flag; there

had never been television like it. I still remember an interview
with one of the marines who was trying to recapture the Citadel.
It went something like this:

"What's it like? Is it rough?" the interviewer asked. The
young marine leaned against a wall, a thousand-yard stare in his
blasted eyes. In the background other marines popped up to fire
over the wall, then ducked down again.

"Real rough," he said. "The worst thing is not knowing
where they are. Could be anywhere—in the gutter, in a house—
anywhere. Everybody just wants to get out of here and get back
home and go back to school."

Get back home and go back to school. I was in school, safe,
when I heard him say it. When I ended up in Vietnam two years
later I realized he had said it all. Those were our goals: stay alive,
get out of here, and pick up our lives again. This war was certainly not our life—that was "back in the world."

But the Vietnamese were home already; this *was* the world,
and there would be no other plans, and no other life but the war,
until it was over. The marine on television, who just wanted to
get home and go back to school, was our typical fighter, and for
all that he did a superb job. The young men who were willing to
live in the jungle and give up seeing their families for fourteen
years, who would defend a citadel against bombs and artillery,
who would hold elections to see who got to go on suicide missions, were their typical fighters. That they fought well should
be no surprise. Fighting was their life.

Ky asked me if I had seen the PBS program *Vietnam: A
Television History*. "Everyone here saw it," he said. "I remember watching American troops throwing grenades into shelters.
I thought of so many places I had seen such crimes. Those poor
people were just peasants and laborers. They only wanted to
plant rice, and they were killed. I could have cried."

As he talked, my own memories came back. In 1970, I had
spent several weeks teaching English at night in Da Nang.
One of my students told me this story: "My parents were
living in Hue in 1968, when the Viet Cong took the city. They

were schoolteachers. The Viet Cong came to the door and took them away. They told my grandmother they had to ask them some questions. My parents never came back. They found their bodies near the Imperial tombs. They had been tied up and strangled."

And I remembered a Viet Cong attack in 1970 on a hamlet south of Da Nang called Thanh My. The Viet Cong had gone from bunker to bunker, throwing in satchel charges. If anyone tried to flee, they were shot—old men, women, young children. When I got there the next morning the mangled bunkers were still smoldering, the bodies were laid out in long rows, and a few survivors with blank faces were poking in the rubble. They were just "peasants and laborers—they only wanted to plant rice." And I could have cried too, and did.

Near the end of my year in Vietnam the Viet Cong attacked a Buddhist orphanage near An Hoa, southwest of Da Nang. They killed the priests and the women in charge, dismembered the children with bayonets, and blew up the buildings. I was at the 95th Evacuation Hospital when the few survivors were brought in by helicopter. Orphaned by the war, they had now been maimed by it. It was the most senseless tragedy I had ever seen.

I stared numbly at the tiny bodies wrapped in bandages, and marked off another of the few days I had remaining before I went home. By then I had run out of tears.

One of the young women brought out shish kebabs of sausage, garlic, herbs, and mushrooms, and showed me how to wrap them in gossamer-thin rice paper. I was their guest, they were taking time out from fighting the flood to entertain me, and they had treated me—as everyone had—with great hospitality. And I still felt I was in Vietnam at the sufferance of my hosts; behind the numbing hospitality, the high walls of the Hanoi Hilton kept reappearing in my mind. But something about Ky's bland self-righteousness—or perhaps I had just heard one too many lec-

tures about American bombings and atrocities—reminded me
that I still took some things about the war personally too.

"I remember two things about Hue," I said. "I remember
your flag flying from the Citadel, and I remember the bodies of
all the innocent people the Viet Cong murdered."

A shadow crossed Ky's face, a fleeting moment of hardness
that made me glad I was his guest and not his prisoner. Then the
smile returned. "That was a total fabrication," he said. "It was
completely to the contrary. We were the people. How could we
kill ourselves? It is impossible."

Having proved to his satisfaction that such a massacre was,
in metaphysical terms at least, impossible, Ky went on: "Since
1959 the puppets had brought the guillotine to every corner of
our country. They tied us up and rubbed chili pepper into our
mouths, noses, and eyes."

He warmed to his theme. "They ran electric current into
women's private parts. They nailed your fingers down and then
tore out the fingernails. They put out your eyes and cut off your
ears and wore them around their necks—for publicity. They
ripped open your belly and tore out your heart and liver. They
cut open the womb and yanked out the baby inside, then stomped
it into the dust."

He paused. "Now *that* was terrible. If they could do that,
they could make up any lie about us."

I asked him if he meant to say the Viet Cong had not executed
any civilians.

"That is correct," he replied, reaching across the table for
some pink seaweed on delicate pastry leaves.

"Then where did all those bodies come from?"

He looked at me with sympathy. "It was a very chaotic time.
A few criminals may have been spontaneously rubbed out by the
people, like stepping on a snake. But most of those bodies—if
there were any—were probably patriots who helped us and were
murdered by the puppets after we left."

He put down his napkin. "You know," he said, "I often came
into Hue during the war. I pretended I was a fisherman, or a

student, or a peasant coming to market. The Americans would come right up to me. They'd pat me on the back and offer me cigarettes."

"And what did you do?" I asked him, as the table was being cleared and the coffee brought.

He looked at me with a sly smile. "I just said, 'GI, GI number one.' " With that he pushed back his chair and said his goodbyes. The flood was rising, the rice harvest was in danger, and they had serious work to do.

We checked out of the hotel, a process that took three employees thirty-five minutes to accomplish. I had to sign seven copies of the bill. Outside, the storm had abated. Already the trees that had been blown over had been cut up and carried away for firewood. Hundreds of people were out in the rain, fishing in the old way. They used nets suspended from one end of a long bamboo pole mounted on a bamboo tripod some ten or twelve feet high. The other end of the pole was weighted with a bag of rocks. Using the tripod as a fulcrum, they would lower the net into the flooded rice paddy, then lift it out again by pulling down the weighted end of the pole with a rope. Around each large tripod were gathered two or three dozen people in conical hats, their plastic slickers wet with rain, waiting patiently to see what the nets would bring up. The nets moved slowly above them, like giant praying mantises bobbing in the paddies.

As we drove back to Da Nang, I was still troubled. "Nothing is more important than independence and freedom," Ho Chi Minh said. Not the loss of hundreds of thousands of soldiers, not the murder of innocent people. But why was it so difficult for my hosts to admit that perhaps they had done evil things in a good cause? During World War II we had bombed Dresden and Tokyo and killed hundreds of thousands of civilians. Was that justified? Was Hiroshima? The answer is not simple, but what makes a nation civilized is that it asks the question.

The Communists' massacre of civilians at Hue and at places

like Thanh My are now inconvenient, so they have been air-brushed out of history; they no longer exist. The Communists stand in the flood of history and pluck from the water only what serves the State. If reality is inconvenient, it can simply be changed. If history falls short of the ideal, it can be transformed into myth.

We had our own myths, of course, chief among them that we were helping the people of Vietnam as we bombed their villages, their crops, and their country into a bloody, soggy mess. And in our own history we have customarily gone to war as the protectors of virtue and morality, battling the evil empires of the Huns, the Nazis, the Communists. Our cause was just, therefore we were just. But in Vietnam we came to terms with history.

What Lieutenant William Calley and his men did at My Lai was a horrible atrocity, but he was tried and convicted for it. A marine in my platoon who murdered a civilian was tried and sentenced to twenty years. In Vietnam the men who perpetrated the massacres of Hue and Thanh My are heroes. We Americans, having lost confidence that our cause is automatically just, now tend to see the worst in ourselves and the best in our adversaries. Our moral sense is exquisitely tuned to My Lai and the effects of our bombing, but we are deaf to the brutalities of our enemies. Before Vietnam we could do no wrong—then we could do no right. History is seldom so simple.

I tried to explain all this to Minh. I told him about the bodies at Hue, about Thanh My, about American soldiers who had been found tied to stakes and skinned by the Viet Cong, their genitals cut off and stuffed in their mouths. I said that in war men do extreme things, of which they are often not proud later, even if they are confident their cause was just. And then I said how troubled I was that in Vietnam there seemed to be a national policy not to discuss such things or even to admit that they might have happened.

Minh thought for a moment. "You should not think we are not self-critical," he said. "Read our newspapers. Every day they are filled with criticism of the Party, of the government, of their policies. And Le Duan himself helped bring to light the excesses [a euphemism for the massacre of thousands of Vietnamese farmers after the defeat of the French] when we first collectivized agriculture. But such matters are not the concern of individuals. They are properly decided by the leadership. Once they have decided, we can discuss them. As Uncle Ho said—"

"I know, I know. Nothing is more important than independence and freedom?"

"Well, yes, of course. But he also said that there are two kinds of people who don't make mistakes: the ones in the grave and the ones still in their mother's wombs."

16

THE GIRL
AT MARBLE MOUNTAIN

The next morning we drove across the river and headed for China Beach, just south of Da Nang. We passed the old Marble Mountain airfield, where the Marine helicopters had been based. It was a reprise of our drive north. Once helicopters had been as thick here as locusts, beating the air with the throaty *whop-whop-whop* which is the trademark sound of the war. Now cattle graze near a few empty hangars, and two abandoned watch-towers, deserted and rusting, look out on peasants drying their rice along the road, at children herding ducks and chickens, and at old men—still, ten years later—patiently sorting through mounds of rusted metal that were once American vehicles or machinery but now are only junk.

During the war American supply depots lined the road, and from a jeep you could see endless pallets stacked with cases of soft drinks and beer. Farther down the road hundreds of thousands of refugees lived in huts made from those beer and soda cans. After we Americans threw the cans away, the Vietnamese would collect them, hammer them flat, and connect them with wire to form the walls of their crude huts. We were there to save them, and they lived in houses made of our garbage.

Today the bases, the supply depots, and the houses made of cans are gone, the Americans are back in America, and the Vietnamese who lived in the Coke and Budweiser houses are back in their villages. And the helicopters—the tiny LOHs, the sturdy UH-1"Hueys," the fearsome Cobra gunships, the CH-47s with their twin rotors, and the giant CH-53s—are forgotten.

It's harder to forget the men who flew them. During the second half of my year in Vietnam I lived with the generals and colonels in permanent houses built on top of Freedom Hill. It was a very different war from what I had known as a platoon commander out in the bush. Each morning we would put on our freshly starched uniforms, leave our dirty clothes and beds to be cleaned by Vietnamese mama sans, and breakfast in the general's mess, where we would check off our orders on pads as if we were in a private club. After the morning briefing we would take the helicopter and fly out to visit some battalion headquarters or other outpost, then return in time for lunch, a nap, some exercise or reading. In the early afternoon we would fly back out to the war again.

The first general I worked for felt that it was his duty to visit every marine who had been wounded, so once a week we would take a sackful of Purple Hearts and make our rounds of the military hospitals or, if it was in the harbor, the Navy hospital ship *Sanctuary*.

There was a precise system to our visits. A marine who was wounded received a Purple Heart. If he had lost one limb (testicles and eyes included), he received a Purple Heart and an automatic promotion to the next rank. If he had been unlucky enough to lose two limbs, he got, in addition to the Purple Heart and the promotion, a Bronze Star. There was nothing extra to be gained by losing three or more limbs. In some cases, there was no unbandaged place left to pin the Bronze Star medal, so the general would affix it to the pillow.

I followed along behind, balancing Purple Hearts, certificates of promotion, and boxes of Bronze Stars. The general would try to talk to each marine, if only to ask where he was from and how he was doing. One badly wounded marine tried to respond to the general's homilies, but couldn't make himself heard. The general continued on, and I stopped and bent over to try to understand what he had said. His voice was barely a whisper.

"Fuck the general," he said, "and the horse he rode in on."

"What'd he say?" the general asked me from the next bed.

"Uh, he said he's proud to be a marine, sir," I replied. The man made a face and closed his eyes. To this day I regret my lie.

We would fly back to Freedom Hill, have a superb dinner—steak or perhaps lobster flown in from the Philippines—and then watch a movie and play some Ping-Pong. My biggest challenge was trying to beat the division surgeon, a Navy captain with a deceptively soft backhand that sliced right off the table.

The second general I worked for, Edwin Simmons, hated the whole thing. He called it the Okinawa syndrome, and thought it symbolized how we had resigned ourselves to immobility and permanence, as if the war would last forever and if we could not win at least we could be comfortable.

We had a regular pilot, usually a Marine lieutenant who had flown hundreds of medevac or other combat missions and was up for some easy duty. Every now and then I would visit the pilots at their base at Marble Mountain. Our tactics of helicopter mobility had made the pilots the indispensable men of the war, a fact of which they were not unaware. When we passed a general I would salute and the pilot would wave and say, "Howdy, General."

The pilots' Officers' Club had the feeling of the wardrooms in old war movies, where you never knew until the end of the day who had made it back in. But there was no Hollywood elegance to it. It was more like an armed fraternity house—decorated with old toilets where almost any hour of the day a drunken pilot would be stationed, his arms on either side, vomiting out his insides.

The chopper pilots weren't like the zoomies, the jet pilots off in another war. They were down there with us, in the firefights, lifting out the wounded, hovering like giant targets, taking terrible fire and losses. It made them basically insane, but they were very brave, and when you had someone wounded and were under fire they would be there, their faces, and their fear, hidden behind their visors.

The pilots waited for their missions in the duty room, where there was only one kind of reading material—huge stacks of war comic books. We were all old men, old men with the minds of fifteen-year-olds. We had crossed the line between the myth and the real, and we knew what the real was like and we were without illusions. But a part of each of us still needed the myth, so we read war comic books without cynicism. Like C rations, they kept us going.

South of the airfield was a large American recreational facility called China Beach. The infantry companies were each given a day there, a little bit of R & R known as Stack Arms. They took our company out of the bush one day and brought us in on trucks. We had hot showers, thick steaks, and all the beer we could drink. We were even given special yellow T-shirts to wear so we wouldn't feel we were still in the war. We built a fire on the beach and sat around playing a guitar and singing old rock-and-roll songs, like refugees from a Frankie Avalon beach movie.

Lifeguard stands, surfboards, and ice-cream parlors seemed to be part of the daily routine of the men permanently stationed at the rear. Some of the officers back there even had sailboats. It was a good life. Vietnamese women were there for the asking, without the difficult emotional demands of American women. Money was there to be made on the black market. And, best of all, it was safe, safer than braving the freeways around Camp Pendleton back in California. No wonder many of the men in the rear signed up for another year, and then another.

The next day, they put our company on trucks again and took us back to the war. We were set up near the old French bunker a few nights later when Harlan, one of my radiomen, came up to talk. I was studying the map and trying to dry out my socks. Hiers was inside our makeshift tent, writing letters.

"Lieutenant," he asked, "why are we here?"

It was the question none of us ever asked. We didn't want to know the answer. Harlan had broken the rules.

"Well, Harlan, we're here to help South Vietnam stay independent," I said.

"Sure, sure, Lieutenant. I know all that," Harlan replied impatiently. "But why are we here, right here?"

"Oh. Well, our mission is to protect the Da Nang vital area."

Harlan thought about that for a minute. "Okay, Lieutenant," he said, "but why is Da Nang a vital area?"

"I guess it's because of all the American support troops back there."

"Yeah, but why are they there?"

"Well, to support us," I said, closing the circle.

"That's what I thought. We're here to save the asses of those REMFs! Hell, they're supposed to be supporting us!" Harlan started to get mad. "They hog all the fucking socks! They hang the fucking nylon blankets from the ceilings of their hootches! They carry all the new fucking M-sixteens! They eat hot fucking chow! They eat cold fucking ice cream! They eat sweet pussy! They—"

"Hey, Harlan," Hiers said, poking his head out of the tent. "Nobody said life was going to be perfect."

On China Beach, where once Red Cross Donut Dollies and Army nurses in bathing suits had drawn the hungry stares of thousands of lonely men, there was only one old woman, gathering seaweed. The free-fire zones around the 1st Marine Regiment's headquarters, an area notorious for its booby traps, have been replanted with thousands of *falao* pines. The government has plans to make this into a resort area, and has built a new restaurant. We went in for a drink. We were the only customers, and we sat and drank Coke while "Mr. Tambourine Man" played on the stereo.

When I was here the marines in this area were commanded by Colonel P. X. Kelley, an intelligent, aggressive officer with a subtle grasp of politics, a dedication to excellence, and even a sense of humor. When I left Vietnam in 1970 he gave me an eight-by-ten picture of himself, signed "Semper Fi, P. X. Kelley." He is now the Commandant of the Marine Corps. On the days when he and the other colonels, the really good ones, were up at division headquarters I would think that there was nothing we couldn't do. But today the area where we did our best for him, for ourselves, and for our country is the domain of fishermen and old women with stained teeth who gather seaweed on the beach.

Just inland from China Beach five huge rocks of solid marble tower out of the dunes like the snouts of whales breaching out of the ocean. Pagodas and Buddhist monasteries are hidden away on the largest, known as Marble Mountain, and its base is ringed with tiny hamlets of marble cutters who patiently carve Buddhas, bracelets, and roaring lions and dragons. On weekends during the war marines would occasionally go there to visit a pagoda and buy some marble souvenirs. But there were several caves and pagodas on the mountain that were off limits. It was thought it would deeply offend the religious sensibilities of the Vietnamese if we were to go there.

I had always been curious about the mountain. It had loomed over our area like a brooding shrine, honeycombed with caves and mysteries. Minh and I climbed up the steep steps to the first pagoda.

The priest wasn't in, so we simply wandered through, scattering chickens and children as we walked. Minh explained all the statuary in great detail.

"Are you a Buddhist?" I asked Minh.

"Oh, no," he said, "I am a Communist."

"But you know all the worship, you observe all the holidays."

"I am the eldest son," he said. "When my father dies I will keep the family altar to honor him."

"But why would a Communist do that? Isn't religion the opium of the masses?"

"Life is complicated," he said. "A man may live by ideals that seem contradictory to another man. To me, it would be wrong to break the long line of respect for my ancestors. It would be to dishonor my parents. My mother and grandparents are Buddhists. My father is a Communist. But he keeps the altar. So will I. As Uncle Ho said—"

"Minh!"

"Oh, yes, I remember. No more sayings from Uncle Ho."

"The point is," I said, "that the spiritual life is important for itself, not because you can graft it onto Marxist theory. That's how you live, no matter what your ideology is. Marxism is supposed to explain how the world works, but it says nothing about man's spiritual life."

"You are right up to a point," he said. "But unless the material life is in order, spiritual life is impossible. If I am starving and oppressed, then that must be put right. Keeping an altar won't do that."

"Yes, but you would keep the altar anyway."

"I would, but I would organize the people at the same time."

"It's a contradiction," I said.

"You know," he replied, ignoring this last comment, "when I was in the fourth grade I met Uncle Ho."

"You did?" I asked. "How?"

"I made one of the two best scores on an elementary school test. We were taken into his study. I wore my white shirt and blue shorts. Uncle Ho was dressed simply, in khaki. He gave us some candy, and then he told us always to obey our parents so that we would be good soldiers in the struggle to unite our country. I will never forget it."

We rode awhile in silence, and I thought of the young Vietnamese boy—his father a Communist, his mother a Buddhist—being ushered into Ho Chi Minh's study. It was one of those moments that shape a life forever.

"You're a strange sort of Communist," I told him.

"I am a Communist," he replied, "but I am also Vietnamese."
We made our way down a narrow path, past gardens kept by monks, and came upon a grotto. Entering, we saw that it opened into a huge cave some seventy-five feet high, dimly lit through a hole in the ceiling. Statues of Buddhas, some as much as twenty feet tall, had been carved out of the rock. Incense burned at several altars. Smaller statues of ancient soldiers, dramatically painted in reds, blues, and yellows, stood guard. In one corner was a small shrine and next to it a plaque, which seemed oddly official amid what was so clearly a religious site.

I asked Minh to translate it, and then I knew why it had been inappropriate for Americans to visit there, even though the cave was only three miles from the edge of Da Nang and squarely in the middle of one of the largest concentrations of American troops in Vietnam. The plaque said that in this cave had been a field hospital for the Viet Cong. Now the cave was empty and the only sound was the water dripping from the hole in the roof. I walked out of the cave and in a few steps could look directly down on the main road that had led to the 1st Marine Regiment's headquarters. We had driven right by here on our way to China Beach. The Viet Cong in the hospital must have heard our trucks, and the helicopters from the airfield, every day. No doubt they could listen to the parties at the airfield or China Beach, hear the Filipino bands singing "Proud Mary" and "We Gotta Get Out of This Place."

How little we knew. And our enemy was so certain of our ignorance, so confident we'd learn nothing, that he had hidden his hospital in plain sight, like Poe's purloined letter. To be defeated was bad enough. To be treated with such contempt seemed far worse.

We were leaving Marble Mountain when I saw her. She was a teenager working at one of the small stands selling marble bracelets, statues of Buddha, busts of Ho Chi Minh, and other souvenirs. For a moment, I didn't know why she had caught my eye, but there was something about her, about the way she stood, about her features, something different.

And then Minh, who didn't miss much, noticed my stare. "So you've seen the Amerasian girl?" he said.

She was the first Amerasian I had seen on the trip. I hadn't been prepared for how powerful the experience would be. I had become conditioned to Vietnam as it had become, but she was a living link to the past. We Americans were gone, but we had left behind a new generation neither American nor Vietnamese—outsiders, wearing history on their faces. They were victims, trapped in an eternal no-man's-land of a war they never knew. But while that war had brought to others death and the wounds of body and spirit, to them it had given their very lives. Without the war they would not exist.

I thought of all the bar girls, all the skivvy houses, all the casual and unremembered assignations in bunkers and rice paddies, and of all the war "marriages" that ended abruptly when the American man's year was up. The scene of the last helicopters leaving the roof of the American embassy, the mockery of all our political commitments, had been acted out many times before by men leaving behind their personal commitments, getting on an airplane and going back to the world, to their "real" lives.

I felt guilt when I saw that young girl, guilt and fascination. The first lecture I had been given when I arrived in Vietnam fifteen years ago was on the dangers of sex with Vietnamese women; how odd that the offspring of such liaisons were all we left behind, as if the fundamental power of sexuality had proved stronger than all our armies, all our weapons, all our technology. The girl at Marble Mountain had been raised a Vietnamese, had spent all her life in a tiny hamlet, but I still felt an immediate bond with her.

Her name was Huynh Thi Dieu Dien. She was fourteen years old, a student in the seventh grade. That afternoon she had been at a meeting of the Good Nieces and Nephews of Uncle Ho. They had talked—as children had everywhere in Vietnam that day—about Nguyen Van Troi and his martyrdom, how his death was a beautiful example of Uncle Ho's precept that nothing is more important than independence and freedom.

We talked at the table inside her house, behind the souvenir stand. There was only one room. Her mother sat on the bed; her grandfather, an old man dressed in white cotton, with a wispy beard, moved slowly about the room, getting us tea, then sat down in the corner and smoked the cigarette I had given him.

Her mother began to talk about Dien's father. "I remember his name, but not his address," she said. "He was in the military police. He returned to the United States in 1971. He wanted us to come with him, but my mother was sick and we couldn't go. I had a letter in 1974, but I haven't heard from him since."

She had applied for a visa for herself and Dien to go to America; they were waiting for it to come through. I asked Dien if she wanted to go to the United States. She looked at the marble bracelet on her arm and said nothing. Tears began to flow down her face. The house had gradually filled up with villagers. More than forty people had crowded into the room, pressing all around us. It was suffocating, claustrophobic. No one made a sound.

I asked her if she was crying because she wanted to go or because she wanted to stay.

"Both," she said. "I have a father . . ." She began to cry again. "And I have my native land . . ." And then she paused. Her mother watched her from the bed. The room was totally quiet. Her dilemma was completely public. I had unwittingly asked her to choose between the country of a father who had abandoned her and whom she had never seen, and Vietnam, the people around her, the only world she had ever known—and to do so in full view of the whole hamlet.

"But I don't know my father . . ." she said, and then she simply began to sob, her shoulders shaking. I squeezed her hand, told her that she would like America, that it would be different but that she would like it. Minh translated as the girl cried. The villagers listened in silence. I might as well have been describing another planet.

On the way back to Da Nang I told Minh that I blamed the father, that he had behaved as irresponsibly with the mother as we had with our allies.

Minh didn't agree. "You can't blame the father," he said. "He was a soldier, far from home. I'm sure he didn't intend to create such a sad situation."

No, I thought, he probably didn't intend to, any more than we intended to make a whole people dependent upon us and then abandon them. But he had done it, and so had we. He had walked away, and so had we.

17

"NUMBER ONE!"

A new group of Russian tourists had arrived at the hotel in Da Nang the day I went to Marble Mountain. These Russians were more stylish than the ones I had met in Hanoi; their clothes were more circa 1970 than 1956. That evening they ate in silence while my driver played my tape of Bruce Springsteen's "Born in the U.S.A." on the stereo in the restaurant. I motioned him over.

"They're Russians," I said, thinking he would understand and show them mercy.

"You're right," he said, and turned the tape up as loud as it would go.

After dinner they danced awkwardly to the single most popular tape in Vietnam—*Disco Hits of 1978*. The next morning, Sunday, they had to endure breakfast while the waitresses played an American gospel program on Voice of America. I never ceased to be amused by how Russian tourists continually found themselves emerged in American culture as they traveled Vietnam, their staunch socialist brother. But the fact that their own culture does not travel well makes the Russians a palatable ally for countries concerned about the "evils" of Western culture. No leader whose power depends on a traditional culture— from Le Duan to the Ayatollah—need worry that an alliance with the Soviets might end up tempting their faithful flock to stray from its old values. They can be confident that no one, by choice, is going to start wearing Russian fashions, listening to Russian music, or adopting the Russian way of life.

Sunday morning I went for a walk, alone, through the streets of Da Nang. Whenever I stopped at a coffeehouse or a sandal shop, I would make it known that I was an American. Immediately a crowd would gather, and one person would be stationed at the door to watch for the police. Everyone would gather around me, examining my camera, checking out the label on my running shoes, feeling my Levi's to see if they were made in America ("Good") or Taiwan ("No good"), inspecting my watch. Or they would show me pictures of their relatives in California and thrust letters for the American immigration officials or their relatives into my pockets or my bag.

At the market in Da Nang a woman heard me speaking English. "Were you followed?" she asked. I replied that I wasn't sure; I couldn't always tell.

She looked up and down the street, then said to me, "I just wanted you to know that we all still love the Americans."

I wandered through the market. Along one aisle were stacks and stacks of conical hats. I asked the woman if she had any Hue hats. She smiled, and pulled out a stack of them. I held one up to the light. Inside, in silhouette, I saw the bridge over the Perfume River and other scenes of Hue. I bought four, and waited while the woman painted them with clear pine resin to make them waterproof. As I left the market a woman carrying a child came up to me.

"Lien Xo?" she asked.

"No," I said, "American."

Her mouth dropped, and she followed me for a block, staring. So intent was she on not taking her eyes off my face that she walked right into an open manhole. I heard a scream, looked back, and saw that she had vanished. With some effort, I pulled her and her child out.

"Americans number one," she said, and then was gone.

As I returned to the hotel, two cigarette girls came running up.

"You American?"

"Yes."

"You lie. You Russian."

"No, I'm American."

"You lie, you East German."

"No, I'm really not."

"American?"

"Yes."

"Okay, you tell America Mai and Lien said hello."

"Tell America you said hello?"

"Yeah, sure. America number one."

"Okay, I will." And now I am.

This instant ability to create a sensation was no doubt partly due to the scarcity of my species. And the way the children would follow the Russians shouting *"Lien Xo, Lien Xo"* reminded me of the war, when they would shout "GI, GI" with the same superficial friendliness edged with contempt. During the war the Russians gave them planes, tanks, bullets, and money to fight their enemy—the Americans. But Americans represent something else in Vietnam now; we stand for a future which everyone, from Le Duan to the simplest peasant, knows the Russians cannot give them.

But on a few occasions I was reminded that we Americans are still, officially at least, the enemy. One night I stopped at a small café—just some stools around two low tables, and a glass case with a few soft-drink bottles. I sat down next to a woman with her young daughter.

She looked at me and said, in perfect English, "You're an American."

"That's right. How did you know?"

But instead of friendliness she looked at me with utter fear.

"If they see me talking to you, they'll kill me," she said. She scooped up her child, ran out of the café, and was gone into the darkness.

Late one afternoon we went to the "atrocity museum" which had taken over the old American compound by the river. Tanks and self-propelled howitzers lined the street. An old "Huey" stood in the courtyard. The rooms around the courtyard were filled with displays of the horrors of the war. There were photographs of smiling American soldiers holding the heads of Viet Cong or just the rags and bones of a body. Dead Vietnamese were shown being dragged by tanks or piled like cordwood, the parts all separated and jumbled up. In some photographs prisoners were being beaten or hung upside down with wire, in others villagers were shown being loaded onto helicopters or trucks.

Tucked into the corners were nicely made dioramas showing strategic hamlets (referred to as concentration camps), search-and-destroy raids with Americans burning villages, and prisons with torture cells, complete with implements. Papier-mâché relief maps showed sites of free-fire zones (known as white zones), B-52 raids, and Agent Orange spraying.

There were many photographs of life on American bases, with Americans towering over tiny Vietnamese women, their arms around their shoulders, their hands up the girls' miniskirts. Heroin addicts lay crumpled in doorways or shot themselves up in alleys. Bar girls sat on the laps of GIs. One caption read: "After a bloody search-and-destroy operation American troops are entertained by sexy dancer."

The last exhibits covered the final hectic days before the fall of Saigon. A photograph of the airlift of orphans referred to babies being "kidnapped." Beneath a series of photographs of Vietnamese desperately trying to get on board ships and helicopters to escape the approaching Communist army the caption read: "The U.S. forced hundreds of thousands of people to flee the country, causing many tragedies." The last photographs were of Vietnamese refugees standing in a welfare line somewhere in America, and the caption read: "Waiting for food in the 'promised land.'"

I spent an hour there, slowly going from photograph to photograph. Minh read in the car. Mien, the young Da Nang guide, stayed a respectful distance behind me, balancing on his platform shoes and interpreting my reactions for the crowd of Vietnamese children that had followed us inside. As I stood in front of some photographs of mutilated children, he came up to me. One of the photographs was of a horribly deformed boy with huge tumors growing on his face.

"That's my friend," Mien told me. "He was taken out to a U.S. hospital ship and injected with special chemicals. It was an experiment. Then they brought him back and kicked him into the street."

I told Mai that the boy in the photograph looked to be suffering from neurofibromatosis, the "elephant man" disease, and that it was not caused by an injection.

"Oh, yes," he said. "The Americans did it all the time."

He said this with the same detached placidity with which everyone discussed the war. I was an American, I had fought here, but in his mind I had no connection to the atrocities, real or imagined, we had just seen. They were as real, no more, no less, as the turtle that handed Le Loi his sword.

That night we talked about Western culture over dinner.

"It is a dilemma," Minh said. "Rock-and-roll music came to Vietnam with the American soldiers and the bar girls and the miniskirts. It was all part of the corruption of our society that the war brought to the South. We had to reform prostitutes, drug addicts, a whole corrupt culture. Some older Party members believed that the music was part of that corruption. We had no foreign music at all in the North during the war, and our society was pure.

"At first we wanted to restore Vietnamese music in the South," Minh continued, "but then we realized, correctly, that the music wasn't the cause of the corruption. So we decided to allow the people to take the best of foreign music and fashion, and combine it with the best of our traditional culture."

"That sounds as if you made a virtue of necessity."

"The Party is very wise," Minh replied.

• • •

After dinner I watched a film on the Ho Chi Minh Trail with a group of West German tourists. One of them came up to me later and we began to talk.

"I was one of the radicals in Berlin in 1968," he said. "I was with Rudi Dutschke and Hans Magnus Enzensberger. Every waking moment was spent working against the American war here."

"So how do you feel now?" I asked him.

"Very strange. Vietnam is not popular with the Left anymore. After the reeducation camps, after the boat people, after Cambodia—the Left feels betrayed. We fought so hard for them, and they let us down."

18

THE BEST WEAPON

The next day we drove to Duy Xuyen district, a once bitterly contested area about twelve miles south of Da Nang. On the way we passed lines of children carrying flags and banners. They were marching to the grave of the folk hero Nguyen Van Troi. Troi's last words were "So long as one American soldier remains on our land, we will not have independence and freedom." His grave is in one of the typical martyrs' cemeteries that are fixtures in every village. We stopped and watched the parades of uniformed children from the young Communist organizations enter the cemetery for the ceremonies. They were singing patriotic songs. On the perimeter, some children from the nearby village where Troi was born tried to get in. The police beat them back with bamboo sticks.

In almost every paddy I saw one or two women standing on a muddy dike, patiently draining the flooded fields, one bucket at a time. The gap between the task and the means to solve it was ludicrously wide—almost as great as sending buffalo boys with rifles to fight the most powerful nation in the world.

The district headquarters was in a low stucco building which I had visited during the war. We were greeted by a delegation of officials and offered tea, beer, and fruit. I began talking to Nguyen Truong Nai, the vice-president of the People's Committee. He had joined the guerrillas in 1964, when he was seventeen. During the long years of the war he had been wounded eight times.

"This one, on my arm, was in 1967," he said, pointing out

each scar. "This one, on my leg, was in 1972. These two, on my hand and my head, were in 1969." His body was like a history of the war, written with M-16 bullets, artillery shrapnel, rockets, and bomb pellets from B-52s.

The worst year was 1969, Nai said, echoing what General Tuan had told me in Hanoi. "The situation was terrible. This whole district was a no-man's-land. The people had been herded into Da Nang. There were thousands of Americans, Koreans, and puppet troops in the area, but only four of us were left out of all the local guerrilla forces. Only four. There was nothing to eat. We were discouraged, very discouraged. We seriously considered surrender. But each time we were tempted we talked about our traditions, about our country, and we kept on fighting."

We were joined by two young men from the rice cooperative, who had been out fighting the flood. One of the men seemed very young, too young to have been in the war. But he had been fighting since 1969, when he was nine years old—one year older than my son is today.

"I went to school during the day, and helped the guerrillas at night," he said. "We were scouts. We watched the Americans, sold them cigarettes and talked to them, and then reported back to the guerrillas. Part of my job was to identify the leaders of the strategic hamlets."

I asked what happened then. Almost idly he pulled away a corner of the veil of platitudes that surrounds Communist accounts of such inconvenient embarrassments as the massacre of civilians in Hue.

"I helped work out ways to kill them," he said, smiling pleasantly, as if he were discussing a school fund-raising auction. So convinced are they that history is on their side, that killing a village official, even if he had been a neighbor, was simply not a matter of much consequence. The village officials were in the way like weeds, they had to be pulled up so that the rice could grow. The men we fought were not limited by what Mao called "silly scruples." History has its necessities—and men of vision fulfill them and don't look back.

As we talked we traded cigarettes, drank tea, and munched on fruit. A crowd had begun to gather and dozens of faces filled the windows. There was much discussion of the problems of improving the rice harvest and of integrating the veterans of the South Vietnamese armed forces and government into the district.

"Of our work force of forty thousand," said Vo Duc Thinh, the People's Committee president, "ten thousand are from the old regime. After Liberation we gave them courses in the correct Party line to make them realize they had committed crimes against the people. Most of them needed only a few days to admit their crimes and begin a new life. Some needed more time, a few as much as two or three years. They're all back now. They belong to cooperatives like anyone else, they get the same rations, their children go to the same schools. Even the Catholics are like everyone else now, and before Liberation many of them had salaries and had forgotten how to work."

As he spoke I was reminded of accounts of religious conversions, in which the new believer must first acknowledge his sins and wickedness, admit he has been down the wrong path and is totally alone, and then come to realize he has only one way to salvation—through Christ in one case, the Party in this one. In the world of the true believers, there is always room for the sinner who comes, even at the eleventh hour, to his senses. But woe to him who remains stubborn too long; for the unrepentant infidel, salvation comes only with the sword.

I asked how these soldiers and officials were received when they returned from their conversions.

"You have to remember," Thinh said, "that they had committed great crimes against the people. These criminals had tortured and killed their relatives—one mother had lost six children. Imagine their thirst for revenge. They would have beheaded all of them had we turned them loose. We had to spend much time explaining to the people the policy of the Party, convincing them that reconciliation was right.

"Of course," he continued, "it helped that the tasks facing us were so enormous. The land had lain fallow for many years. We had to organize cooperatives, clear the fields of mines and bombs, develop irrigation and electric projects, plow and plant and begin to harvest. We had to build houses and schools and clinics. We had, in truth, to start over. It has taken us a long time, and we are far from finished. But already rice yields in some cooperatives are over twenty tons per hectare [a hectare is 2.47 acres], which is better even than the Philippines."

He looked around the room at the other officials watching him respectfully. "But we only have so much strength," he said. "If we had not used up so much defending our fatherland through thirty years of destructive war, we could have made far more progress."

I listened through most of this in silence. I had spent a good deal of time in Duy Xuyen during the war. A large portion of its area is known as Go Noi Island, which when I was in Vietnam had been cleared of all signs of life, like an apple peeled of its skin. Nothing, literally nothing, was left. No trees, no cemeteries, no houses, no fields, no people. It was the paradigm of a free-fire zone.

The very term "free-fire zone" has come to stand for the extraordinary brutality of the Vietnam War. In fact, it meant only that the area was a battlefield, a no-man's-land between opposing forces where anyone moving was presumed to be the enemy. Most battlefields are like that. What made Vietnam different is that normal people tended to live on the battlefield, and the usually clear definitions of war didn't apply. Who was the enemy? Was it only the North Vietnamese soldier in uniform, or was it also that old man and woman transplanting rice, or that boy on the water buffalo? In a free-fire zone everyone was presumed to be an enemy. And after a while, idea being father to reality, they probably were.

The solution to the problem of people cluttering up the battlefield was clear: move the people. Consider this remarkably frank account of one of the first such actions, the evacuation of a hamlet near the Da Nang air base in 1965, as described by the Marine battalion commander who carried it out:

"I did not want my defensive posture to include Pho Nam, yet I did not want the VC to have those people. The people were hesitant to move—reluctant to give up their homes; apprehensive about the rice harvest to come; and fearful that association with the government would mark them for retaliation by the VC. So I directed that H and I [harassing and interdiction] fire be brought close in to the hamlet, night after night. The attitude of those people about relocation 'improved' and the relocation was scheduled."

When I was here in 1970 we evacuated some villagers out of a hamlet called Phu Lac 6. Everyone was loaded onto CH-46 helicopters. An old man was pushed on, reluctantly, pulling his water buffalo by the rope through his nose. As the helicopter climbed into the sky, the water buffalo panicked and ran out the opening in the rear. There was a moment of silence, cries of "I don't believe that!" from the door gunners, and then the old man got up and walked out the back after the buffalo, his body tumbling through the blue sky.

In 1970 we began resettlement work on Go Noi. Land was set aside for villages, and some of the old residents were brought back and lodged in rows of houses with tin roofs set beneath the merciless sun. We had destroyed their homes and farms and told them it was for their own good. And then we came with all our machinery and enthusiasm and organization and were building it all back—also for their own good. We were, in short, using the same can-do spirit to rebuild that we employed to destroy, and we wanted them to love us for it.

Still, it was hard to mock all the sincere effort that went into the project. A Marine engineer officer even moved to Go Noi to be with his bulldozers, which were kept busy from first light until the night brought the threat of ambushes. He and his men wanted to help, and they believed they were. But after the bulldozers were finished and the marines had left, the Viet Cong returned and imposed, by a combination of fear and allegiance, their nocturnal rule on the hapless peasants. Go Noi had been destroyed and then rebuilt, but nothing had changed.

Not only were we trying to solve a terrible situation by applying Band-Aids, we were also playing into the hands of the corrupt South Vietnamese bureaucracy. The Vietnamese province chief had instigated the entire Go Noi resettlement project by telling the Marines he would take it to the Army if the Marines refused to do it. And if there is anything that motivates the Marines, it is the thought that the Army might get credit for something within their area. So the project was approved, greatly enriching the province chief, who among other things charged the people for the building materials we gave them. As always, they understood us better than we understood them, and perhaps even better than we understood ourselves.

But even with such callous and imperfect means we did succeed in pushing the Viet Cong out of much of Duy Xuyen—with only four men left in the local forces they were hardly a military threat. And when the war was pushed away from the villages, the people were able to plant and harvest rice in peace and send their children to school. But that freedom depended on us, on foreigners.

I spent a month working with what we called "Vietnamization," our term for our effort to end the dependency of the local officials on Americans and get them to assume more responsibility for their fate. Vietnamization clearly puzzled the Vietnamese. Why, if we had been helping them, were we going to stop? Why, exactly, was that for their own good?

My work centered on rice production, particularly the introduction of improved strains of rice.* We also helped form cooperatives to purchase pumps to drain and fill paddies. I took the general down to meet the chief of a village where we had helped buy a tractor.

"So you've done all this yourself?" the general asked him.

Oh, absolutely, he replied.

"Isn't it better to be standing on your own feet again?" the general asked.

Oh, absolutely, the village chief replied again.

"So you will be fine when we depart?" the general said.

The village chief turned pale and began to chatter. He tore off his cap and wrung it in his hands. He beat his chest. The interpreter listened for a while, then put out his hand to get the village chief to stop. No luck.

"What's he saying?" the general asked.

"He says," the interpreter replied, "that if the Americans leave, the Viet Cong will come and they will all die."

In Vietnam, power really did come out of the barrel of a gun. And the village chief knew that if our guns left, the Viet Cong guns would still be there. His fear was the fear of a man who knew that in the end his government could not protect him. In 1975 that fear became panic, and in a few dramatic days destroyed the South Vietnamese army, an army we had trained and equipped for almost two decades, an army we had given everything but a reason to fight.

At that moment, in 1970, I knew—that no matter how many victories we celebrated, how many villages we pacified, and how many new strains of rice we introduced—we would win the war only if we were willing to stay in Vietnam forever.

• • •

*During the war, American antiwar activists attacked the use of these new strains of rice as destructive of Vietnamese culture. Today the new rice is everywhere, and the Vietnamese point to it with pride.

Around the table in Duy Xuyen the talk turned to the weapons we had used during the war. I said that most of the marines I knew preferred the Communists' AK-47 rifles to their own M-16s. The M-16s were badly made, like toy weapons, and their defects were legend. Every Marine unit had stories of men killed while they desperately tried to repair their M-16 during a firefight.

"You could bury an AK-47 in a rice paddy for a month," I said, "dig it up, wipe it off, and start firing it. If we got a speck of dust in our M-16s, they jammed."

"The AK-47 was a good weapon," Hien, the former Viet Cong company commander, said, "but most of us carried M-16s."

"You did? Why?"

"It was so much easier to get ammunition. You were always dropping magazines full of it, or we could buy it from the puppet forces."

I asked him if we Americans had any weapon he had found particularly effective.

"The M-79 grenade launcher," he replied. "We were very frightened of it. In an ambush, we always tried to get the M-79 man first. It allowed you to throw grenades a hundred, two hundred meters. A terrible weapon."

"What was your best weapon?" I asked.

He smiled.

Then he pointed to his heart.

19

MY ENEMY, MY SELF

At Duy Xuyen, when we began to share war stories, the children were cleared out and the beer was poured. The old saying among soldiers is that the difference between a fairy tale and a war story is that the fairy tale begins "Once upon a time" and the war story begins "This is no shit." It's meant as a joke, but it makes a deeper point. War stories, in fact, are like fairy tales. There is something primal about them. They have a moral, even a mythic truth, more than a literal one.

War stories reach out and remind their audience of their place in the world. They are the primitive stories told around the fire in smoky tipis after the pipe has been passed. They are all, at bottom, the same.

Some of the best war stories out of Vietnam are in Michael Herr's *Dispatches.* One of Herr's most quoted stories goes like this:

"But what a story he told me, as one-pointed and resonant as any war story I ever heard, it took me a year to understand it:

" 'Patrol went up the mountain. One man came back. He died before he could tell us what happened.'

"I waited for the rest, but it seemed not to be that kind of story; when I asked him what had happened he just looked like he felt sorry for me, fucked if he'd waste time telling stories to anyone as dumb as I was."

It is a great story, a combat haiku, all negative space and darkness humming with portent. It seems rich, unique to Vietnam. But listen, now, to this: "We all went up to Gettysburg, the summer of '63: and some of us came back from there: and that's all, except the details."

That is the complete account of the battle of Gettysburg by one Praxiteles Swan, onetime captain in the Confederate States Army. The language is different, but it is the same story. And it is a story that I would imagine has been told for as long as men went to war. Its purpose is not to enlighten but to exclude. Its message is not its content but to put the listener in his place. I suffered, I was there. You were not. Only those facts matter. Everything else is beyond words to tell.

There are two constant themes: death and comradeship. "When we were in the jungle and in the mountains," one of the former Viet Cong said at Duy Xuyen, "the bonds of comradeship weren't only in fighting, but in everything. The strong would help the weak. We carried each other's burdens, cooked each other's meals, did everything together. If one of us was wounded, we would risk our lives to bring him back."

Thinh, the district president, remembered the time he was hit in a B-52 raid. "I was knocked unconscious. They thought I was sure to die, but they carried me for two days through the mountains to the hospital. Another time, near An Hoa, we were hit by waves of B-52s. And then helicopters brought in hundreds of marines. For a month we were surrounded. When you have gone through such things together, you have a bond that can never be broken."

Hien had been sitting quietly. He took one of my 555 cigarettes, lit it, and said, in a soft voice, "It was a pure world. Those who had more gave to those in need. We shared the same bamboo bed, we shared the same shirt or blanket. That kind of sentiment, so pure, was even more than I have for my blood brother. And when we lost our comrades, when they sacrificed, the pain gave us strength in fighting."

I asked Hien if he still saw his old comrades.

"At Tet or other feast days we still try to get together," he said. "We drink and eat and talk about the war. We have a lot of memories."

"What kind of memories?"

For a long moment after the translation Hien said nothing, then the words poured out. "When we had to fight an enemy ten times stronger; when we were so hungry we had to chew uncooked rice; when we were overrun and had to carry our wounded on our backs; when we were weak from hunger and being bombed, but we kept going; when we were surrounded and had to fight for weeks against constant artillery and bombs and helicopters firing rockets and the days and nights ran together in hails of fire and fatigue, but we never gave up. We can't forget any of those things. But above all we will never forget the day we came into Da Nang as victors, the day we liberated our home. How all the people cheered us. That will be with me always."

I had sat through his memories with my own memories coming back, of ambushes and booby traps and days and nights in the jungle looking for an enemy we never seemed to find, of all my men, so young and brave, being wasted for nothing. I remembered coming home and walking the streets of Georgetown in my PX cotton trousers and my jungle boots and my short haircut, feeling I was invisible or the carrier of some terrible disease, a caste enemy, unclean.

It was as if we had fought in two different wars: in spite of all their years of fighting, my former enemies seemed to burn with a simple belief in honor and sacrifice and patriotism—the way Rupert Brooke wrote about World War I in 1914, when to die for England was still glorious. And even though I had fought so little compared to my enemies, my own memories were more like Wilfred Owen's poems of 1918, exuding the heavy air of the trenches, of disillusionment and death without meaning.

And then I realized that I was back on the bloodiest battlefields of a long and brutal war, sitting around a table with my old enemies, and we were consumed with nostalgia. We hated the war, but we missed it. After I returned from the war I did my best not to talk about it, and on the rare occasions when I did I would always begin by saying that of course war was a great evil, and that I hated it. It was the proper thing to say. And it was true, but it wasn't the whole truth.

In 1983, a year before I returned to Vietnam, I encountered my old radioman, Jeff Hiers, by accident at the Vietnam Veterans Memorial in Washington. I had not seen Hiers since 1970, when we said goodbye in a paddy in Vietnam. He invited me to Killington, Vermont, where he and his wife, Susan, run a bed-and-breakfast place. On the first morning we were up at dawn trying to save five newborn rabbits whose mother was blissfully unaware of her maternal responsibilities. Hiers built a nest of rabbit fur and straw and positioned a lamp to provide warmth against the bitter cold.

"What people can't understand," Hiers said as he gently picked each tiny rabbit up in his hands and placed it in the nest, "is how much I loved Vietnam. I loved it, and I can't tell anybody."

Men have always loved war, even as they hated it. But to admit such feelings about Vietnam seems inappropriate. The war was brutal and morally complex, fought by Americans who carried the terrible burden of knowing that the country which sent them didn't believe in what they were doing. We were fighting an enemy whose entire society was organized for war, and who would do anything to win. Our enemy didn't hate war any more than George Washington or Winston Churchill did—it was the only way they could get what they wanted. But nothing about the life we Americans knew and cherished would be affected whether we won or lost. When the horrors of war seem without purpose, it is natural to hate them.

And today Americans have to hate war more than most other peoples, because we have our fingers on the nuclear trigger. For us, war will never again be a simple matter of the nation giving its all to win. We can't get worked up. We have to stay cool. But while that logic is inescapable for the nation as a whole, it produces a painful paradox in the heart of the soldier. For him, after all, the concept of limited war is absurd. When your own life is on the line, all war is total war.

I am a peace-loving man, fond of children and animals. In high school I was in the history club instead of on the football team. I believe passionately that war should have no place in the affairs of men, and that the existence of nuclear arsenals means that the emotions that lead to wars can no longer be indulged. But on the way back from Vermont in a driving snowstorm, my children asleep in the back of the car, I realized that Hiers had given words to an emotion I had been unable, or unwilling, to recognize. A part of me loved war, and at Duy Xuyen I discovered my old enemies felt the same way.

I don't mean we had some romantic notion of war. That was ground into the mud at Verdun and Passchendaele; honor and glory do not survive the machine gun. And I don't mean the sort of nostalgic longing among men my age who didn't go to war— as if it were something they missed, some classic male experience, the way women their age who didn't have children worry that they may have missed something basic about being a woman, something they didn't value much at the time they could have done it.

We loved war for many reasons, not all of them good. The best reason we loved war is also its most enduring memory— comradeship. A comrade in war is a man you can trust with anything, because you trust him with your life. Philip Caputo described the emotion in *A Rumor of War:* "[Comradeship] does not demand for its sustenance the reciprocity, the pledges of affection, the endless reassurances required by the love of men and women. It is, unlike marriage, a bond that cannot be broken by a word, by boredom or divorce, or by anything other than death."

Comradeship isn't a particularly selective process. Race, personality, education—anything that would make a difference in peace—count for nothing. It is, simply, brotherly love. War is the only utopian experience most of us ever have. Individual possessions and advantage count for nothing; the group is everything. What you have is shared with your friends. No one is allowed to be alone.

And in war loneliness is the greatest enemy. The military historian S. L. A. Marshall did intensive studies of combat incidents in World War II and Korea and discovered that at most only 25 percent of the men under fire actually fired their weapons. The rest cowered behind cover, terrified and helpless—all systems off. Invariably, those men had felt alone, and to feel alone in combat is to cease to function; it is the terrifying prelude to the final loneliness of death. The men who kept their heads felt connected to other men, a part of something, as if comradeship were a collective life force, the power to face death and stay conscious.

That sense of comradeship was what the Viet Cong veterans kept coming back to when I talked with them about the war. They shared the same meager rice ration, passed around a single cigarette, slept in the same bamboo bed. They took almost superhuman risks to recover their wounded and their dead—we almost never found them. They lived together for years in the jungle, enduring our terrible firepower. Their comrades counted on them to guard the flanks, to pull their load, to be there. They believed they were fighting for a great goal, one worth dying for. Instead of working in the paddy, they were riding on the wind of history. They called each other brother, and they meant it to mean more than blood.

Men also love war because it is a game, a brutal, deadly game, the only game that counts. War is the thrill of a great challenge, to your courage and endurance and, yes, to your intellect. Nothing I had ever studied was as complex or as creative as the small-unit tactics of Vietnam. No sport I had ever played brought me to such close awareness of my physical and emotional limits.

The first time I was under fire, my mouth immediately went dry. I could not speak; not a sound would pass my lips. My brain erased as if the plug had been pulled—I felt only a dull hum throughout my body, a low-grade current coursing through me like a power line. I was terrified, I was ashamed, and I couldn't wait for it to happen again.

Talking to the men and women in North Vietnam about the war against the American bombers brought out not only their fear and suffering but also something else. As the long ceremonial meals wore on and the night grew longer, we would begin to talk about how they loved the game of it, the incredible intensity of wheeling around in the seats of those antiaircraft guns, trying to shoot down the hurtling F-105s or F-4s. When one of their jet pilots described shooting down a B-52, his eyes burned at the memory, and all of a sudden he was back in the night sky, one machine against another, one pilot against another, in the deadly thrill of a great game.

For the former Viet Cong I met in the South there was joy in eluding our patrols, joy in setting ambushes, joy in infiltrating our bases and destroying our tanks and riverboats. And that joy was magnified because we Americans appeared so invulnerable. For men who had mounted commando raids on big American airfields, who had crawled through the barbed wire at American combat bases, who had been surrounded and escaped, war was the transcendent challenge. War was an initiation into the power of life and death. Women touch that power at the moment of birth; men on the edge of death. It is like lifting off the corner of the universe and peeking at what's underneath.

As anyone who has fired a bazooka or an M-60 machine gun knows, there is something to that power in your finger, the soft, seductive touch of the trigger. It's like the magic sword, a soldier's Excalibur—all you do is move that finger so imperceptibly, just a wish flashing across your mind like a shadow, not even a full brain synapse, and poof!—in a blast of sound and energy and light a truck or a house disappears, everything flying and settling back into the dust.

There is a connection between this thrill and the games we played as children, the games of cowboys and Indians and war, the games that ended with "Bang! Bang! You're dead!" And then everyone who was "dead" got up and began another game. That's war as fantasy, death without consequences, and it's the same emotion that war movies toy with. When President Reagan spoke in the fall of 1984 at the Vietnam Veterans Memorial, his voice choked when he told stories about veterans cradling their mortally wounded comrades in their arms.

But it rang false. He hadn't been there. What did he know about it? It was as if he were describing the filming of a movie where the actors died movingly and then went into the commissary for lunch.

War isn't like that. It bears no resemblance to the patriotic fantasies of ex-actors who made training films in World War II. The blood doesn't come off. It flows from fragile bodies out into the mud. And the wounded take a long time healing and the dead don't get up. They stay dead.

After one ambush my men brought back the body of a dead North Vietnamese soldier. I found the dead man propped against some C-ration boxes. He had on sunglasses, and a *Playboy* magazine lay open on his lap. A cigarette dangled jauntily from his mouth, and on his head was perched a large and perfectly formed piece of shit.

I was repulsed and outraged. But I felt something else, welling up from a deeper part of me, a part of me I wanted to keep hidden, didn't want to know. Somewhere inside I was . . . laughing. I laughed, I believe now, in part because of some subconscious appreciation for this obscene linkage of sex and excrement and death. And in part I laughed because of the exultant realization that he—whoever he had been—was dead and I—special, unique me—was alive. He was my brother, but I knew him not.

In war the line between life and death is gossamer thin. There is joy, true joy, in being alive when so many around you are dead. And from the joy of being alive in the presence of death to the joy of causing death is, unfortunately, not that great a step.

I don't know if I killed anyone, even that man in the tunnel. I fired at muzzle flashes in the night, threw grenades during ambushes, ordered artillery and bombing where I thought the enemy was. I don't know if I killed anyone, but I know that killing is what I tried as hard as I could to do.

As I sat and talked at Duy Xuyen with the flesh-and-blood men who had been the abstractions I had tried to kill, I thought back on that man whose body had become such an obscene joke on Death. I felt guilt, yes, but I also knew that the men around me had thought of me and my comrades as abstractions, had perhaps mutilated the bodies of Americans. Did I remind them of some terrible things they had done and then never spoken of again?

What were they thinking, seeing me there?

I asked the men around the table in Duy Xuyen what else they remembered about the war.

Nai's eyes lit up and he began to talk about a quality not often associated with war—its beauty. "When we sent our sappers in against an American base we were all filled with terror. But I remember one attack when we breached the wire and were running from bunker to bunker with our satchel charges. The bunkers were exploding like giant firecrackers, and I could see the shadows of my comrades in silhouette against the flames. And then the Americans began firing at us from all directions. I thought I would be killed, but I remember also thinking what a beautiful place to die."

Other Communist veterans talked lyrically about a line of trucks moving at night along the Ho Chi Minh Trail, like a parade of dark elephants trunk to tail. And in Hanoi men and women marveled at how the city had looked under the bombing, the SAMs launching in bursts of flame, the searchlights, the antiaircraft guns with their tracers reaching for the planes.

For me, nothing was more beautiful than a firefight at night. The red tracers from the M-16s and M-60 machine guns would go out into the blackness as if we were drawing with light pens. Then little dots of lights would start winking back, and green tracers from the AK-47s would begin to weave in with the red to form brilliant patterns that seemed, given their great speeds, oddly timeless, as if they had been etched on the night.

And then perhaps the AC-130 gunships we called "Spooky" would come in and fire their incredible guns like huge hoses washing down from the sky, like something God would do when he was really ticked off. And then the flares would pop, casting eerie shadows as they floated down on their little parachutes, swinging in the breeze, and anyone who moved in their light seemed a ghost escaped from hell.

Daytime offered nothing so spectacular, but it had its charms. Many men loved napalm, loved its silent power, the way it could make tree lines or houses explode as if by spontaneous combustion. But to me napalm was greatly overrated, unless you liked to watch tires burn. Far superior was white phosphorus, which would explode with a fulsome elegance, wreathing its target in intense and billowing white smoke, throwing out glowing red comets trailing brilliant white plumes.

Even though I had met Kim Phuuc in Hanoi, and listened to her talk about being napalmed as a child, I could not get the beauty of it out of my head. Even during the war I knew, rationally, what white phosphorus would do: it would transform human flesh into Roman candles, spontaneously bursting into puffs of flame. I knew that, but I still marveled, transfixed. I had surrendered to an aesthetic divorced from that crucial quality of empathy that lets us feel the suffering of others.

But war is not simply the spirit of ugliness, although it is that, the devil's work. But to give the devil his due, it is also an affair of great and seductive beauty. The carved cannons at the

Invalides in Paris and the armor at the Metropolitan Museum of
Art in New York are examples of how war was once thought to
be worthy of the same artistry that built the great cathedrals,
the instruments of destruction as fitting objects for beauty as
the instruments of worship. And there is an aesthetic elegance
to a Huey Cobra helicopter or an M-60 machine gun. They are
without artifice, form as pure function.

Almost none of the former Viet Cong I met would talk about
how lonely they had been or about what they did for companion-
ship with the opposite sex. If I pressed, they would turn the
question into a joke. In front of their comrades, they would not
admit romantic—and certainly not sexual—feelings.

Since so much of their popular appeal was based on a puritan
attitude toward the moral corruption of the Americans and their
Vietnamese allies, during the war the Communists did their best
to appear celibate. But the short stories written by the Viet Cong
and North Vietnamese veterans both during and after the war
reveal more of the truth than do political slogans. Most of these
stories are in some way about love. A man keeps trying to find
a woman he met on the Ho Chi Minh Trail. A woman waits at
night for a guerrilla to return. A wounded North Vietnamese
soldier courts and marries the Viet Cong nurse who cared for
him in a jungle hospital. They were not, I suspect, that different
from us.

Most men who have been to war, and most women who have
been around it, remember that never in their lives was their
sexuality so palpable. War cloaks men in a costume that conceals
the limits and inadequacies of their separate natures. It gives
them an aura, a collective power, an almost animal force.

War heightens all appetites. I cannot describe the ache for
candy, for taste; I wanted a Mars bar more than I had wanted
anything in my life. And that hunger paled beside the force that
pushed us toward women, any women. Even the homeliest

women floated into our fantasies and lodged there. Too often, we made our fantasies real, always to be disappointed, our hunger only greater.

But there's also the agonizing loneliness of war, the way a soldier is cut off from everything he holds dear. The uniform did that too, and all that heightened sexuality is not much solace late at night when the emptiness comes.

There were many men for whom this condition led to great decisions. I knew a marine in Vietnam who was a rarity, an Ivy League graduate. He also had an Ivy League wife, but he managed to fall in love with a bar girl who barely spoke English. A peasant girl trying to support her family, she was not particularly attractive. But my friend fell in love with her in an awkward, formal, but total way. At the end of his twelve months in Vietnam he went home, divorced his beautiful, intelligent, and socially correct wife, then went back to Vietnam and proposed to the bar girl, who accepted. It was a marriage across a vast divide of language, culture, race, and class that could only have been made in war.

After I ended my tour in combat I came back to work at division headquarters and volunteered one night a week teaching English to Vietnamese. One of my students was a beautiful girl—the girl whose parents had been killed in Hue during the Tet Offensive of 1968. She had fallen in love with an American civilian who worked at the consulate in Da Nang. He had left for his next duty station and promised he would send for her. She never heard from him again.

I found myself seeing her after class, then I was sneaking into the motor pool and commandeering a truck and driving into Da Nang at night to visit her. She lived in a small house behind the consulate with her grandparents and brothers and sisters. It had one room divided by a curtain. When I arrived, the rest of the family would retire behind the curtain. Amid their hushed voices and the smells of cooking oil and rotted fish we would talk and fumble toward each other.

I didn't see her as one Vietnamese, I saw her as all Vietnamese. She was the suffering soul of war, and I was the soldier who had wounded it but would make it whole. I wrote her long poems, made inquiries about staying in Da Nang, built a fantasy future for the two of us. I wasn't going to betray her the way the other American had, the way all Americans had, the way all men betray the women who help them through war. I wasn't like that.

But then I received orders sending me home two weeks early. I started to drive into Da Nang to talk to her, to make definite plans. Halfway there, I turned back.

At the airport, I threw the poems into a trash can. When the wheels of the plane lifted off the soil of Vietnam, I cheered like everyone else. And as I pressed my face against the window and watched Vietnam shrink to a distant blur and finally disappear, I felt sad and guilty—for her, for my comrades who had been killed and wounded, for everything.

But that feeling was overwhelmed by my vast sense of relief. I had survived. I was going home. I would be myself again.

When I was in Da Nang in 1984, I tried to find that young woman I had loved almost fifteen years before. On a rainy Sunday afternoon I walked to the compound that had been the consulate. I peered through the bars. The building looked deserted. I tried to see the house in back where she had lived, but the bushes had grown up and I could see nothing. I couldn't look up her address. There are no phone books in Da Nang. And besides, she had worked for the Americans. She had most likely fled. Perhaps she had been drowned in the Gulf of Thailand, or murdered by Thai pirates. Or perhaps she had finally made it to America.

I didn't know. I couldn't find her. Like everything connected to the Americans in Vietnam, she had vanished. It was as if we, and she, had never been.

20

THE ROAD TO HILL 10

By my third day in Da Nang, the floods had receded enough so that we could drive out in the direction of Hill 10, my old battalion base. At Cobb Bridge we crossed the Tuy Loan River and stopped the car on the other side. Sweet potatoes and manioc were drying in the sun. Sugarcane stalks had been strewn along the road so that the traffic would crush it. The air smelled sweet like syrup.

I walked onto the bridge. It was new; the Viet Cong blew up the old one in 1974. On the north bank, where our bunkers had been, there was now a brick kiln. On the south bank, where I had my command post, two men were sitting under a shed patiently sawing logs. Across the road, near where we set up our 106mm recoilless rifle, was a small roadside stand selling tea, cigarettes, and drinks. Everything had changed, and for a moment I thought I was in the wrong place. But the bend in the river was as I remembered, and so were the mountains in the distance.

I looked for the familiar rice paddy, the tree line, and, beyond it, the hill with the old French fort on top. In the map of my memory they are vivid and immense, spread out across a vast expanse, a day's march from each other. But to my surprise the French fort rose up in the foreground no more than a mile or two away. Vietnam was so much smaller, and so much closer together, than I had remembered. When I fought here Da Nang was a world away; today, the drive had taken fifteen minutes. The old French fort had seemed miles from the bridge; now it clearly was only a short walk, just across the paddies and along a tree line.

But then I realized why it had seemed so far. That paddy had meant booby traps and mines and being caught in the open, and that tree line had meant ambush and death. Who lives in war and who dies is decided by inches: walking down a paddy dike, you step over a mine that kills the man behind you. And when inches are everything, the measure of distance goes out of whack. Then I measured with the yardstick of fear. But now the same scene was only a small, peaceful Asian landscape, a nice place to have a picnic. Then it had defined my entire world; now it was only a Chinese watercolor of river, paddies, and foothills in the shadow of the mountains—just another piece of Vietnam.

Hien, the former Viet Cong company commander who had fought against the marines here, smoked a cigarette while he leaned against a placid water buffalo and talked with the boy on the buffalo's back. I walked up to an old man drinking tea at the roadside stand.

"The Americans had a position here," he said, gesturing at the bridge. "We attacked it constantly." I remembered that, although "constantly" was a bit of hyperbole.

"The Americans spent all their time destroying our gardens and our village and desecrating our graves. The village next to the bridge was very damaged," he said.

I did not, however, remember that. But in Vietnam the legends of the war are now its facts, and history is at the service of the state.

I remembered at Tet in 1970 a delegation from my platoon was invited to a feast in Hao Phung 2, the village next to the bridge. With great earnestness—uncluttered by irony—I spent several hours trying to teach my nineteen-year-old marines how to use chopsticks. I didn't want us to seem insensitive to the village culture. We took our places in the hamlet meeting place, and were served a ceremonial meal along with many glasses of beer and rice wine. After many toasts to "friendship" I looked around the table—all the marines were dutifully struggling with chopsticks, but all the Vietnamese were scooping up their food with plastic spoons. I was now hearing the same hamlet described to me as a "heroic hamlet," a center of the revolution, a thorn in the side of the Americans.

The Vietnamese have a phrase that describes why they embrace a whole range of religious beliefs, from animism and geomancy to Buddhism and Catholicism; the phrase is "just in case." We follow these precepts, they say, "just in case" they might work, and we are polite and hospitable to Americans "just in case" they might never go home. But we also maintain contacts with the Viet Cong "just in case" they might win. Now that the Viet Cong have won, clarity reigns: everyone was with them all along. Without exception every single person I stopped at random claimed to have been in the Viet Cong.

We got back in the car and drove south, down the road my battalion had swept for mines each morning. The gravel road that turned off Route 540 was still there. We followed it down amid the rice paddies, flooded and green. Two old men came walking down the road. One of them, Nguyen Van Pham, had been the president of the Viet Cong in a nearby village.

"All this was a no-man's-land," he said, gesturing around the paddies and hills I knew so well.

"We were very strong here. We worked right under the nose of the U.S. base up this road. We knew everything—we knew of every sweep operation. We lived in tunnels right over here, next to the district headquarters, and in Bo Ban hamlet across the road. Our best fighters worked on the base. They pretended to serve the Americans, but at night they joined us."

Pham and his comrades had lived in tunnels under our noses. They had worked with us and been our "friends." One of them might well have been the man I had encountered in that tunnel on the riverbank. But as I stood in the bright sunlight, that dark passage seemed only a dream.

Then a woman came up the road. Her name was Dong Thi San. I asked her if she had been here during the war.

"Of course," she said. "I was the wife of a guerrilla, and our home was a center of the revolution."

I asked her what her husband did now.

"He was killed," she said, "killed by an American Marine patrol in 1969, right over there by Bo Ban hamlet. And he left four children."

She looked at me with steady eyes. I had been here in 1969, patrolling these rice paddies, and I had been through Bo Ban hamlet, and set out ambushes there. It is not inconceivable that my platoon killed her husband. Perhaps he had even been that corpse my men decorated with the cigarette and the *Playboy* magazine. Then, he was the enemy, an abstraction; now I saw him as a man with parents, a wife, children—a man like me.

"But the war is over now," she said. "We have much to do. Life goes on."

We drove up the red dirt road toward Hill 10. It was the spoke from which radiated all my memories, as my patrols had radiated from there fifteen years ago. And now, after all those years, after so much history in between, it was, once again, just around the next bend.

We passed a crumbled gate that led to the old headquarters of Hieu Duc district. During the war I became friends with the American adviser to the Vietnamese district chief. My friend was an Army captain who lived in the headquarters compound —although the chief himself spent the nights in the security of Da Nang. One afternoon the captain opened his refrigerator, offered me a beer, and together we sat down to do his pacification report.

"What about the Bo Bans?" he asked me.

"Terrible. Awful. A nest of VC," I told him.

"I don't know. I drove by there the other day. It looked more secure to me. I'm going to upgrade it."

After a few more beers, we had upgraded about half of the hamlets in the district, information that as it sped away from the dusty little hamlet would become more and more reliable, until the Pentagon's computers spewed it back out as hard evidence of our progress.

"See?" the Army captain said to me. "We're winning the war."

Near the top of the hill a ditch had been cut across the road. I got out of the car, crossed the ditch, and walked up to the top of the hill. There were no interlocking rings of barbed wire, no mines, no gates, no bunkers, no jeeps, no buildings, no weapons, no noise, no people. Where the base had been was only a rough field of red dirt. I'm not sure what I had expected, but it wasn't this empty space and this silence.

I walked over the hilltop, and I could remember perfectly where everyone had lived and worked, where everything in that little world had happened. I paused where the command post had been, where the Filipino bands had sung, where the PX and the Enlisted Men's Club had stood, where the showers and the mess hall had greeted us when we came in from the bush and enjoyed the luxury of civilization. This hill had been a piece of America, our connection to the world, to reality. Now there were only the paddies, the mountains beyond, and the sounds of birds singing, brought on a gentle breeze.

Hien, the former Viet Cong company commander, my old enemy, the man we had built all our bases to kill, walked quietly up and stood at my side as I stared toward the mountains. My preoccupation with the past amused him; he had other problems now. With a stick, he drew diagrams in the dirt of how his company could have attacked Hill 10. I watched with interest, but there was really nothing left to say. In the end, he didn't have to attack it. He simply had to survive until we left, and then the country would be his.

The next day I was sitting at the airport with Minh and Hien waiting to board the plane to Saigon. I asked Hien how it felt, after all those years in the jungle, to have returned in victory.

He looked out the window, toward the mountains rising out of the paddies, toward where he had lived and fought for so long. "I just felt such joy," he said. "Such joy and happiness. I saw the puppet government disintegrating and I just walked the streets in happiness. None of us thought it would take so long."

He paused, his long lashes hiding his eyes, his hands resting in his lap. "You did it. It was your stubbornness and all your troops and aid. We would have won years earlier, without all the bloodshed."

As always, we Americans were the ones who stood in history's path, with the choice to prolong or to end the war. It was pointless to say that they could have stopped the war anytime as well. The concept of their quitting simply doesn't penetrate; they would have kept fighting for five, ten, twenty years more —for as long as it took.

Hien asked me how the airport had changed since I was last here.

"It's a lot quieter," I said. "And it's yours."

21

THE SAME SAIGON

I first saw Saigon in the spring of 1970, its late baroque period. The graceful French city had by then been smothered beneath a sprawling, energetic American one. Saigon was of the war but not in it. Going there from the real war was almost the same as going to Bangkok or Manila, only there was a curfew and more barbed wire in Saigon. Life in Saigon was like life back in the world—a wierd, bizarre variation, but the same basic idea. Thousands of Americans lived in houses and worked in air-conditioned offices where they put in eighteen-hour days fighting the war with computers and reports. There was a Yale Club, whose members gathered to sing "The Whiffenpoof Song." I felt naïve and unwashed when I first came to Saigon. I was a hick with mud on my boots from the combat zone.

On my way in from the airport that first time, I stopped at the PX to buy some civilian trousers, a shirt, and some shoes. Without my fatigues and my pistol I felt like a deserter, helpless and out of place. As I left the PX a swarm of hustlers and taxi drivers descended on me, imploring me to change money, buy them cigarettes, come meet their sisters. I picked a taxi and asked the driver to take me to the Continental Palace—I could not be in Saigon without paying homage to Graham Greene—but instead he took me to a whorehouse and insisted I go in, to the point of casting aspersions on my manhood. We argued for ten or fifteen minutes.

Exasperated, I got out, caught another cab, asked for the Continental Palace, and was driven back to the PX, where the driver spent ten minutes trying to get me to buy him cartons of Salems. I gave up and bought him two cartons. For the rest of my week in Saigon I could not leave my hotel without his following me in his cab, trying to sell me on some new scheme.

After I bought the cigarettes he drove me to the Continental Palace. I ordered a gin and tonic from the Vietnamese waiter—a waiter! in the war!—who wore a white shirt with a black bow tie and seemed in every bone of his being to long for the days when his clients were French. A Vietnamese woman at the next table examined precious stones with a jeweler's loupe. A large, red-faced American civilian bent closely over a Vietnamese woman in an *ao dai*. Her tiny hand disappeared into his. She looked straight ahead as he whispered into her ear. From the terrace bar I looked down on Tu Do Street, which was filled with prostitutes, cyclo drivers, bicycles, jeeps, and an incredible din.

Everywhere I saw Saigon cowboys, the Vietnamese draft dodgers with long hair, sunglasses, and pegged trousers who roared about the city on motorcycles. The war seemed very far away, and the reasons we were fighting farther still. I was filled with anger: young Americans had been dying for five years in Vietnam, supposedly to protect these young men who lounged about the sidewalks combing their hair and hustling GIs. At that time the Thieu government still refused to enact a tough draft law; it was easier to dodge the draft in Vietnam than it was in America.

I got to know one of the cowboys. His name was Khanh. He was twenty, but his forged ID said he was thirteen. His hustle was changing money. I asked him why he wasn't in the Army.

"Why should I die for the Americans?" he said.

To Khanh, and to much of Saigon back then, the war was an American concern, and they would get the most out of it while it lasted. Saigon's concern was opportunity and intrigue. When I returned in 1984 I found that some of Saigon's most blatant excesses have been suppressed, but opportunity and intrigue still make it tick. Beneath the surface, it is the same Saigon.

Saigon is a direct challenge to the Communists' ideology and morality. It is the symbol of what they see as the corruption, immorality, and consumerism of the West—as well as the last stronghold of the new regime's opponents. Still, the Communists need Saigon almost as desperately as they hate and fear it. Even they recognize that beneath Saigon's "antisocial" exterior are the most efficient and successful economic institutions in the country. It's a dilemma: as if a fundamentalist minister had taken over Las Vegas to reform it, but had to live on its winnings.

To enter Saigon from North Vietnam is like going from Moscow to Los Angeles. The place is loud, raucous, colorful; it spills onto the street—more discreetly now, of course, but its basic energy has yet to be sapped. Everything is still for sale—everything. Within five blocks of my hotel I was offered Buddhas plundered from Cambodia, rare Chinese antiques, gold jewelry, sex with male or female prostitutes, heroin, and, my favorite, a stamp collection (which I bought). I was asked to change money, buy cigarettes, get my shoes shined, sell my camera. I saw markets offering everything from U.S. Navy silverware and American weapons to the latest cameras and stereos.

In the Majestic Hotel the shop sells every kind of liquor—except the Russian brands that alone were available in Hanoi. Foreign cigarettes are sold openly. But, more impressive, everything works. The clerks at the hotel speak good English. The elevator goes up and down. I could combine hot and cold water in my bathroom. My air conditioner—American, not Russian—sent me searching for a blanket. In the restaurant on the roof the waiters still dress in the black trousers, white shirts, and black bow ties of the French era. The orange juice in the morning is freshly squeezed, the croissants hot and newly baked, the coffee pungent and rich.

If not for the other foreigners beginning their conversations with me by saying, "I saw they had two cops following you today," I could almost have believed I was in a normal place. In Saigon one meets many cultured people, familiar with the West, good conversationalists. Unfortunately, they aren't the people who won the war.

And then there is the matter of the new name: Ho Chi Minh City. The renaming of things is the essence of conquest—not only did the Communists take over the city, they wiped out its memory. Hotels, streets, landmarks, all have new names—and some, new uses. Graham Greene's Continental Palace Hotel is now a Communist Party billet, closed to the public. Mimi's Bar, like all the bars on Tu Do Street, is gone, replaced by the ubiquitous antique shops. The Vietnamese Air Force Officers' Club was one of the best examples of the corruption of our war. It was so dark you couldn't see your table, so cold you immediately began to shiver. But then you discovered there was a woman on duty under each table, and once you sat down she immediately went to work. It's gone, and good riddance. Soul Alley, where dark-skinned Cambodians and métis fathered by African soldiers of the French war catered to black Americans, is just a neighborhood now.

The American embassy, taken over briefly by the Viet Cong in the Tet Offensive of 1968, is the headquarters for the government petroleum agency. The Cercle Sportif has become a workers' recreation club. The Majestic Hotel is the Cuu Long, Tu Do (Freedom) Street is Dong Khoi (Uprising) Street, and so on. The old names continue to be used, but Tu Do Street was more often called by its French colonial name: Rue Catinat. Unless I was talking with a high-ranking functionary, I almost never heard the name Ho Chi Minh City. Granted, it was written on all my documents and I could say Ho Chi Minh City and be understood; but the city is still Saigon.

The old Caravelle is still a hotel, and as I emerged from its elevator my first afternoon in Saigon I was surprised by an extraordinary sight: an American car pulled up, and four American Air Force officers in green fatigues got out and strode purposefully past two American MPs guarding the entrance. They were greeted by a beautiful young Vietnamese woman in a miniskirt, who took the arm of one of the Americans as they entered the hotel. It was as if nothing had changed, as if the last fifteen years had been a dream, and I was watching it all happen again. I stared at them, openmouthed.

And then I saw the cameras. They were making a movie, it turned out, about a "heroic" attack on the Americans in the Caravelle during the war. The Air Force officers and American MPs I had seen were Russians wearing American uniforms. And they looked just like us.

The Russians weren't the only people in Saigon who looked like us. One entrance to the Majestic was blocked off with an iron grating that looked into the hotel lobby. Night and day the children stood at that grating, their faces pressed through the bars, watching the foreigners sip cocktails or purchase cigarettes and toiletries in a small dollar shop. Almost all of them had American fathers. Lulu and Huong and Minh and Mai were the regulars. Mai was the leader, an irrepressible, resourceful teenager whose sharp eyes missed nothing, and whose equally sharp tongue gave no quarter. Her intelligence system was better than the police's—perhaps *was* the police's. Nothing happened on the lower end of Tu Do Street around the Majestic that she didn't know about.

Five minutes after I arrived they knew I was an American. Every time I left the hotel they would dog my every step, trying to get me to to buy them things, to lend them money, to notice. When all else failed they sold me peanuts and cigarettes. I came to know them as the Peanut Gang. The first morning I walked out of the hotel to take a look around, Mai was on me at once. Naturally she knew my name, although I had told it to no one.

"Hey, Bill," she called. "You buy me shampoo. My hair so dirty."

"Look, here's some dong. You buy it."

"No way. Vietnamese shampoo number ten. You buy for me at hotel."

"I'm really a little low on money," I said.

"Hey, I'm the one poor," she replied with a grin. "You not poor."

She had me there. So I went back into the hotel, but the shop was out of shampoo. I bought some soap instead, and walked back into the street and gave it to her. Immediately I was confronted by Lulu, whose large brown eyes flicked up and down in constant warfare with her cheekbones, as if her face was unsure whether it was American or Vietnamese.

"Hey, you buy Mai soap," she upbraided me. "What's the matter? You no like me?"

I went back into the shop, bought some more soap, and gave a bar to Lulu.

Two days later my car broke down in the Saigon suburbs. For an hour we tried to fix it, with not the faintest sign of progress. I decided to take a cyclo, and was sped off silently through the wet streets of the city. We stopped at a traffic jam in Cholon, the Chinese quarter miles from the Majestic. Some children came running up. I had never seen them before.

"Bill! Bill!" they yelled. "You give us soap too, okay?"

When I got back to the hotel I went for a walk. Little Minh, from the Peanut Gang, fell in step with me. Little Minh (no relation to Minh, my interpreter) was short and looked about ten years old, but in fact was fifteen.

"Hey, Bill," he said, "you number one. You help me, right? I need money for English lesson."

The Canadians who come regularly to Saigon had told me about Minh. He was, one of them said, "the least favorite. He used to follow us around and when we didn't give him money he'd kick us and call us Cheap Charlies."

During the war I had made friends with a young girl who lived near Cobb Bridge. Every evening when I walked up to eat at the 7th Engineers' headquarters, I would pass her at a small pagoda by the road. When I brought her an apple or some bread she would hold my hand, but whenever I forgot she would follow down the road, throwing rocks at me. And then there was GTO, a twelve-year-old boy who essentially ran Cobb Bridge. He untangled traffic jams, settled disputes between bus drivers and Marine convoys, and regulated the sale of Cokes, ice—and, I am sure, drugs and prostitutes—to the marines on the bridge.

GTO once gave me the most succinct explanation I ever heard of what the Americans did to the economy of Vietnam: "Before you come here everybody work rice, fix tires, weave baskets. Once or twice a week, buy a Coca-Cola for a few piasters. Marines come—they pay fifty cents for Coca-Cola, five dollars for skivvy girl. Now nobody who work rice, fix tires, weave baskets can afford buy Coca-Cola anymore. So everybody sell Coca-Cola and skivvy girls now. Old way gone. . . . Hey, I hear you go R and R. Want to borrow hundred bucks? Low interest."

I heard later that GTO had been killed in a sapper attack on the tank battalion headquarters up the road. He apparently was guiding a Viet Cong unit through the wire.

When I came to Saigon during the war I spent some time browsing among the stalls of booksellers. I began talking to a young girl who was sitting in front of her family's stall reading *Les Misérables.* She was fourteen years old and dreamed of going to Paris to study. I sat down and for two hours we talked about Balzac and Hugo. She was friendly, open, Western—so different from the children I had met in the villages. For several years we wrote to each other, and when I returned to Saigon I went looking for her book stall. No one there or at the address where she had lived remembered her or her family.

During the war most of the children in Saigon who sought out Americans were fronts for pimps or con artists. On a spring morning in 1970 I was using my movie camera and a boy came up.

"You sell camera?" he asked.

"No, thanks."

"My brother give you two hundred dollar."

"No, I don't think so," I said, although that was twice what I had paid for it.

"Okay, you nice guy. I know he give you more. Two-fifty."

"I really don't want to sell it."

"Final offer. Three hundred."

"Well—" I said, thinking I could buy another camera and have two hundred dollars left over. If they wanted to pay me so much, then why not?

"You meet in alley back of Mimi's," he said. "Fifteen minutes."

I went to the alley, but I was nervous. We had been told such transactions could be dangerous—and besides, they were illegal. The boy was in the doorway of a small building. He motioned me over. A man was standing there. He flashed me a roll of twenty-dollar bills. Just then the boy hissed at us, and motioned down the alley.

"Police!" the man said. He pressed the money into my hand, grabbed the camera, and was gone. I stuffed the money into my pocket and darted down the alley, made it safely to the street and caught a bus. When I was sure no one had followed me I pulled out the money. I peeled off the top twenty-dollar bill—and inside was nothing but a stack of all but worthless piaster notes. I had "sold" my camera for about twenty dollars and fifty cents.

The Peanut Gang was refreshingly innocent by comparison. When I paid too much for a haircut Mai came running down the street with my change. When I lost my key in front of the hotel during a monsoon rain, they all helped me search through the flooded gutters.

"C'mon, Minh," I said, when he asked me for money to take English lessons. "You speak English really well."

"No way. My mother sick. Need money for doctor too."

I gave him five dollars for basic creativity.

"Hey, Bill, thank you very much," Little Minh said, tucking it into his pocket with a big grin. "And be careful. Your cyclo driver a police informer. He tell them wherever you go."

22

BOATS ALONG
THE MEKONG

The next day we went to Ben Tre, a river town on the Mekong where in 1959 the Viet Cong first revolted against the government of South Vietnam. I had been to Tan Trao, in the North, where the war against the French began. In Ben Tre the war against the Americans began.

The car broke down twice on the way to meet the ferry at My Tho, and we arrived too late to catch it. Minh and I and Viet, the guide from Saigon, had *pho* in a café and waited for the next ferry. Women were selling *petit pain* from racks in the street, so I bought a couple of loaves and soaked up my *pho* with the bread.

Minh told me why the lotus was such a special flower.

"It grows from the mud," he said, "but is not of the mud. Its flower is pink, its odor clean and fresh. Whenever I see a lotus, I know that beauty can grow from ugliness. It is like our country, the lotus. We are growing from the mud of the war, and our new blossoms are beautiful."

Viet smiled at this story. He wasn't exactly a cynic, but he had seen more than he let on, and certainly he had seen more than Minh. He seemed tolerant of Minh's romantic streak, but his mind ran more to the practical, to the mud in which the lotus grows. Viet was in his early fifties. His mother was killed by an American soldier. His wife's parents had been separated in 1954 and did not see each other again until after the fall of

Saigon, twenty-one years later. He married at forty-two, after the war.

Viet had been a member of the Communist Party for twenty years, Minh only for three. I asked how I would become a Party member if I lived in Vietnam.

"First you would have worked hard in youth organizations, or been a cadre doing the real work of the Party," Viet said. "Then you would be nominated by another member, probably where you work. If your cell believes you are a worthy prospect, you would become a provisional member and be judged over a period of time by your knowledge of ideology, your deeds for the Party, your dedication to the country."

If once admitted, was I in for life?

"Oh, no," Viet said. "The Party is a living thing. In the past few years we have admitted many new members and removed a number of old members whose views had not—had not, well, matured. Minh is our new generation."

"It's really like a patriotic organization," Minh said. "We all have regular jobs, and we do our Party work on our own time. My boss at the Foreign Ministry, for example, is not a Party member. I often don't know if my colleagues are members or not. No one asks. It doesn't matter."

"Ah, but we should not talk of such things," Viet said, reminding me that, in fact, it mattered a great deal—that it meant everything.

By then the ferry had arrived, and we joined the wave of cars, buses, bicycles, and pedestrians who surged on board. At My Tho the Mekong is not so much a single river as a great wide flood bound for the sea, interspersed with islands large and small.

A few minutes after we left My Tho we rounded an island and passed the abandoned headquarters of the coconut cult. The South is the land of strange cults, from the Cao Dai, with their worship of Jesus Christ and Victor Hugo, to the warlike Hoa Hao, to smaller cults like the coconut cult, whose members ate only coconuts and worshipped a coconut god. The defunct coco-

nut cult's world headquarters was a tiny river village, sur-
mounted with strange, spidery metal sculptures several stories
high, like skeletons of an abandoned amusement park.

We arrived late at Ben Tre and went straight to the provincial
headquarters on the banks of a small lake. During the French
war the young half-breed Colonel Leroy built the lake and placed
in its center a small pagoda in imitation of the Lake of the
Returned Sword in Hanoi. In the winter of 1951–52 Graham
Greene went to a party given in Ben Tre by Colonel Leroy, on
a barge stocked with brandy and dancing girls. Greene rode back
to Saigon with an American attached to the economic aid mission, and the American talked the whole way of the need for a
"third force" between the French and the Communists. On that
ride, Greene recalled, "the subject of *The Quiet American* came
to me."

That "third force" proved to be somewhat more elusive than
expected. Sixteen years later, we Americans—who once had contempt for French incompetence—were bogged down just as the
French had been. When the Viet Cong attacked Ben Tre during
the Tet Offensive of 1968, American jets and artillery virtually
razed Ben Tre to root them out. For block after block along the
canals not a single structure remained. An American major,
commenting on the destruction, voiced one of the most famous
comments of the war: "It became necessary to destroy the
town," he said, "in order to save it."

We stopped at Colonel Leroy's old headquarters only long
enough to pick up some province officials who would be our
guides, and then drove to a large barge moored on the banks of
the river. I wondered if it was the same barge that had seen
Greene's party, with the dancing girls and the brandy. From the
barge we transferred to a small dugout with a tiny lawn-mower
engine that actually went *putt-putt-putt* as it took us downriver
at a speed I estimated to be slower than if we had simply drifted
in the current.

The river was filled with traffic. Sampans passed us, filled within an inch of the gunwales with rice, sugarcane, coconuts, cement, and, in some cases, people. On the banks, boys repaired nets and women counted their money from market day. We passed the hulk of an American river-patrol boat. Above the noise of the engine, one of the officials described how they would set ambushes along the river.

"We mined the banks and dug shelters in the mud," he said. "We usually had two B-40 rockets, one for each end of the boat, and a machine gun to rake the middle. We would put a lookout up in a coconut tree to watch for the enemy and then we would sit in the mud and wait. Sometimes we'd wait a week, and no boat would come by. The enemy would bomb us, and the rain would soak us. Our skin would wrinkle like old leather. I still smell the mud. But when the enemy's boat would finally come, we would fire our rockets and machine gun with great joy. When the boat burned and sank I never knew such happiness."

As we made our slow way downstream I remembered that I and my friends were the "enemy" he was discussing—that it was our deaths that had brought my companion such "happiness." I tried to imagine being on a patrol boat and staring into the riverbanks, trying to spot the ambush before I became a target. But the vegetation was so thick, the bank so opaque, that even a few yards away I could see nothing.

After a couple of hours we got out at the hamlet of Luoang Hoa, the home of Madame Nguyen Thi Dinh, one of the leaders of the Ben Tre insurrection of 1959 that began the war against the government of South Vietnam and the Americans. We made our way from the boat past huge mounds of crushed sugarcane, pungent in the heat.

Inside a windowless brick shelter with portraits of Marx, Engels, and Ho Chi Minh on the wall, I met the local officials, who gave me the usual briefing along with tea and cookies and tiny bananas.

We then toured the tiny shops of the local trading cooperative, where members could buy homemade cola, soy cakes soaked in soy oil, a large metal cooking pot for 150 dong, and the bargain of the week—ten bowls for 51 dong. To buy the pot and the bowl, even at the artificially low prices of the cooperative, would take almost a month's salary. On our way to the tiny war museum we passed a huge bomb crater which had been converted to a fish pond. The museum consisted of tables filled with the primitive weapons from the early years of the war—handmade rifles, concrete mines, sharpened bamboo sticks. On the wall was an honor roll of martyrs from the village who were killed in the war. I counted 328 names.

We said our farewells and climbed back into the boat. On the bank I noticed a tall, beautiful young woman. She had an indefinable quality, the sort of magic which every now and then will touch a young woman in a small town anywhere. If she hadn't lived in Vietnam that magic would have meant that she was going to leave this little village on the banks of a river and make the world notice. But we were in Vietnam, and I felt a powerful urge to invite her to come along, to give her a ride to Saigon and whatever destiny might be hers. But the boat was already pulling away. She stood on top of a pile of sugarcane, staring at me, until we reached a bend in the river and I could see the village no more.

The heat on the river was inescapable. After half an hour we pulled onto the bank and scrambled up into a grove of coconuts. An old man came out, a métis from the days of the French with a Ho Chi Minh goatee and round, bright eyes. He knocked off a few coconuts and my companions took knives and cut off the tops and scraped out the meat. A soft rain began to fall. We stood in the shade of the coconut trees, eating the meat and drinking the cool clear milk from the shells.

"Just think," one of my guides said, "ten years ago this was nothing but a desert soaked in Agent Orange. And now we are eating coconuts here."

Suddenly I wasn't certain how much I was enjoying my coconut. The day before, I had visited Tu Du Hospital in Saigon to talk about Agent Orange. If our soldiers might have suffered from casual contact with the pesticide, how might the Vietnamese have been affected by living with it? In Hanoi I had spent an afternoon at the East German hospital talking to Dr. Ton Duc Lang, currently the leading Vietnamese expert on this problem. I was shown photographs of deformed fetuses born to women whose husbands had been in sprayed areas. The doctors had performed some rudimentary statistical studies, and had discovered that cases of liver cancer and major birth defects were much higher than average. It was a very calm, very organized, very quiet presentation.

In Saigon, I didn't see photographs of deformities. At Tu Du Hospital, I was led into one of the main stops on the media tour of Saigon—a room filled with jars from floor to ceiling. In each jar was a grotesquely deformed fetus: Siamese twins joined in every conceivable manner, fetuses with one huge eye like a cyclops, parasitic twins with one baby growing out of the other's chest, fetuses with heads like vultures, and jars containing a shapeless fleshy mass from which protruded an arm or a leg. My guide, Dr. Nguyen Thi Ngoc Phuong, insisted that the incidence of these problems was strikingly high.

"Take Siamese twins," she said. "At this hospital alone we have had thirteen cases out of our last fifteen thousand births, and four in the last six weeks."

I walked from bed to bed in the wards upstairs, meeting young women—teenagers or in their twenties—who had choriocarcinoma, a type of cancer of the reproductive organs normally seen after menopause. They were all from areas heavily sprayed with Agent Orange. In the delivery room we caught up with the hospital director. I asked him about the choriocarcinoma cases.

He slowly shook his head and said, "Too young, too young. They are too young to have this."

As yet, at least, there is no solid proof that Agent Orange

caused these problems. There is only a crudely measured statistical correlation that may or may not be valid.

"They try to lay this on Agent Orange," an American doctor sympathetic to the Vietnamese told me. "Choriocarcinoma has a higher incidence among *all* Asian women—not just Vietnamese. They have anecdotes. They don't have evidence."

During my trip in the South I passed through a number of areas that had been heavily sprayed during the war. In Quang Nam province I could see no lasting effects; everything seemed to have grown back. As we ate the coconuts in Ben Tre, my hosts were neither alarmed nor outraged; they were proud that the new coconut trees were already bearing fruit. But I remembered those women I had seen at Tu Du Hospital, and the American veterans I knew with skin lesions whose children had birth defects, and the coconut milk didn't taste quite so sweet anymore.

When we finally returned to Ben Tre, the barge was filled with hundreds of people attending a briefing. The speaker fanned himself with his papers, and much of his audience seemed to be looking out the windows at the river. The subject was the topic of universal discussion in Vietnam, Resolution Six. Resolution Six attempted to introduce a measure of local planning and initiative into the economy—not to the extent practiced in Hungary or, recently, in China, but in terms of Vietnam's Russian-style central economy a major change in direction.

One of my hosts had been to Hanoi twice to be lectured on the implications of Resolution Six. All the ten thousand members of the Communist Party in Ben Tre province had attended courses on it, as had all the Party workers and cadre and some 80 percent of the ordinary workers, including the ones I had just seen on the barge. I found it mildly ironic that a program designed to encourage initiative was being driven so relentlessly into everyone's head. I was assured that such education was vital so that the entire country could move forward, as one, with local initiative.

My hosts in Ben Tre, at least, seemed pleased at the prospect of managing their own small businesses and their own foreign currency accounts. (And no wonder—these local foreign currency accounts have become a lucrative part of the black market.) I read numerous accounts in *Nhan Dan*, the Party newspaper, about the success of the new program. There was testimonial after testimonial from enthusiastic Party bureaucrats about how they had "accumulated capital" and how an "investment" would "pay for itself in fourteen months"!

Unlike some Eastern European countries where Western publications are sold routinely, Vietnam has no independent news. But *Nhan Dan* routinely publishes horror stories about corruption and mismanagement, about abuses of the peasants and the people, about failures of the government and the Party. Its picture of Vietnam is tough-minded and realistic, and it gives old-line members no more quarter than the newest cadre. Case studies of the problems of establishing cooperatives and collectives openly discuss opposition from peasants and failures of leadership. In one account, the cooperative leader, an old guerrilla, was picketed by peasants who believed he was practicing arrogant, one-man rule. There are stories of excessively zealous tax collectors seizing personal property, of Party members running smuggling rings, of payoffs for jobs, permits, apartments.

Two themes run through these accounts. The first is that the power of the central government is far from absolute. A deputy minister in Hanoi confirmed this for me, in words that sounded exactly like the complaints we Americans used to make about how hard it was to get anything done in Vietnam.

"The old saying that the power of the Emperor stops at the gates of the village is still true," he said. "Even on the province level, they basically do what they want to do. Cables get lost, orders get 'misunderstood.' In most cases of practical government, we cannot simply give orders and expect they will be followed. We have to persuade. At the level of the village and the cooperative that is even more true. We cannot command allegiance; we must earn it."

The second theme is that the transformation of the South into the socialist model of the North has been far more difficult than the regime ever expected it to be. Ten years have passed since "Liberation," and still the North and the South might well be two countries. "The Politburo believes that so far as the South goes, it's now or never," a senior Western diplomat told me. "And they've decided that it's never."

In Vietnam, ideology has always come in by the back door. "We inspired the people to fight out of patriotism," Xuan Oanh had said in Hanoi. "Then, when we had their allegiance, we could convince them of our ideology."

That strategy worked against the French, and it worked against the Americans. The goals were transcendent: drive out the foreigners, unite the country. If Communist ideology was the price that had to be paid for that—and if it would get rid of the landlords in the process—then the people would pay it. But there are no more epic battles for independence and freedom to be won. Now the only incentive is the Party's own authority: you will follow this ideology, not because it is the only way to liberate the country, but because we say so.

"After the war," I was told, "we expected the same spirit of sacrifice and patriotism to continue. We expected it to pervade the South. We overestimated the fervor. It was a serious mistake."

Having organized this culture to drive out the foreigners and unite the country, the leadership seems incapable of uniting everybody to live a normal life and to improve the common lot. Part of the problem stems from the legacy of one of the longest and most destructive wars in history. But the single biggest drag on mobilizing the country's naturally industrious and entrepreneurial people has been the tired, bankrupt Marxist-Leninist ideology whose primary virtue is as a method of social control and which has little to offer a country wishing to create a modern economy.

Without the drama of Deng Xiaoping's headlong dash away from Marxism in China, the Party leadership have begun to disengage themselves from the centralized state-planning approach to economics. The talk is still of three incentives: for the state, for the collective, and for the individual—but almost all the attention is going to the last two. The pragmatists in the leadership have discovered that the desire for personal betterment—the capitalist vice of acquisitiveness—is a much more effective motivation for hard work and economic growth than exhortations for social good. The evidence is undeniable: the countryside is better off than the cities because the peasants have been allowed more opportunity to produce for themselves; the South is better off than the North because in the South there still exists the desire to create wealth.

The loosening of economic ties to allow individuals to produce more has inevitably loosened social ties as well. To the casual visitor North Vietnam seems almost a religious state. Public morality is pervasive and governs all behavior; the individual must sacrifice for the good of the society. The mechanism for enforcing this morality is all but invisible. With the exception of Saigon, there are few police in the cities, and they are almost never armed. In the villages I never saw a policeman or a soldier. And although there is a pervasive network of informers, much of the behavior seems not imposed but internal, built in. But even in the North the belief that society is more important than the individual is no longer so automatic.

Vietnam today is a society accustomed to sacrifice, on the verge of having sacrificed enough. To ease those sacrifices the country must grow economically, but to grow economically means opening the door to all the Western social effects that the old Party members find so threatening. They are puritans, uncomfortable with suggestiveness in speech or dress. They are deeply suspicious of the corrupting influence of "addictive" Western music. They hate drugs. They believe in patriotism and family values. They want to get tough on criminals, and have no problem with enforcing the death penalty. They see military service as the crowning glory of the individual's relationship with the state, and they believe that a country's leaders, from the schoolhouse to the very top, should be given respect and considerable leeway to carry out their responsibilities.

As I heard Vietnamese embrace these values, over and over again, I began to believe that the American politician they would be most comfortable with is Ronald Reagan. Like him, they have a pervasive nostalgia for a simpler past, with all for one and one for all, when the complexities and temptations of modern life didn't deflect their countrymen from their basic values. There is, of course, a great gulf between Ronald Reagan and Truong Chinh, the Party's staunchest ideologue, but on many matters about which they both care deeply I suspect they would agree.

In Vietnam the true social contract is on matters of morality anyway, not economics. The Vietnamese are amateur Marxists at best. So far, the Westernizers like Le Duan are winning, but the purists are watching and waiting. On several occasions I heard them mutter, "Did we fight the war for this?" And until the leadership can convert their warrior culture to peace, until they can live by Ho's words about independence and freedom, their victory will remain bittersweet.

23

DANCING IN THE DARK

The next evening I met with Nguyen Huu Hanh, one of the highest-ranking South Vietnamese generals still in Vietnam. He fought with the French against the Viet Minh, and in the 1960s was the deputy commander of IV Corps and then II Corps in the Highlands. He spent two tours in the United States studying at American military schools. General Hanh was an old ally of Duong Van Minh, known to Americans as Big Minh. Big Minh had been one of the plotters who overthrew President Diem, with American support, in 1963. For a few months, during the period when South Vietnam changed leaders the way Paris changes fashions, Big Minh had been President. But when Thieu came to power he carefully kept Big Minh, and allies of his like General Hanh, on the sidelines.

Throughout the war, there were persistent rumors that Big Minh had close connections to the Viet Cong. As the Communists tightened the ring around Saigon in 1975, they insisted they would never negotiate so long as Thieu was in power—but Big Minh would be acceptable. Two days before the Communist forces entered Saigon, after Thieu had fled, Big Minh once again became President. And he brought General Hanh into the presidential palace with him, as deputy chief of staff of the armed forces.

Today General Hanh's wife runs a coffee shop in the garden of their villa near the cathedral in Saigon. Hanh himself is retired, but, in contrast to most of the North Vietnamese generals I met, has the bearing and dignity of a lifelong military officer. As rock-and-roll music blared from the café in the garden, we talked about what had gone wrong.

"You Americans repackaged the British experience in Malaya, but the Vietnamese were not like the Malayans. They weren't poor, and they didn't live in huts on rubber plantations. They had brick houses. When you rounded them up and sent them to live in straw huts, they couldn't understand why it was for their own good. The essence of counterinsurgency—and I learned this myself at Fort Leavenworth, at your Command and General Staff College—is to dry up the sea where the guerrilla swims. But instead of drying up the sea, you simply moved it around, and ended up making it larger.

"The Viet Cong would say to the people that they had to fight the Americans the way they had fought the French—until not a single foreigner remained on Vietnamese soil. Drive the foreigners out, unite the country. It was a powerful message. And then we would come along and say, 'Yes, but . . .'

"At first, the people would listen to us, but then they would look at how we lived and at how the Communists lived, and that would speak more eloquently to them than all our words. The Communists made more sacrifices; they had an ideal, and they fought for it to the death. They left their families and lived in great hardship. We were fighting for ideals too, some of us, but most of us were fighting for a living. The people could see how Ho lived, that pure simplicity, and they saw how Diem and Thieu lived. They saw how our officers bought their commands, how they sold off their military supplies on the black market, how they kept mistresses and Swiss bank accounts. The people weren't blind.

"In the end, they saw that we cared more for ourselves than for our country."

I asked him why, if he felt this way, he had fought against the Communists for so long.

"We thought we were fighting for our country," he said. "We relied on you to stand firm, to help us, the way the Soviet Union and China helped the Communists. But you insisted on doing things your way. All those coups d' état, from Diem on, that was simply because the CIA was trying to get a government that would do what you wanted. And then in the end you wouldn't stand with us, as you had in Europe and Korea. You made us dependent, and then you abandoned us to our fate."

I asked him why he hadn't fled the country, as had almost all of his fellow senior officers.

"I am a Vietnamese," he said. "And I have fourteen children. This is my country, even now."

General Hanh's mind often wanders back to the day when the North Vietnamese tanks burst through the gates of the presidential palace. Waiting in his office, General Hanh could hear the footsteps of the Communist soldiers echoing down the empty hallways—President Thieu had already fled—with, it is rumored, a fortune in gold. General Minh, his successor, was on his way to the radio station to announce the surrender. A squad of young North Vietnamese soldiers, breathless, burst into Hanh's office, waving their AK-47s.

"Where is the flagpole?" they asked.

General Hanh told them, and heard their footsteps clambering up the stairs. He waited in his office a few hours more, until General Tra, the Viet Cong commander, arrived. Then he walked home.

He had given the young soldiers good directions. From the flagpole of the palace flew the flag of North Vietnam. The Republic of Vietnam was no more.

One relic of the old Saigon still tolerated by the government is the Rex nightclub. During the war it was one of the more elegant centers of Saigon's corruption. Everything was for sale, from women to influence, but the cheapest prices were put on such devalued commodities as honor, patriotism, sacrifice. War always exalts the sexual, and at the Rex, sex was not so transparent a commodity as at the barbershops, bars, and whore-houses. At the Rex a certain grace and decorum prevailed.

Only three months after the fall of Saigon, the leaders of the Viet Cong's Provisional Revolutionary Government, who for years had lived in the jungle under B-52 strikes and the constant threat of capture or death, met at the Rex. It should have been a happy event, but it was not. Throughout the long years of the war, through separation and suffering, the Viet Cong had been fighting for their country. But because of the great strength of the Americans, their final sweet victory came on the backs of North Vietnamese tanks, and they were escorted back to Saigon by the North Vietnamese Army. At the victory parade in May the Viet Cong divisions, which had fought the Americans so hard, were disbanded and not allowed to march.

Throughout the war the North had insisted that reunification would be a long process based on mutual agreement. Harrison Salisbury asked Pham Van Dong in 1966 whether the North wanted to annex the South. The Premier became angry: no one in the North had this "stupid, criminal idea." Le Duan, the Party First Secretary, gave a speech in which he called for "socialism in the North, democracy in the South." Salisbury, no fool, believed that the National Liberation Front was perhaps the best chance for a stable, viable government in the South. Most of the Viet Cong's own government believed the same thing.

The idea that the North wanted to annex the South may have been "stupid" and "criminal." It also happened to be true. Ho's saying that nothing was more important than independence and freedom was on everyone's lips. But once the victory was won, nationalism was revealed as merely the means; the end was a Soviet-style state, controlled rigidly from the North. And the Viet Cong and their nationalist allies, who had fought Diem and Thieu and the Americans for so long, went unceremoniously into the rubbish heap.

The Viet Cong gathering at the Rex in July 1975 was a funeral: a wake for the dreams and goals of patriots who happened not to be doctrinaire Communists. Truong Nhu Tang, the Viet Cong Minister of Justice, was there, and described the scene: "We ate without tasting, and we heard without listening as some revolutionary music was cranked out by some sad little band. . . . We even managed to choke out a few of the old combatants' songs. But there was no way to swallow the gall in our mouths or to shrug off the shroud that had settled on our souls. We knew finally that we had been well and truly sold."

The Viet Cong were not the last items sold at the Rex. It's still open for business. I rode up in the elevator with two Russians who were busily combing their hair, turning up their collars, and checking each other's clothes in an uncanny re-creation of the Dan Aykroyd–Steve Martin *Saturday Night Live* parody of "wild and crazy guys." The Rex is a classic nightclub, dark, with discreet waiters who whisper, "Would you like a taxi girl, sir?" after they take the drink order. A woman named Cam Van sang basic Las Vegas lounge act songs in perfect imitation of Linda Ronstadt. The women were fashionably dressed, friendly, and spoke good English; they were even good dancers.

"Many men have fallen in love here," my American companion told me. Officially, everything is chaste; the girls all go home alone. But I spoke with several men who had managed to arrange private meetings; as with everything else in Saigon, anything is possible. I asked one of the women to dance. The first thing she said was: "Can you help me get to America?"

Throughout North Vietnam, and even in Da Nang and Hue, I felt I was in a basically stable culture, beset with problems and apprehensive about its future, but committed to it. In Da Nang I had encountered on my walks a few people who asked me to help them get out. But Saigon—well, as always, Saigon was totally different. Saigon had the feel of an occupied city. Everyone seemed to be whispering to me—about the government, about the police, about how bad things are, and, most of all, about how they wanted out. Even the wife and children of the government press coordinator in Saigon live in Los Angeles.

"Sometimes I think that all anyone does here is plot to leave," a European visitor from Hanoi told me over breakfast.

Robert Minnich, an American who interviews applicants for entry visas, met me at the hotel and talked about how badly people want to leave. "The worst is with the Amerasian kids. Their face is like a ticket out. We've seen them kidnapped and even bought and sold. You'll see a twenty-five-year-old woman claiming to be the mother of a seventeen-year-old kid. And then the same kid will come in later with a seventy-five-year-old woman who says that it was all a mistake, that she's the mother."

I asked him if there was a chance that any of the Peanut Gang might get out.

"Sure," he said. "You know Minh? Mr. Cheap Charlie?"

"How could I not?" I said.

"He's going out this week. On your plane."

"But I just gave him five dollars for English lessons," I said.

"Doesn't surprise me a bit," Minnich said. "Minh's going to do just fine."

I went out of the hotel and found Mai.

"Where's Minh?" I asked her.

"He at home," she said. "He no sell peanuts no more. He lucky. He go America. We all go airport to say goodbye. Hey, I almost forget. You give him five dollar! What's the matter? You no like me? Give me five dollar too!"

I did.

I met a number of people who qualified for exit visas but didn't want to leave. A métis nurse in one of the New Economic Zones designed to reclaim marshland for farming shrugged and said simply, "I am Vietnamese. This is my home." I met a former prison guard who qualified for departure but had decided to stay, he said, "because I am making up for my mistakes by helping to rebuild my country." I looked around his modest hut on a barren bit of salt marsh, and asked him what he would do if I gave him a ticket to California today.

"Today?" he asked, a smile on his face.

Dr. Phuong, my guide through Tu Du Hospital, is the most famous Vietnamese who could leave but doesn't. Her husband lives in Paris and has repeatedly tried to get her to join him. Her refusal, transformed into a propaganda film, has made her a national hero.

"I am needed here," she told me. "The people here are my family. I cannot leave them. I could have many things in Paris, live a good life—but that's not what is important, is it?"

Against this anecdotal evidence is the stark fact that more than a million Vietnamese have fled their country since the fall of Saigon, and another million are on file as wanting to get out by legal means. When the news spread in Saigon that I was an American, I became a walking mailbox. Wherever I went, people would stuff letters into my hands, my bag, my pockets. The desperation was very real: they wanted out, and they wanted help to make it. There were letters to relatives, letters to congressmen, letters to President Reagan, but above all, there were letters to perhaps the most famous American in South Vietnam —Don Colin. Don Colin. His name was on the lips of shopkeepers in Da Nang, hotel clerks in Hue, and virtually everyone I met in Saigon, from cooks and cyclo drivers to nurses and antique dealers.

As it happened, I knew Don Colin, which made me an even bigger attraction. Don Colin was the administrator of the Orderly Departure Program, which was established in 1979 to stem the tide of Vietnamese boat people, the desperate refugees who were dying by the thousands in the South China Sea and at the hands of Thai pirates. The ODP is officially a program of the United Nations High Commissioner for Refugees, but the countries that are the most common destinations—the United States, Canada, France, and Australia—run their own programs.

The ODP office is down an alley next to the USIA compound in Bangkok, about two miles from the American embassy. Once in the door, the visitor sees . . . files. Hundreds of file cabinets, stretching in rows and rows, filling up a huge room. On top of the file cabinets are stacks of files; stacks of files cram the aisles and pour off the desks of serene Thai office workers. As of September 1984 there were 125,000 files, representing more than 500,000 people trying to leave Vietnam. And two thousand new letters in support of old cases or requesting new ones arrive each week—all addressed to Don Colin.

Don Colin is a veteran of the war's civilian-run pacification programs, an old Vietnam hand who married a Vietnamese nurse who helped him recover from his injuries in an auto accident. He was one of those Americans who became absorbed in the culture, who dressed in black pajamas and slept on bamboo beds in village huts, who squatted in rice paddies talking politics to farmers, the country in his blood. He talks about Vietnam today the way an exile would, as if he were cut off from the piece of land that meant the most to his life. On the wall of his office was a blackboard with the words from the Armed Forces radio station which began each day of the war: "Goooooood morning, Vietnam."

The Vietnamese government has been the crucial link in making the program work. Eager to erase the image of the boat people, they have processed tens of thousands of exit visas for Vietnamese citizens with relatives abroad or for Amerasian children. But the problem arises when the exit visas they have approved do not match the entry visas we have approved—which is often the case. There is a good deal of variation in how the different provinces cooperate with the program.

"We get almost no one from Da Nang. They're very hardline," Colin said. "From Hue we get some mandarins and members of the old Imperial family. We get a few from the countryside. But the great majority come from Saigon. And if you're Chinese they'll practically hand you your exit visa when you apply; they want the Chinese out.

"We're in the people-moving business. We have very specific criteria. People either meet them or they don't. I can't let my staff get too involved in a poignant case; if they do, twenty other poignant cases get delayed. Our job is to move the files. It's a technical problem."

He paused, then said it again, as if he were trying to convince himself. "A technical problem. That's what it all comes down to, the whole war. Just moving files."

About fifteen thousand people make it out each year. At that rate, to clear every person in the current files would take thirty to forty years, not to mention all the new cases which come in each year. Even the Vietnamese government complains. I met with the head of their ODP staff in Saigon.

"We have thirty thousand exit visas approved for the United States that have yet to be acted upon," he told me. "These people have made the difficult decision to leave their native land. Their relatives are waiting for them abroad. It is inhumane not to process these matters more quickly."

Many of these people trying to get out were committed to us, worked for us, risked their lives for us. When we left in such inexcusable panic in 1975, we left them behind. They are our responsibility, and they are being treated as if they were illegal aliens trying to swim the Rio Grande. The entire weight of the federal bureaucracy has come down upon them, and the result is all those files, which represent hundreds of thousands of real human beings—the terrified people, their woeful stories melting into each other, who accosted me each day in Saigon. The gate could be closed at any time, as it was in Berlin, as it has been in every other Communist country. In the meantime, the American government continues to do the bureaucratic slow shuffle.

When I had finished my talk with Don Colin he escorted me out a different way, through a small room where two Thai secretaries sat gossiping to each other. On one desk was an out box with three or four files in it. "These are the ones that are completed," Colin said.

I looked back over my shoulder, at that room of the hundred thousand files with their half-million desperate people all neatly ordered inside. It was a scene from George Orwell or Kafka: every individual a case, every case a file folder, every file folder to be processed in due course.

Nightlife in Saigon is somewhat different than in Hanoi, where there are only two restaurants—in which, at times, the dogs outnumber the people. Saigon has dozens of restaurants. I met a European friend from Hanoi at Cola. Tables spilled out onto the sidewalk. The place was packed. Crowds of people waited for tables. A platoon of chefs stirred their woks over the flames of what appeared to be welding torches. The burners roared like gas wells being flared in an oil field. We ate sea slugs and shared the latest gossip from Hanoi.

Most Westerners end up having a meal at Madame Dai's, a French restaurant in the library of a villa near the cathedral. Madame Dai is a tiny woman, educated in law in France. She is a member of the National Assembly and sponsors a school for disabled children. She also seems to know every journalist who has ever been to Vietnam. Michael Flaks and I ate there several times, surrounded by Madame Dai's law books and ancient pottery, while portraits of her mandarin ancestors gazed down from the walls. Michael and Madame Dai talked in French about the old days.

"I did not want to open a restaurant in my home," she said. "But I had to, in order to survive."

"Oh, you love it," Michael said. "You get to see everyone."

"Yes," she said, "you are wonderful. But it's not the same."

I took my guides and drivers to a restaurant near the Majestic. A five-piece orchestra played dance tunes while slides of vacation spots in Eastern Europe flashed on the curtain behind them. The bill for the four of us was 3,000 dong, or about what each of them makes in a year. The restaurant had more than two hundred seats, and was completely full. I was the only Westerner. All those Vietnamese were making a great deal of money,

and something told me it was not from their salaries as com-
missars.

I spent the next morning at the University of Ho Chi Minh
City talking to a group of professors about the nature of Vietnamese society and history. I asked them how they had kept up
intellectual life during the war.

"It wasn't always as grim as you think," one professor told
me. "I remember while I was being bombed by B-52s at Cu Chi
I received a package from America—*Leaves of Grass*, by Walt
Whitman. It was very comforting."

The rest of the meeting was not a great success. Each of the
professors seemed intent on being the most ideologically correct, on not giving a colleague the slightest excuse to doubt his
loyalty to the party line. This one-upmanship ended when one
professor concluded his monologue on how outsiders exagger-
ate the influence of Confucius in Vietnam by saying, "And therefore, we see that the culmination of thousands of years of Vietnamese culture, its greatest achievement, is"—he paused for
dramatic effect; I leaned forward, pen ready—"the Communist
Party of Vietnam."

The professor leaned back, with what seemed to be a slightly
ironic smile on his face, although I couldn't be sure. In any case,
that remark was untoppable, and all the other professors knew
it. The discussion quickly came to an end.

I had tea with Nguyen Van Binh, the archbishop of Saigon
and the leader of that city's 450,000 Catholics, at his official
residence. The archbishop, a tall, stately man, was ordained in
1937 and has clearly seen everything.

"At first," he said, "things were difficult. We were suspicious
of the regime. The regime was suspicious of us. We had to give
up our schools, our hospitals, our orphanages to the state. But
our worship was allowed to continue. Now we understand each
other. There are still tensions, but there is also peace between
us."

Archbishop Binh is a man of considerable diplomatic skills.

When I asked if there was discrimination against Catholics in jobs and education, he replied, "There is no problem at the central level. Out in the countryside there may be some cadres who still believe Catholics are allied with the CIA, and that may cause problems."

I tried to get the archbishop to talk about how the regime was choking the Church by controlling the selection of new bishops and consolidating the seminaries to limit the supply of new priests, but he would only say that the Church and the regime had a constant "dialogue." There was, of course, no reason for him to be candid; I would soon return to the safety of America and he would still be in Saigon.

As I prepared to leave, the archbishop had a parting comment.

"Tell the world," he said, "that our churches are open, our people are worshipping, and mass is being said." I half expected him to add, "Life goes on."

I walked to the door. The archbishop took my arm and said, in a low voice, "Pray for us."

24

A MY LAI SURVIVOR AND THE WHITE VIET CONG

As I wandered about Saigon, my thoughts kept returning to Da Nang. I was still regretting that the floods had kept me from going to Khe Sanh and My Lai, and when I was offered a chance to go to Cambodia for the weekend, I decided I would rather go back to Da Nang. In two days I could only scratch the surface in Cambodia, while in two more days in Da Nang I could visit two of the most important scenes of the war. It would be time well spent. I began lobbying my hosts to return. Phone calls were made. Cables were sent. To my surprise, the officials in Da Nang, famous even among the Communists for their recalcitrance, invited me back, and offered to help set up my trips to Khe Sanh and My Lai with the province officials in each area.

The night before we were to leave, I met with Phuong Nam, the coordinator of press relations in Saigon. He regaled me with stories of the Ho Chi Minh Trail. He had spent years going up and down it as a journalist, taking pictures, talking to the troops. He was bombed many times, but he feared the bombs less than the AC "Spooky" gunships, whose Gatling guns could fire six thousand rounds a minute.

"The bombs would come and be gone," he said, "but the gunships would hover for an hour or two. As they fired, it was like the long scream of a cow being slaughtered—there was no sound like it."

He showed me stacks of pictures—of truck drivers posed jauntily at the wheels of their vehicles, of antiaircraft gunners, of men stringing telephone wire, of bomb-disposal teams with their flags to mark unexploded bombs, of troops posed self-consciously at a junction with arrows pointing to the South and to Quang Nam—the province I had fought in. The men I fought had turned left there, and headed for me. The photographs that stayed with me were of North Vietnamese soldiers reading letters, playing the guitar, or relaxing over a game of chess. They looked so young, and so innocent.

Here, I thought, was the mysterious enemy who had been hidden deep in the mountains I gazed at each night from our lonely outposts. I had imagined that enemy many ways, but I had never imagined him playing chess or strumming a guitar. After I saw those photographs, I wondered why I hadn't. Of course they would relax, just as we did. And of course they would play the guitar or chess, just as some of us did. They were, after all, like us—young men sent to war, trying to stay alive, savoring anything that reminded them of home.

"My favorite story of the trail," Phuong Nam told me, "is the one about the eleven girls of the Dang Loc junction. It was a pass on the trail through tall mountains. The Americans bombed it night and day. The eleven girls were in charge of leveling the craters so the trucks could get through. They marked the time bombs and the magnetic bombs with flags, for the engineers. They were very young—their leader was under twenty-one—but they were filled with enthusiasm.

"One day a plane dropped a five-hundred-pound bomb right in the middle of the trail. They went out to fill in the crater, and another bomber flew over. But they were determined to open the trail for the midnight convoy, so they kept working. The plane dropped its bombs and buried them all—all eleven sacrificed at once."

I asked Minh if he had heard this story before.

"Of course," he said. "They are heroes of the fatherland. Everyone knows their story."

"Yes," said Phuong Nam, "but I saw the girls. I knew them. They were so young, so young."

Phuong Nam was called to the telephone. It was raining in Da Nang again. Perhaps, it was suggested, I would rather go to Cambodia after all. No, I said, I came all this way to see Khe Sanh and My Lai, and I would take the chance. The next morning we left Tan Son Nhut airfield and flew back to Da Nang. The weather was beautiful—not a cloud in the sky. And then, just a few miles south of Da Nang, the land disappeared into a roiling mass of clouds. Our plane began to be tossed around. We landed at Da Nang in a driving rainstorm. Another typhoon had struck.

Hien met us at the airport. "You are unlucky," he said as I got off the plane. We drove to the hotel through flooded streets. Khe Sanh and My Lai were isolated again. It seemed I had come for nothing. But one of the West German activists had given me the name of a survivor of My Lai—she worked at a military museum in Da Nang. A few hours later, we were on our way to see her. Her name was Vo Thi Lien, and she was a beautiful young woman of twenty-seven. Like Kim Phuuc, she became a hero by being a victim—but unlike Kim Phuuc, she is sophisticated and articulate.

When I was in Vietnam during the war I believed that the My Lai massacre was a result of the system of privilege that kept educated young men out of the military. William Calley, the lieutenant in command of the Americal Division platoon that did the killing, was a dropout and a loser—he should never have been an officer, and would not have been had his more talented peers been drafted. When the military fights a war without popular support, men like Calley end up with responsibility they can't handle.

And the responsibilities of an officer in Vietnam, where the enemy and civilians intermingled, could be complex beyond the scope of any military handbook. When my platoon was at Cobb

Bridge, for example, I woke up at dawn one morning to the sound of an explosion. Outside the wire a young Vietnamese man lay next to a motorcycle. He was bleeding from dozens of shrapnel wounds. At first I thought he had hit a booby trap. And then I heard a commotion at one of the bunkers. Three or four of my men were beating one of my squad leaders.

"Hey," I yelled, "what's going on?"

"We're going to kill this motherfucker, Lieutenant," one of them said. "He just blew up that pimp."

I pulled the squad leader out.

"What did you do?" I yelled at him.

He mumbled something.

"What?"

"She gave me the clap," he said.

"She what?"

"She gave me the clap."

Guarding Cobb Bridge was nothing like being in the bush. Out in the jungle the danger seared away everything like a purifying flame. No drugs. No racial problems. No prostitutes. Back at the bridge everything fell apart. Drugs were everywhere, and cheap. Girls could be bought for five dollars, for twenty dollars all night. Or they could be bought for C rations. The first time I went to Cobb Bridge we kept running out of C rations. I had to keep reordering with every supply.

"I can't understand this," I told Hiers. "We're using twice as many C rations as we did in the bush."

Hiers looked at me. He couldn't believe I didn't know what was going on. But the essence of a subordinate's function in any bureaucracy is to conceal unpleasantnesses from his superior.

"Well, Lieutenant," he said, "back in the rear there's more time to think about food. And the men get real, real hungry back here."

I finally figured out what was going on. But no matter how hard I tried, I couldn't stop the flow of drugs and prostitutes. And now one of my men had just killed another man because a prostitute had given him gonorrhea. The rest of the platoon knew what he had done, which is why they wanted to kill him. In part they were simply outraged by the callousness of the murder. But it was also something more. He had broken the code.

I described the code in my journal: "It is an axiom in my platoon that 'if you fuck with the villagers, they'll fuck with you.' Everybody knows to leave the people alone, if only to avoid getting hit. We've seen it happen too many times: a villager gets raped, a sampan gets stolen—and the unit that did it gets hit."

The murderer had put everyone in danger, and it didn't take long for danger to appear, not in the form of the Viet Cong, but of our South Vietnamese allies. An hour or so after the murder, the brother of the pimp, a South Vietnamese ranger, came to the bridge with a dozen of his comrades, each carrying an M-16, and demanded that I give them the killer. I refused, and we had a tense confrontation before he finally backed down. The brother then became convinced that I had helped plan the killing, and for weeks kept trying to get my men to lure me into a trap so he could kill me.

By then I was used to the idea that people wanted to kill me. But it was different, somehow, when there was one person out there who wanted to kill, not Americans, but me, just me. Finally, he was transferred south, and I put him out of my mind. The pimp's killer was charged with premeditated murder, put on trial, and sent to prison for twenty years.

Even now I can close my eyes and see the pimp lying in the road, his body perforated with hundreds of pieces of grenade shrapnel, his life flowing out into the dust. A soldier in wartime makes a pact with death; it is his secret sharer, his constant companion. He kills, and risks being killed, for reasons of national purpose that remove the moral and legal sanctions against killing. But even though in war the line between killing and murder is not always easy to define, any soldier knows the difference. Murder is different from killing. I saw many people killed, but I saw one man murdered, and I will never forget it. My Lai was like that—not killing, not warfare, but murder.

"I was a young girl then," Vo Thi Lien said. "My parents were with the Liberation forces, so I lived with my grandparents. The Americans would come once or twice a month. They would bomb first, then move through our village. They were nice—they gave me gum and candy. But this time they were different. It was morning. Everyone had gone to work or school. Then the helicopters came. They went first to Thanh Yen hamlet, about two kilometers from my hamlet. We could hear firing and grenades.

"Usually they would come and go in half an hour. But this time two hours went by, then more. And we still heard the firing. Only later did I learn about the ditch where they herded in a hundred and seventy people and then shot them all. Two of them survived—they told me blood ran in that ditch like a river.

"After three hours, they moved on to my village. Some of the people decided they would come out of their shelters to show the Americans they weren't Viet Cong. They were all shot. I could see two Americans coming to our shelter. My grandmother started to come out to talk to them. They shot her in the chest, then threw in a grenade. The explosion threw her back on me and her body blocked the entrance. The whole shelter fell, and my grandfather and I were buried alive."

Her voice had gradually risen, until it filled the room. A tear formed in the corner of one eye.

"I knew they were going to kill us all. And they did. They killed everyone. Then they burned down the houses, killed all the animals, and cut down the trees. It was dark when they left. Then the guerrillas came back and helped me out of the shelter."

The tears were running down her cheeks as she talked. She stopped, and the room was silent. Then she swallowed, and began again.

"I lost thirty-five relatives that day. Ninety-seven people

were killed in my tiny hamlet, five hundred and four altogether. There were bodies everywhere. Six-year-old girls had been raped and then shot. Unborn children had been ripped from the wombs of pregnant women. Old men had been burned alive or beheaded and thrown down a well. I couldn't understand how such a thing could happen."

She was no longer looking at me. Her face was soaked in tears. As she talked and stared in distant focus, she twirled a strand of her black hair.

I thought of telling her about Hugh C. Thompson, an Army helicopter pilot who saw what was happening and landed. Some soldiers were about to kill a group of sixteen children they had rounded up, but Thompson stopped them by threatening a shoot-out if they tried it. Someone, at least, amid all that frenzy, had kept his moral compass. And I thought of telling how Calley's company had been cut to pieces by booby traps all around her hamlet, how they had bled and died while the villagers watched impassively. And I thought of retelling the stories of the massacre at the Buddhist orphanage and the innocent village destroyed by the Viet Cong, the children and the old men and women slaughtered as heartlessly as Calley's men destroyed the people of My Lai.

But none of that made any difference. It wouldn't bring anyone back, or erase the horror and the shame of what happened. There was nothing for me to say, except that I was sorry, and that I wished to God it had never happened. She looked at me steadily as I said it, but even as I spoke the words rang hollow.

From the commander's viewpoint, My Lai was a symptom of the failure to fight guerrillas with total war. General William Westmoreland has written in his memoirs: "So closely entwined were some populated localities with the tentacles of the VC base area, in some cases actually integrated into the defenses, and so sympathetic were some of the people to the VC that the only way to establish control short of constant combat operations among the people was to remove the people and destroy the village. . . . That it was infinitely better in some cases to move people from areas long sympathetic to the Viet Cong was amply demonstrated . . . at a place called My Lai."

The Americal Division soldiers knew My Lai as "Pinkville." To them it was the enemy. If it had been cleared and destroyed as Ben Suc was in the Iron Triangle, as were the Phu Lacs and Go Noi Island where I fought, then the massacre would never have happened. No people, no massacre—the logic is brutal, but correct. The flaw is that as a solution it has no end. If we had evacuated and destroyed every village sympathetic to the Viet Cong, we would have had to remove millions of people and virtually destroy the country. This logic works only if the people are the enemy. And if they were, then whom were we fighting *for?*

My platoon did its best to keep straight whom we were fighting. I knew some men in the rear, clerks and supply officers, who hated all Vietnamese—they were all "gooks." But in my platoon we used the word "gooks" only to mean the enemy. One day we were on patrol and saw a line of people walking along a path in a free-fire zone.

"Are those gooks?" the point man asked. The squad leader pulled out binoculars and studied the line of people.

"No," he said, "they're just Vietnamese."

When we were back at Hill 10 they would greet the young woman who cleaned our area by saying, "Good morning, Linda. How many rockets did you fire at us last night?"

We did our best to separate the people from our enemies, but the hard truth was this: that line of people *could* have been Viet Cong, and Linda quite possibly *was* firing rockets at us at night. It is hard to keep making the distinction when the very people you are supposed to be helping stand by and watch your men being killed and mutilated by ambushes, mines, and booby traps.

"I sent them a good boy," the mother of one of the Americans at My Lai said later, "and they made him a murderer."

As I listened to Vo Thi Lien, I was thinking of the Marine training village in the woods at Quantico, Virginia. It had been

constructed to look peaceful, but each time my officer class tried
to patrol it, we were blown up and ambushed. The lesson was
driven home again and again: trust nothing, for the smallest
child and the oldest woman can kill you.

We were taught always to be alert, never to relax. The war
could erupt anytime, anywhere. We were trained to be soldiers,
but we never learned who our enemy was. If anyone could be our
enemy, then why not everyone? It was a small—if false—step,
logically. But morally it led to the abyss—it led to My Lai.

Almost every American who fought in Vietnam went
through the booby traps, the ambushes, the frustrations of
never seeing the enemy—what Calley's platoon had been
through before the massacre. With only a handful of exceptions
in a long war, they didn't respond by slaughtering unarmed old
men, women, and children. Calley's platoon committed this horror. But the blame lies ultimately with the men who sent Americans like Calley to Vietnam in the first place, who put them in
a war they could not win, where their only victory was not to die.

While I talked to Vo Thi Lien, a co-worker, a Major Be, listened
in silence. As we were preparing to leave, he casually mentioned
that he had led a scout unit near Da Nang and that he had spent
a good deal of time with American POWs.

"Robert Garwood was with me for a year," he said. "He was
with us as a Liberation fighter. He lived better than my other
men, but he was always sick. We kept trying to send him to the
North, but he refused."

Marine Private Garwood disappeared under mysterious circumstances outside Da Nang in 1965 and then turned up again
at the Thang Loi Hotel in Hanoi in 1979. He became the only
American POW to be tried for desertion and aiding the enemy.*
In 1984 Garwood told *The Wall Street Journal* that he knew of

---

*The charges of desertion were dismissed; Garwood was convicted of collab-
oration.

at least seventy Americans still held captive—a claim he chose to withhold until five years after he returned. When Garwood was negotiating his departure from Vietnam, he said he knew of other captive Americans, but he later said he had made up the story to encourage the Americans to get him out.

Garwood has consistently claimed that he did not collaborate with the Communists, that he was a prisoner like all the other Americans, but that his ability to speak Vietnamese forced him into a no-man's-land where he was not trusted by the guards or the prisoners. But I had just been told casually that he had participated in operations, had actively worked with the Viet Cong.

When I was fighting in Vietnam everyone talked about the white Viet Cong. It was accepted, on faith, that Americans were out there, fighting with the enemy against their countrymen. I had always dismissed the story as legend. It seemed impossible that an American could be fighting us. Our enemy was so mysterious, so different, so much "the other," that the journey to his side would have been too vast. Now I was not so sure.

I remembered a story I had heard in Hue from the vice-president of the provincial People's Committee. "We had young women who worked as prostitutes," he said. "They opened up lines of communications with Americans. I would send them pamphlets and letters. After many months, I had convinced seven to join us. They left their posts and were traveling with us to the North, but we were caught by B-52s and six were killed. The seventh fled back to the American lines. I heard he was severely punished, but I never saw him again."

Were there others like these men? Like Garwood? What happened to them? Are there any left? I had dozens of questions, but I got no more answers. It was as if the curtain had been raised for an instant, and I had seen a shadow of what lay behind it—but no more.

25

AT THE END OF
THE TUNNEL

The next morning I was told that the flight from Da Nang to Saigon had been canceled. My visa was about to run out, so there was only one solution: we would rent a car and drive. At first the car rental authority wanted $1,000, but we settled on a still outrageous $700—in advance. It took almost all the money I had, and even so, the car rental commissar refused to accept one of my hundred-dollar bills because a bank in London had stamped it with its name and the date. I argued that the bill was perfectly good, and besides, it was the last I had—take it or leave it. The rental commissar left with the bill and went to consult with the economic advisers to the province. An hour later, he was back. The money was acceptable. No problem.

So we loaded a new Toyota with our bags and six large cans of gasoline and set off for Saigon, a thousand kilometers to the south. We passed the Que Son Mountains, where Donald Sparks became an MIA in 1969. I had the driver stop the car. I walked to the edge of the road and looked west, to the hills where Sparks had disappeared. I would get no closer, on this trip, to the mystery of his disappearance. I got back in the car, and we resumed our journey south.

But I kept imagining the scene—the ambush, his comrades pinned down, the terrible silence when they pulled back, that first knowledge that he was a prisoner. And I kept thinking of

Vo Thi Lien at My Lai, a ten-year-old girl huddled in a bunker
with her grandparents, watching the faces of the American soldiers who were methodically massacring everyone she had ever
known. Vo Thi Lien. Donald Sparks. So many victims.

Vo Thi Lien insisted that she was looking to the future. She
was worried about the Chinese and about Pol Pot working new
massacres in Cambodia. But Donald Sparks kept pulling me
back into the past. If I thought he was alive, I would volunteer
in an instant to help bring him back. But I became convinced on
this trip that if any POWs had remained alive in Vietnam, they
were probably dead now. Live American POWs have long since
lost any value to the Vietnamese, would, in fact, be an embar-
rassment—how, after all these years of denials, would they
explain why POWs were still there? And despite their inability
to throw anything away, their determination to hang on to everything until, someday, it had a use, even the Vietnamese recognize when something has outlived all possible value. And
when they realize that, like anyone else, they get rid of it. That
is my rational conclusion.

But the day I left for my second visit to Da Nang I learned
that the Vietnamese had "discovered" a tourist from Hong
Kong whom they had captured in 1975, and who—unknown to
the world—had been lost in their prisons for almost ten years.
Who else, came the nagging thought, is in there?

We drove south on Route 1, the highway that links North and
South Vietnam. For miles we did not pass another vehicle. With
so little traffic between the two parts of the country, it is no
wonder ten years have passed and they still seem like separate
nations. We spent the night in Nha Trang. Since my visa did not
include a visit to Nha Trang, the local security forces told me I
had to stay in the hotel. Minh and the driver went out on the
town; I ate in the dining room, alone except for a small army of
cats.

We reached Saigon late that night. The next day my plane was to leave in the early afternoon. That morning we drove out to Cu Chi, the fortified tunnel complex next to the Iron Triangle, the Viet Cong stronghold only fifteen miles northwest of Saigon. It was my last drive through Vietnam. Women were hanging coils of freshly dyed purple yarn on racks and setting out large circles of transparent rice paper to dry on woven mats. A young boy followed three cows along the road, picking up their droppings with a wooden shovel and putting the valuable fertilizer in a basket. Other boys herded ducks, lazed on the backs of water buffalo, fished in the rice paddies. Crowds of men sat on low stools in outdoor cafés, sipping their morning *pho*.

We passed a funeral. The coffin was on three-wheeled Lambretta. The funeral party followed along on foot, singing, everyone dressed in white. I almost didn't notice all the bicycles anymore, but they were everywhere, loaded with rice, old shock absorbers, even, in a tour de force of balancing, a large chest of drawers. I tried to remember the smells—excrement and mud and charcoal.

I'm going to miss this, I thought to myself.

Cu Chi was the center of one of the most ambitious tunnel complexes in the history of warfare. Begun in French times, the tunnels were expanded against the Americans until they covered two hundred miles or so. There were kitchens, meeting rooms, dormitories, hospitals, schools, and munitions factories—all underground. In certain areas the tunnel went directly under the base of the 25th Infantry Division at Dong Du.

The war in the tunnels was the most dramatic example of the success of primitive methods against modern, highly technological warfare. The tunnels were dug by hand, and the dirt smuggled out, bit by tiny bit, in jars and baskets. Some systems had as many as four levels, connected by interlocking trapdoors and water traps that sealed off each section in case the Americans tried to enter or to flood them with water or gas. The air was rancid and foul, and the tunnels also became home to rodents, poisonous snakes, mosquitoes, and painful parasites.

The Americans tried everything to destroy the tunnels and to flush out the Viet Cong who lived in them. The Limited Warfare Laboratory in Maryland and other government labs turned out the Olfactronic Personnel Detector, which was designed to "sniff" the body odors of tunnel dwellers; the Air-Delivered Seismic Intruder Device, which measured movement; and the Portable Differential Magnetometer, which detected soil differences where tunnels had been dug. None worked. They tried special pumps that filled the tunnels with water and gas. That didn't work either.

The only method that proved at all successful was to send a soldier down into a tunnel with a pistol and a knife—to fight the Viet Cong hand to hand, in the dark. It was the trip I had made, into that tunnel near Da Nang where I had felt the presence of my enemy. The Americans near Cu Chi, atop a burrow of tunnels, developed special teams of "tunnel rats" who specialized in going underground.

To stop the tunnel rats the Communists booby-trapped the tunnels with grenades and poisoned stakes. They hid behind false walls and speared the American as he crawled by, or they waited by the trapdoors and slit his throat as he came through. It was nightmare combat, the kind of warfare that shakes loose every primitive fear. The very earth became the enemy. And fighting the earth was a battle we would lose.

In 1967, in Operation Cedar Falls, one of the largest operations of the war, the Americans used B-52s, fighter-bombers, helicopters, artillery. Giant bulldozers called Rome Plows did their best to collapse the tunnels. What couldn't be dug up was pumped full of water and acetylene gas. Among the documents discovered were the plans to send Nguyen Van Troi to assassinate Robert McNamara the year before, and lists of Viet Cong sympathizers—which included all the barbers at the 25th Infantry Division base. The Americans boasted that the whole region had been transformed into "a military desert": "a strategic enemy base was decisively engaged and destroyed."

No, it wasn't. The tunnels were quickly repaired and a few

weeks after Cedar Falls, the Iron Triangle and Cu Chi were once again dominated by the Communists. Less than a year later the tunnels were the headquarters for the most dramatic offensive of the war—the attacks on Saigon and the assault on the American embassy during the Tet Offensive of 1968.

The Cu Chi district has six "heroic villages." I examined the roll of martyrs for two of them. In Phuoc Hiep village, out of 724 households, 829 people died; in An Nhan Tay, out of 717 households, 873 "sacrificed." At that casualty rate, a city like Austin, Texas, would have had some 200,000 people killed—or more than three times the total American deaths in the whole war. On the Communist side, the heroes of the tunnel battles are known throughout Vietnam. The surviving heroes on the American side, the many tunnel rats who braved the booby traps and the horrors in that dark, dank, alien world, have blended back into America, their pride and their nightmares a private affair.

I stood above the tunnel entrance. I didn't want to go down there —it brought back too many memories, too many fears. It seemed too real, that tunnel, too close to what I remembered. But when my guide let himself down slowly into the blackness, I followed him. The tunnel had been carved out a little to accommodate foreigners, but as we descended into its blackness I immediately felt a horrible claustrophobia.

The flashlight of the guide barely flickered. I was on my hands and knees. Water flowed along the dirt floor. A furry body brushed my hand. The air was hot, stifling. We crawled up and down, through switchbacks, up ladders, down ladders, all in the dark. I kept feeling that I was back in the war, back in that terrible tunnel. I was underground for about fifteen minutes; it seemed like an hour.

This time I hadn't found a mysterious, alien presence—my enemy. Instead, I was down in a tunnel with a friendly and quite normal young man who kept cursing at his flashlight when it went out. He had fought in the tunnels during the war and now led regular tours through them. When we came out at last into the sunlight, I tried to talk to him about the tunnels. I had encountered someone like him in a tunnel fifteen years ago. Now, at last, I could learn what that encounter had meant.

"What was it like to be down here, under the earth, for so long?"

"It was difficult," he said.

"But what was it like when B-52s bombed you? How did you sleep? How did you breathe? How did you cook?"

"All that was very difficult."

"But what was it like when an American came down in the tunnel, trying to find you? What was it like to meet another man, your enemy, down there?"

"It was quite difficult."

I had wanted so much, but I was getting nothing. Or perhaps I was getting everything. I wasn't sure. I tried one more time.

"How do you feel now?" I asked him. "Do you think about all those years in the tunnels?"

He thought for a minute, then replied, "No."

I asked Minh to try again, to find out if the man understood my question. How did he feel about his years in the tunnels? Didn't he think about them a lot now?

Minh asked him again.

"He says, yes, he understood your question," Minh said to me. "And no, he doesn't think about it anymore. He says the war is over."

"Life goes on?" I asked Minh.

"Life goes on."

We drove back to Saigon, picked up my bags, and headed for the airport. I was nervous about the few antiques I had bought. I had been told there could be "difficulties" at the airport. It was the same feeling I had had when I first changed money on the black market. They know, I kept thinking, and they've been waiting until the last minute to arrest me. Perhaps sensing my nervousness, Viet had been reassuring.

"Don't worry about customs," he had said. "There will be no problem."

When we arrived I looked for the Peanut Gang, but they were nowhere to be seen. The Amerasian children and their families who were traveling on my Air France flight had arrived hours before. The customs officers were patiently going through every bit of their luggage—opening each tube of lipstick, unfolding each sock, poking at the sole of each shoe. Viet slipped the customs director a note, and I was waved straight through into the departure lounge. I was out!

In my relief I almost forgot to say goodbye to Minh, who was standing awkwardly among all the uniformed officials. We had been together for a month, from mountains near China to the delta of the Mekong. We had argued politics, religion, poetry, rock and roll. He had translated illiterate tribesmen, poets, farmers, fishermen, bureaucrats, soldiers, and victims of napalm and My Lai. We had laughed together, shared many meals and a few tears. He had become my friend.

"Goodbye," he said. "I hope you come again."

"Goodbye, Minh," I said. "I will miss you. You are a good guy —for a Communist."

"And you," he said with a smile, "for a capitalist you are almost human."

We shook hands, and I went through the curtains into the departure lounge, which to my surprise seemed filled with Americans. There were girls dressed in red corduroy pants, plaid shirts, and circle earrings, as if they had just been shopping at the Northpark Mall in Dallas. There were black kids in floppy hats, walking with a loose roll as if they were checking out the action on the Grand Concourse in the Bronx. There was a boy who could have been a homecoming king at Modesto High School, another who could have stepped out of South Boston.

Everywhere I looked, I saw Americans. The war may have

been over every place else I visited, but here, in this waiting room, it was not; among these children it would never be over. They carried the war on their faces, would transmit it, in their genes, to new generations of Americans. It would live forever. But except for Little Minh not one of those kids spoke a word of English, and not one had ever talked to an American before their first interview to qualify for departure. Where, I wondered, had those girls got that look and those boys that walk? It was as if they carried American teenage style in their genes, or else had received it through some vast special network invisible to adults.

A woman who fled without her son eleven years ago had come back to get him. She was dressed in designer jeans and a silk blouse; her hair had a permanent; there were gold bracelets on her wrists and a gold chain around her neck. A few days before, her son had been riding a water buffalo in a paddy. He sat stiffly, looking straight ahead, afraid to talk.

An older boy next to him, Dao Ngoc Tuan, had lived in a Buddhist monastery since 1975, when his mother disappeared. He looked a little like Matt Dillon. The monks had taught him watch repair, so he had a trade. But like all the other kids, he could not name a single city in the United States, and he had not the slightest idea where he was going or what he would do when he got there. They would all spend several days in Thailand being processed, and then most of them would go to transit camps in the Philippines to learn English and obtain sponsors for the final journey to America. A few would go directly to America.

Each family is interviewed one last time by ODP officials who come with the flight from Bangkok and then return. There were three interviewers: a black man, a woman, and a bearded white man in Christian Dior white shoes. They were young. The woman had a kind face; everyone wanted to be interviewed by her. I asked about Little Minh. He had already cleared his interview. I found him sitting quietly in a corner.

"Minh, what about those English lessons I gave you the money for?"

"I no lie. I take English lessons when we get to Philippines."

"Yeah, but they're free there."

"I got expenses," he said with a smile, but the old spirit wasn't in him. He kept looking nervously at the door that would lead to the plane.

I left him and went over to a group of kids. I put the Bruce Springsteen "Born in the U.S.A." tape in my Walkman and showed them how to listen to it. None of them had ever seen a Walkman before. At first, they were afraid to put on the earphones, but once they did, huge smiles would spread across their faces and I couldn't get them to give it back. They wanted the volume up all the way. The mothers watched—confused, shy; their children were being transformed before their eyes. After a while, one kid began to move, slowly, tentatively, to the music —began to dance.

At last the flight was called, and all the Vietnamese stood up for one last check of their documents by the Vietnamese officials. "This is the moment," said one Canadian ODP worker. "They've waited years for this moment."

They walked out onto the tarmac to a waiting bus. Up on the next level hundreds of their friends and relatives were shouting and waving as they left. I looked for Mai and the Peanut Gang —so did Little Minh—and finally spotted them waving madly and wiping tears from their faces. As they boarded the bus, each person turned and waved, waved farewell to everything he had known. They were on their way to America.

We boarded the Air France plane. Western travelers are automatically put in first class; the Vietnamese emigrants filled the rest of the plane. The stewardess offered me caviar, champagne, and newspapers. I felt different already. For a moment I couldn't decide why. Then I realized it wasn't the champagne or the caviar. I felt as I had when I got off the train in West Berlin after visiting East Germany. I felt free.

In 1970 I was part of a planeload of marines going home after our year in the war. When the plane's wheels left the ground, a great cheer went up. This time, on a plane full of Vietnamese leaving their native land forever, the only sound was of quiet weeping.

I found Little Minh squeezed into the corner of his seat. It was his first trip on an airplane. He looked so much younger and smaller than the little street kid who had conned me out of money for English lessons, who had terrorized the other foreigners. He looked like the young boy he was. I asked him how he felt.

"Scared," he said. "I am so scared."

And he turned and stared out the window, until Vietnam was only a gray haze beneath the clouds.

EPILOGUE

I went back to Vietnam to answer the question: "What does it mean to go to war?" I went back to find a man I never knew—my enemy. I went back to find the pieces of myself I had left there, and to try to put the war behind me. For four weeks I traveled almost three thousand miles by plane, car, jeep, bus, ferry, and sampan from provinces on the Chinese border to the Mekong Delta. I met hundreds of Vietnamese, from mountain tribesmen, fishermen, and Amerasian children to Communist Party officials, professors, and generals. I also met with the former Viet Cong and North Vietnamese soldiers who had been my enemy.

The men and women I had fought against had been bombed by B-52s, shelled by battleships, pounded by artillery, incinerated by napalm and white phosphorus, and drenched in defoliants. They had been strafed by jets, rocketed by Huey Cobras, and, perhaps worst of all, attacked by "Spooky" gunships. They had lived in tunnels and caves, coming out only at night. Few soldiers have ever seen so much war. Yet I was constantly amazed at how unmarked they seemed by the experience. I could no more find evidence of war in them than I could in the streets of Hanoi or in the paddies of Quang Nam province; the scars all seemed to have healed.

The Viet Cong veterans talked with me for hours, their eyes and their voices apparently untroubled by doubt or guilt about what blood might have been on their hands, and unmarked with anger or bitterness about what blood might have been on mine.

They did not look into their selves and see angst or guilt or confusion, if they looked into their selves, in our Western self-infatuated way, at all. They had done their duty, like everybody else. For them the war was long, bitter, terrible—and over. The past is past, they kept saying to me. They were sustained then, and are now, by simple ideas, believed without question. Nothing is more important than independence and freedom. Life does go on.

Those simple ideas were a powerful weapon: they excused much. The Communist veterans I met refused to accept any responsibility for the mass graves at Hue, the mutilated orphans of An Hoa, the many atrocities and massacres they committed. They were engaged in total war, and they did what was necessary to win. Victory has a way of imposing its own morality, and the most enduring reward of victory may well be a clear conscience.

The Communists have what Milan Kundera has described as their "kitsch"—the images of happy workers giving their best for the fatherland. The millions of Vietnamese who have fled their country after the war have helped puncture that fantasy. Our own kitsch was of the "destroy the town in order to save it" school, which in result if not intention came uncomfortably close to the kitsch of the Communists. In each, beneath the rhetoric, the individual had to bow before the necessities of the state.

On neither side did the people win: the war won, and kept on winning. That is the price of a war in which the people, not land, are the battleground. To win that kind of war requires a special weapon—a moral certainty so strong as to make the suffering of individuals invisible. A million, two million might die, said General Giap, without a qualm. To our great dishonor, we played that game too long. But to our great credit, we learned we had to stop.

For millions of Vietnamese who fought on our side, the end of the war has meant suffering, imprisonment, exile, even death. But for the North Vietnamese and for most of the Viet Cong and the people of the South, the end of the war has meant they could live and work in peace, if not in freedom and prosperity. The dead are buried. Life goes on. It is not a society I could live in, but I was not on the winning side. They won, we lost, and it is their country now.

I left Vietnam with a sympathy for my old enemies I had not had before. I found myself wanting to share in their war experience, since it seemed so much better than mine. But there are times when one must choose who one is. I kept thinking of the prisoner-of-war experience of Admiral James Stockdale. In his book *In Love and War*, Stockdale seems stiff-necked, proud, uncompromising, and unforgiving. I am not sure I would enjoy his company. But he survived almost eight years of captivity and terrible torture, and he gave away nothing. Stockdale never wavered; he was willing to die for his beliefs and, yes, for his country. If I had been captured, I would have wanted to be like him.

In fact, the Vietnamese today have a fascination with the Americans who fought them, and particularly with the POWs, who displayed in their captivity the qualities of dedication, inner strength, and sacrifice the Vietnamese celebrate in their own heroes.

On occasion I would ask my hosts what they would have done if they had been Americans during the war. Invariably they began by saying that they would have joined all "peace-loving peoples" in opposing our "imperialist aggression." But after we had talked for a while the answer was different.

"I am a patriot. I would have fought for my country," Bui Tin told me. "Or if I truly had courage I would have hoped to have been like the hero Morrison and sacrificed for peace."

The antiwar activists were their allies of convenience during the war, but toward them the Vietnamese attitude of official respect has a patronizing tone, the sort reserved for children.

The antiwar activists were like the non-Communist Viet Cong: their idealism made them useful—for a time.

In Hanoi I told General Tuan, whose Viet Cong troops I had fought in Quang Nam province, that when I returned home I demonstrated against the war.

"All of Vietnam is grateful for what you did for our country," he said.

I was offended. "I didn't do it for your country," I said. "I did it for mine. I wasn't sure whether you would be good or bad for Vietnam, but I knew that Vietnam was bad for us."

He smiled, patted me on the knee, and said, "It is right for you to say that. Americans should love their country too."

He was trying to be polite and generous. But he made me angry. Who did he think he was?

A week after I returned from Vietnam I went to the Vietnam Veterans Memorial in Washington, D.C., for Veterans Day. The men I saw in Washington could not have been more different from our old enemies. Each man's face seemed clouded, haunted. They wore some bit of the war—a jungle hat, a field jacket, a camouflage shirt. A part of them was still out there. A part of them was still frozen in time, back where I had just been.

One Navy corpsman sat in the lobby of the Marriott Hotel in full uniform, the Navy Cross on his chest, trying to talk about the war to anyone who would listen. There were too many men like him, men with chips on their shoulders and pain in their hearts. For them, life didn't go on. For them, the war wasn't over, and its emotions kept battling inside them, the pride, the anger, the guilt, the comradeship, all mixed up.

The essential morality of the soldier is that he is willing to give his life for something larger than himself. The principle that some values are worth dying for is what finally underlies patriotism—but the hard part is, which values? Vietnam was a war of great moral confusion—we were fighting for the people of Vietnam, but we never knew which of them was our enemy and which our friend. All we had was each other, and our pride. A soldier alone and without moral clarity—no matter how good his weapons—is a soldier crippled.

We had been willing to give our lives for our country, no less than our fathers had been at Normandy and Iwo Jima. This war, however, was different. We lost. And the country that sent us did not take us back into its arms. It either hated the war or simply wanted to forget it.

But if the war had no value, then what were the men who fought it worth? Too many American veterans thought of themselves as losers, outcasts, suckers. They blamed everyone: protesters, the government, the media, their friends who didn't serve. Or they blamed themselves and wallowed in guilt.

Of course, most veterans came home, put the war behind them, and proceeded with their lives. That's what I tried to do. But for us too, the war wouldn't quite settle into our memories. The image was fuzzy and troubling. Even as we climbed the ladders of success and acceptance, we never were quite sure how to think about the war. The media was no help. Throughout the 1970s Vietnam veterans were routinely portrayed in movies and on television as crazed drug addicts, psychopaths, or pathetic cripples. But that image was no more accurate than the current rip-'em-up post-Grenada macho fantasies of Rambo. We are, in fact, ordinary men. We are the doctor, the lawyer, the plumber, the trash collector. And instead of blaming the war for our problems, many Vietnam veterans now give it credit for their success.

The best example of what Vietnam taught its veterans is the Vietnam Veterans Memorial. On July 4, 1979, Jan Scruggs, who had been an Army private in Vietnam, announced to the press that he had raised $144.50 toward establishing a memorial for Vietnam veterans in Washington. It was the perfect beginning. A memorial for all of us, announced not by a grateful President but by a buck private ("How do you talk to a private?" asked one general on the way to a fund-raising meeting) who refused to abandon his comrades and soldiered on until his mission was accomplished.

After building their own memorial, the veterans decided to give their own parade, a full-scale ticker-tape parade down the canyons of lower Manhattan, a hero's parade. They had remembered, finally, what they learned in the war: no one cares, really, except the men you are with; if you want anything, you have to do it yourself.

The parade began on the Brooklyn side of the Brooklyn Bridge on a bright May morning, Memorial Day, 1985. More than 25,000 of us—an ageing army in blue jeans, Brooks Brothers suits, and faded combat fatigues gone tight around the waist —milled about, preparing to cross the bridge on one last mission. Back at the parade headquarters, and at a fund-raising dinner the night before, we had all been apprehensive. We didn't know what we would find on the other side of the bridge—whether we would be cheered or booed or just ignored as we had always been. We didn't know what America thought of us. But when we crossed the bridge the next morning we were singing "Born in the U.S.A." at the top of our lungs. By then, if no one had been there, it wouldn't have mattered. We were marching for ourselves.

I was with Jeff Hiers, my radioman during the war. Hiers has a hearty manner that deflects sentimentality about the war. He calls it his invisible M-16. It protects him. When the emotions get too close he blows them away. Gary Beikirch, a counselor from Rochester, New York, joined us. Beikirch won the Medal of Honor as a Special Forces medic. Wounded himself, he braved heavy enemy fire again and again to help his wounded comrades. He was the first Medal of Honor winner I had ever met. He wasn't an actor playing a hero. He was the real thing. But because he had been a hero in Vietnam he had kept his Medal of Honor in a drawer. For years he tried to forget about it. Today he was wearing the medal on a ribbon around his neck.

The parade passed City Hall. More than a million people crowded the streets, standing four and five deep on the sidewalks, with many others in windows overlooking the street. They were waving flags. The policemen and sanitation workers lining the sidewalks applauded as we passed. Beikirch waved to the crowd. So did Hiers.

Then some bystanders recognized the Medal of Honor around Beikirch's neck and broke through the barriers to embrace him. The noise was deafening. Hiers began to cry. His invisible M-16 had jammed.

All along the sidewalk people were shouting to us.

"Welcome home!"

"Welcome home!"

"We love you!"

Thanks, I thought. Better late than never.

I came home from the parade with my mind filled with faces—faces of the men I had fought beside, of the women and children who had watched my platoon pass through their villages, of the woman I had loved and the men who had died. The faces at the parade showed the battles of time. We were all older, and another generation, ignorant of the reality of what we did, stood on the sidewalk and cheered us with unlined, innocent faces.

I kept thinking of the men and women I had seen in Vietnam when I returned—a man I had fought against, smoking a cigarette and leaning against a water buffalo; a woman whose husband I might have killed, her eyes clear and untroubled. I thought of Pham Tuan talking about the thrill of flying MiG-21s, of Kim Phuuc with her long-sleeved shirt, and of Vo Thi Lien, the tears streaming down her face as she talked about My Lai. And I thought about the Amerasian children I had met, the girl at Marble Mountain and the Peanut Gang in Saigon, children who carry the war on their faces.

And I kept thinking about Hill 10, my old combat base. I was only there a few months, but it remained the hub of all my memories of the war. And when I returned to Vietnam it was at Hill 10 that I found what I had been seeking.

Just outside Hill 10 I stopped at a Viet Cong veterans' cemetery. The headstones are simple markers, the dead having been buried near the battlefield or, in many cases, never recovered. Each headstone bears the word "Hero."

This cemetery had been built where my men and I had once set out ambushes and been ambushed. I came upon a marker bearing the name Ngo Ngoc Tuan, with the dates 1944–1969. It was the grave of a man born the year I was, and killed the year I arrived in Vietnam. I stood there in silence, the wind rustling through the ripe strands of rice that surrounded the graves.

I never knew Tuan, but his grave bore the same dates mine might have, if only an AK-47 round or a mortar had taken a slightly different course, or if my footsteps down a slippery paddy dike had fallen an inch or two differently and set off the mine waiting beneath the mud. By a similar accident—some intersection of his body with force and matter—and by the ultimate accident of birth, he lay here in a muddy paddy, where boys sang songs to water buffalo as he no doubt had done, and his ancestors before him. And I stood, a tourist from the land of his old enemy, and looked upon his grave and thought how it might have been my own.

I had felt this way when I first visited the Vietnam Veterans Memorial and saw my own face reflected from the names of my comrades who had died.

Why them, I thought, why did they have to die? And then I thought, why me, why did I have to live?

Four months before my trip to Vietnam, Americans of another generation revisited their battlefields on the beaches of Normandy. President Reagan spoke, his voice quavering. The veterans and their relatives cried. The American flag flew over the cemetery where crosses stretched as far as the eye could see. It was a powerful, patriotic moment, a reminder of the great national crusade of World War II, the good war. I thought of that moment in Normandy as I stood on Hill 10. I did not feel patriotic. I simply felt sad.

"It is easier to start a war than to end one," the North Vietnamese general had told me. A valuable lesson, seldom learned. The cost of that lesson is beyond calculation: the long black wall in Washington, with all its names of young Americans who died so far from home; the cemetery just down the road, with its headstones bearing the word "Hero"; the grief of the woman whose husband I may have killed; the grief of every family who lost someone because of Vietnam. There are times when such costs must be paid. We had to fight the Nazis. We did not have to fight here.

I stood on Hill 10 and looked around the deserted base one last time. I could imagine a line of marines making their way across the paddies, bound for the hill. It was an image from a dream I often had before I returned to Vietnam. My old platoon is returning to Hill 10, and in its shadow, on the football field where I had led my first inglorious patrol, we are ambushed. The firing is terrible. Help is only a few yards away, but no one comes to our aid. We are cut to pieces. I am the last one left alive. I try to fire my M-16, but it jams. I am surrounded by the enemy. As their fingers tighten on the triggers of their rifles, they are smiling at me.

This time, however, there was no ambush. This time, the men just kept coming, heading for home, together.

As I turned to go, I noticed an old empty sandbag lying half buried in the dirt. I picked it up and took it back as a souvenir. When I returned to New York, no matter how much I washed that sandbag, I could never get it to come clean.

On the other hand, I never had that dream again.

•   •   •

I had gone back to Vietnam with the war still raging in my head. I was looking for the world I had known then. But the men and women I had known, loved, and too often lost, the vast bases, the tunnels, the free-fire zones—everything I remembered from the war—had vanished into the past. The war was only a memory now.

I did find the grave of an enemy I never knew—the man I could have been. And I discovered that I had more in common with my old enemies than with anyone except the men who had fought at my side. My enemies and I had shared something almost beyond words. We had been through war, and by accepting our memories of it honestly we were able to greet each other in trust and friendship, hoping that we would never see war again.

We had tried to kill each other, but we were brothers now.

ESSAY ON SOURCES

This book is a personal narrative, not a work of scholarship. It is based primarily on my interviews and experiences during the month I spent in Vietnam in late 1984, and on my memories of the year I spent there during the war, in 1969–1970.

To give that narrative depth and breadth, I also drew on other sources. I conducted dozens of interviews before and after my return to Vietnam, and consulted hundreds of books and articles. Most of these appear in the standard bibliographies about the war. I see no point in duplicating those lists here, but I would like to mention those works which I found most useful in writing this book, even though some of the best books about Vietnam are not among them.

For general reference I relied on Stanley Karnow, *Vietnam: A History* (Viking, 1983); Michael MacLear, *The Ten Thousand Day War* (St. Martin's Press, 1981); David Halberstam, *The Best and the Brightest* (Random House, 1972); Bruce Palmer, *Summons of the Trumpet* (Presidio, 1978); Frances FitzGerald, *Fire in the Lake* (Atlantic, Little, Brown, 1972); John T. McAlister, Jr., and Paul Mus, *The Vietnamese and Their Revolution* (Harper & Row, 1970); U.S. Department of Defense, *The Pentagon Papers* (Quadrangle, 1971); and several volumes of *The Vietnam Experience* (The Boston Publishing Company, various dates).

The published proceedings of two recent conferences on Vietnam were of value: Peter Braestrup, ed., *Vietnam as History* (The Wilson Center, 1984), and Harrison Salisbury, ed., *Vietnam Reconsidered* (Harper & Row, 1984). No one who writes about Vietnam should be without two excellent books—Philip Beidler, *American Literature and the Experience of Vietnam* (University of Georgia, 1982), and John Clark Pratt, *Vietnam Voices* (Viking, 1984)—and a subscription to *Indochina Chronology*, edited by Douglas Pike and published by the Institute of East Asian Studies, University of California at Berkeley.

As reference sources on weapons I used various Army and Marine Corps field manuals, as well as Anthony Robinson et al., *Weapons of the Vietnam War* (Bison Books, 1983), and Ray Bonds, ed., *The Vietnam War* (Crown, 1979).

What follows is a discussion of the other works I found most useful, arranged, somewhat idiosyncratically, by chapters.

Chapter 1

In preparing to return to Vietnam, I consulted a number of books by Americans who had visited North Vietnam during the war, especially Harrison Salisbury, *Behind the Lines: Hanoi* (Harper & Row, 1967); James Cameron, *Here Is Your Enemy* (Holt, Rinehart & Winston, 1966); Staughton Lynd and Thomas Hayden, *The Other Side* (New American Library, 1966); and Susan Sontag, *Trip to Hanoi* (Farrar, Straus and Giroux, 1968). Wilfred Burchett, *Viet Nam: Inside Story of the Guerrilla War* (International Publishers, 1965), was useful as an account from the Communist side, of the early years of the guerrilla war and the Ho Chi Minh Trail. Accounts of Vietnam after the war are few, although William Shawcross, "In a Grim Country," *New York Review of Books*, September 24, 1981, was particularly helpful.

Chapters 2, 5, 6, and 7

Several books helped me in writing about the air war over North Vietnam: Jack Broughton, *Thud Ridge* (Lippincott, 1969), a pungent and irreverent book, one of my favorites; Dewey Waddell and Norm Wood, eds., *Air War—Vietnam* (Arno Press, 1978); James N. Eastman, Jr., et al., eds., *Aces and Aerial Victories* (Headquarters, USAF, 1976); John Trotti, *Phantom over Vietnam* (Presidio, 1984); and Tom Wolfe, "Jousting with Sam and Charlie," in *Mauve Gloves, Madmen, Clutter & Vine* (Farrar, Straus and Giroux, 1976).

In describing the North Vietnamese response to American bombing,

I relied on the already-mentioned reports by Americans who visited Vietnam during the war, as well as Jon M. Van Dyke, *North Viet Nam's Strategy for Survival* (Pacific Books, 1972), and Gerard Chaliand, *The Peasants of North Viet Nam* (Pelican, 1969).

Chapter 7

The discussion at Phat Diem about the nature of Vietnamese peasant life was informed by my reading of Gerald Hickey, *Village in Vietnam* (Yale, 1964), and Samuel L. Popkin, *The Rational Peasant* (University of California, 1979).

Chapter 8

In wrestling with the dilemmas of going off to war, I drew on the World War I memoirs of Robert Graves, *Goodbye to All That* (Doubleday, 1957), and Siegfried Sassoon, *Memoirs of an Infantry Officer* (Collier, 1969), as well as on the single best volume about men and war—J. Glenn Gray, *The Warriors: Reflections on Men in Battle* (Harcourt, Brace, 1959).

The extremes to which some Americans went to avoid the draft are shown in Andrew O. Shapiro and John M. Stubin, *Mastering the Draft* (Little, Brown, 1970), and, with considerable drama and moral subtlety, in James Fallows, "What Did You Do in the Class War, Daddy?," *Washington Monthly*, October 1975. The best study of who went to war, who didn't, and why is Lawrence M. Baskir and William A. Strauss, *Chance and Circumstance: The Draft, the War, and the Vietnam Generation* (Knopf, 1978).

Chapter 9

My discussions about the war with Vietnamese generals benefited by reference to Harry G. Summers, Jr., *On Strategy: A Critical Analysis of the Vietnam War* (Presidio, 1982), and "The Bitter Triumph of the Ia Drang," *American Heritage*, February 1984; Herbert Schandler, *The Unmaking of a President* (Princeton, 1977); Theodore Sorensen, *Kennedy* (Harper & Row, 1965); Henry Kissinger, *White House Years* (Little, Brown, 1972), and *Years of Trial and Hope* (Little, Brown, 1982); Leslie H. Gelb and Richard K. Betts, *The Irony of Viet Nam: The System Worked* (Brookings, 1970); Denis Warner, *Certain Victory* (Sheed Andrews and McMeel, 1978); and John E. Mueller, "The Search for the 'Breaking Point' in Viet Nam," *International Studies Quarterly,* December 1980.

William C. Westmoreland, *A Soldier Reports* (Doubleday, 1976), is an invaluable resource on the early years of the American war. In addition to my discussions with General Edwin Simmons and other military historians at the Marine Corps Historical Unit, I also used several volumes of the excellent Marine Corps history *The U.S. Marines in Vietnam,* Edwin Simmons, ed., particularly Jack Shulimson and Charles M. Johnson, *The Landing and the Buildup: 1965* (Headquarters, U.S. Marine Corps, 1978).

Among the best sources on how Vietnam affected the American military are Douglas Kinnard, *The War Managers* (University Press of New England, 1977); Richard A. Gabriel and Paul L. Savage, *Crisis in Command* (McGraw-Hill, 1978); the already-mentioned Harry G. Summers, Jr., *On Strategy;* and Drew Middleton, "The American Military and the Legacy of Viet Nam," *New York Times Magazine,* January 10, 1982. Affidavits in the libel trial of General Westmoreland versus CBS et al. in the U.S. District Court, Southern District of New York (82 CIV 7913 PNL), were also invaluable, particularly those of George Christian, Joseph McChristian, George W. Allen, Gains B. Hawkins, Donald W, Blascak, and John T. Moore.

On the South Vietnamese side, I consulted Nguyen Cao Ky, *Why We Lost the Viet Nam War* (Scarborough, 1978); Tran Van Don, *Our Endless War* (Presidio, 1978); and Hoang Ngoc Lung, *Strategy and Tactics* (U.S. Army Center of Military History, 1979)—one of a series of valuable monographs by former South Vietnamese officers.

For more insight into the North Vietnamese view of the war, I read many issues of the *Viet Nam Courier* and *Vietnamese Studies,* both published through the Foreign Language Publishing House in Hanoi, as well as two books by Vo Nguyen Giap, *People's Army, People's War* (Praeger, 1962), and *Dien Bien Phu* (Foreign Language Publishing House, 1984), and the memoir by General Van Tien Dung, commander of the North Vietnamese forces in the final offensive in 1975, *Great Spring Victory* (Foreign Broadcast Information Service, 1976).

Chapter 10

For background on Tan Trao, I referred to Archimedes Patti, *Why Vietnam?* (University of California, 1980); Lucien Bodard, *The Quicksand War: Prelude to Vietnam* (Atlantic Monthly Press, 1967); and Jean Lacouture, *Ho Chi Minh* (Random House, 1968). Two books by Bernard Fall, *Street Without Joy* (Stackpole, 1961) and *Last Reflections on a War* (Doubleday, 1967), are indispensable for understanding Ho Chi Minh and the French war in Indochina.

Chapter 13

The account of the Oakland antiwar demonstration—and other excellent reporting of the time—is in John Gregory Dunne, *Quintana & Friends* (Dutton, 1978).

Chapter 15

The best sources for the Tet Offensive and what happened at Hue are Don Oberdorfer, *Tet!* (Doubleday, 1971); Douglas Pike, *The Viet Cong Strategy of Terror* (U.S. Information Agency, 1970); D. Gareth Porter, "Bloodbath: Myth or Reality?," *Indochina Chronicle*, September 15, 1973; Keith William Nolan, *Battle for Hue* (Presidio, 1983); Robert Pisor, *The End of the Line: The Siege of Khe Sanh* (Norton, 1982); and Peter Braestrup, *Big Story* (Westview Press, 1979), a comprehensive, and controversial, account of the role of the press during Tet.

In writing about the effects of the war on village life, I used Stuart A. Herrington, *Silence Was a Weapon* (Presidio, 1982); Jeffrey Race, *War Comes to Long An* (University of California, 1972); and F. J. West, Jr., *The Village* (Harper & Row, 1972).

Chapter 19

The discussion about men and war at Duy Xuyen drew upon the already-mentioned J. Glenn Gray, *The Warriors;* Paul Fussell's superb book on World War I, *The Great War and Modern Memory* (Oxford, 1975); and John Keegan, *The Face of Battle* (Viking, 1976). A more technical book, Anthony Kellett, *Combat Motivation* (Kluwer Nijhoff, 1982), was also useful, as were various military handbooks, among them *Guidebook for Marines* and Department of the Army Field Manual 21–75, *Combat Training of the Individual Soldier and Patrolling.*

Michael Herr's *Dispatches* (Knopf, 1977) captures with perfect pitch the war's strange blend of violence, comradeship, drugs, and rock and roll. The account of Gettysburg by Praxiteles Swan is contained in Ernest Hemingway, ed., *Men at War* (Crown, 1942).

The musings about why men fight were informed by the best book on that subject, S. L. A. Marshall, *Men Against Fire* (Morrow, 1947). As noted in the text, Philip Caputo, *A Rumor of War* (Holt, 1977), is particularly good on the emotional bonds men form in war; so are several novels, most notably James Webb, *Fields of Fire* (Prentice-Hall, 1978); Winston Groom, *Better Times than These* (Summit, 1978); John Del Vecchio, *The Thirteenth Valley* (Bantam, 1982); and Jack Fuller, *Fragments* (Morrow, 1984). Also useful were an oral history edited by Al Santoli, *Everything We Had* (Oxford, 1978) and Bernard Edelman, ed., *Dear America* (Norton, 1985), a collection of letters from American soldiers in Vietnam.

Of Vietnamese short stories set during the war there is an abundant supply, all published by the Foreign Language Publishing House in Hanoi. Nguyen Khac Vien and Huu Ngoc, eds., *Vietnamese Literature,* is the standard work, but there are numerous story collections, my favorites being *The Ho Chi Minh Trail* (1981), *The Revolution in the Village* (1984), *After So Many Years* (1983), *White Sand* (1981), and *Two Old Men in the Plain of Reeds* (1984).

Two publications which also helped me understand my old enemies were Douglas Pike, *Viet Cong* (M.I.T., 1966) and Konrad Kellen, *Conversations with Enemy Soldiers in Late 1968/Early 1969* (Rand, 1970).

Chapter 22

Graham Greene's account of a journey to Ben Tre and the origins of *The Quiet American* is in his autobiography, *Ways of Escape* (Simon and Schuster, 1980). The discussion of Vietnam's current eco-

nomic situation and the importance of Resolution 6 was reinforced by
reference to Nayan Chanda, "Viet Nam in 1983," *Asian Survey*, January 1984, and Ton That Tien, "Viet Nam's New Economic Policy,"
Pacific Affairs, Winter 1983–84.

Chapter 23

For the account of the disillusionment of the non-Communist Viet
Cong I relied on Truong Nhu Tang, *A Viet Cong Memoir* (Harcourt,
Brace, Jovanovich, 1985), and the already-mentioned Harrison Salis-
bury, *Behind the Lines: Hanoi.*

Chapter 24

About My Lai I used Seymour Hersh, *My Lai 4* (Random House,
1970); The Peers Commission, *The My Lai Massacre and Its Coverup*
(Free Press, 1976); John Sack, *Lieutenant Calley: His Own Story*
(Viking, 1971); Richard Hammer, *The Court Martial of Lieutenant
Calley* (Coward, McCann & Geoghegan, 1971); and Tim O'Brien, *If I Die
in a Combat Zone* (Delacorte, 1973), a riveting account of combat in
the My Lai area. For information on the case of Robert Garwood I relied
primarily on Winston Groom and Duncan Spencer, *Conversations with
the Enemy: The Story of PFC Robert Garwood* (Putnam, 1983), as well
as on an article about Garwood in the *Wall Street Journal*, December
4, 1984, page 1.

Chapter 25

A fine account of the war in the tunnels as viewed from both sides
is Tom Mangold and John Penycate, *The Tunnels of Cu Chi* (Random
House, 1985).

Epilogue

The account of Admiral Stockdale's POW experience is from Jim and
Sybil Stockdale, *In Love and War* (Harper & Row, 1984). The story of

the Vietnam Veterans Memorial, along with a complete listing of all the names carved upon it, is in Jan C. Scruggs and Joel L. Swerdlow, *To Heal a Nation* (Harper & Row, 1985). There are many books about the Vietnam veteran and the importance of the war to an entire "Vietnam generation." I found particularly useful A. D. Horne, ed., *The Wounded Generation* (Prentice-Hall, 1981); John Wheeler, *Touched with Fire* (Franklin Watts, 1984); Arthur Egendorf, *Healing from the War* (Houghton Mifflin, 1985); and Joe Klein, *Payback* (Knopf, 1984). The basic statistics on Vietnam veterans are contained in *Myths and Realities: A Study of Attitudes Toward Viet Nam Era Veterans* (U.S. Veterans Administration, 1980), and some fascinating comparisons are provided by consulting similar surveys of World War II veterans in S. A. Stouffer et al., *The American Soldier: Combat and Its Aftermath* (Princeton, 1949).

As always, the best source was being there.